BLACK HILLS FOREST RESERVE
Ex. Orders. Feb 22 1897. Sept. 19 1898

RAWLINS

C A R B O N

A L B A N Y

L A R A M I E

LARAMIE

CHEYENNE

Francis E. Warren, November 14, 1929. Harris and Ewing photograph courtesy University of Wyoming Library.

WYOMING

A POLITICAL HISTORY, 1868–1896

by Lewis L. Gould

NEW HAVEN AND LONDON, YALE UNIVERSITY PRESS

1968

TO MY MOTHER AND FATHER

PREFACE

In 1955 Earl Pomeroy wrote that "the history of western politics in the middle years of the nineteenth century needs further study and clarification." Over the last decade, scholars have begun to investigate the workings of political life in the West, but Pomeroy's generalization is still basically correct and, with much accuracy, can be extended to cover the whole experience of western politics in the nineteenth century. Such crucial states as California, Colorado, and Nebraska have only recently become the subjects of sustained scholarly activity.

Because of its association with the range cattle industry, the territory and state of Wyoming has, to some extent, escaped this historical neglect. A diverse array of amateur and professional scholars have labored to explain the development of the social and economic institutions of the state, and such men as Gene Gressley, W. Turrentine Jackson, and Ernest S. Osgood have demonstrated the larger importance of the cattle business for American economic history. Exciting episodes like the range war in Johnson county have also attracted students of frontier violence and law enforcement.

Despite all this work, the political history of Wyoming from the creation of the territory through the 1890s has remained cloudy and mysterious. To be sure, some writers have attributed large influence to the Wyoming Stock Growers Association, while others have noted the power and prestige of the Union Pacific Railroad. These hypotheses about the nature of politics within Wyoming, however, have been untested and have gained acceptance more through repetition than verification.

This study seeks to supply an analytic narrative of the

course of Wyoming politics from the first settlement near Cheyenne in 1867 through the controversial election of 1896. Unlike other western states, Wyoming did not possess a stable political organization when statehood came in 1890; it required six more years of factional contention to demonstrate that the Republican party, under the leadership of Francis E. Warren, would attain a position of supremacy. At the same time, the study attempts to show how this single western state was affected by the broader trends and patterns of national political history. Furthermore, certain generalizations and theories about western politics are tested. How important was the role of the federal government in political and economic life? Were politics dominated by personality, by ideology, or by economic interests like the cattlemen and railroads? How complex and sophisticated were the operations of western politicians? Finally, what effect did the personalities and politics of the national parties and their leaders have on local events?

In answering these questions, I quickly discovered that the most fruitful approach, in the case of Wyoming, lay in focusing on the emergence of a single politician as the preeminent leader in the state. From his arrival in 1868, Francis E. Warren gradually expanded his role in politics, until by 1896 he exercised undisputed sway in the Republican party and thereby secured power in the state at large. Because his private papers have been preserved, unlike those of other politicians of this period, a decision to concentrate on Warren was inevitable. An examination of the Warren manuscripts underlined the wisdom of this choice. His personal letterbooks are an unusually rich source for Wyoming political history, for his compulsion to supply his lieutenants with every scrap of useful information makes his letters virtually a daily record of Wyoming history in this period.

Considerations of substance as well as convenience dictated a detailed examination of Warren's career. His ability to construct a political machine dedicated to the efficient acquisition of federal subsidies set him apart from his colleagues. While everyone realized that Wyoming could not rely solely on its own economic resources for growth, Warren alone perceived that federal appropriations could be obtained only by professional politicians able to build up influence and power in Congress through seniority and persistence. Thus over two decades Warren systematically reduced the chaotic state of Wyoming politics to a condition of order and tranquillity.

The record of this process sheds light on why western politics has been, as Earl Pomeroy has noted, less radical than historians have believed. In Wyoming, settlers were more concerned with economic development than with social protest and as a result favored policies designed to increase their stake in society. They saw the federal government as a potential source for the promotion of their prosperity, and they tailored their actions to speed the flow of government monies to their state. For this reason, issues like land reform, irrigation, the location of military posts, and conservation were not peripheral and inconsequential, but constituted the heart of western politics. This symbiotic relationship between the national government and the West put a premium on conservatism and stability, and residents of Wyoming found Warren's program readily acceptable.

Wyoming's small population limited its importance in national elections after it became a state. This is not to say, however, that its three electoral votes were ignored by leaders of both major parties or that problems like land policy, free silver, or Populism did not affect it. While not engendering the level of excitement that these issues met in other states, such questions did influence politics in Wyoming. On matters like the relationship between the American Protective Association and the Republican Party or the connection between the McKinley campaign and middle-of-the-road Populism, a look at the Wyoming experience reveals much. Thus an examination of political struggles in the state discloses a great deal about the way in which public life was carried on in the West in this period. It also demonstrates that politics had a life of its own, with its own rules, demands, and rewards. Hopefully, the following narrative will bring some order and coherence to Wyoming political history and offer other scholars a firm basis from which to generalize about Wyoming and the West in the latter part of the nineteenth century.

L. L. G.

New Haven, Conn.
April 1967

ACKNOWLEDGMENTS

It is a pleasure to acknowledge the kindness and help of the individuals and institutions without whose assistance I could not have written this volume. In Wyoming, my primary debt is to Professor Gene Gressley and his able staff at the Western History Research Center, University of Wyoming, who made my two research visits there so rewarding and enjoyable. Professor Gressley also generously shared with me his knowledge of Wyoming and the West, took time out from his hectic schedule to drive to Cheyenne and uncover a significant addition to the Francis E. Warren Papers, and improved several chapters of the manuscript with his suggestions and criticisms.

Mrs. Katherine Halverson and the gracious ladies at the Wyoming State Historical Society extended me every possible courtesy and responded efficiently to every request for an obscure record. Mr. and Mrs. Charles D. Carey, Mr. William R. Dubois, and Mrs. Herbert V. Lacey, all of Cheyenne, Mrs. W. H. Barber of Greeley, Colorado, and Mrs. Agnes Wright Spring of Denver, granted me interviews, allowed me to examine personal letters, and displayed unfailing kindness and generosity. Mrs. Laura Ekstrom, of the Colorado State Historical Society, and Mrs. Alys Freeze, of the Denver Public Library, facilitated my work in Denver. The staff of the Iowa Department of History and Archives, Des Moines, made my work in the Grenville M. Dodge Papers most profitable.

The dedicated workers at the Manuscripts Division, Library of Congress, and at the National Archives went out of their way to aid my investigations. Mr. Winslow B. Van Devanter of Washington allowed me to consult his father's

ACKNOWLEDGMENTS

papers, helped me locate other possible sources, and cooperated unstintingly with my efforts to understand Wyoming and Willis Van Devanter.

Mrs. Sandra Whedbee and Mrs. Anne Granger typed various drafts of the manuscript with skill and efficiency. Mr. Barry Seltser of Yale College, 1970, saved me from many errors.

I have also enjoyed the assistance of numerous friends and colleagues. F. Duane Rose, by mail and through conversations, imparted the insights gathered from his study of the career of Francis E. Warren. William Lilley of Yale broadened my knowledge of irrigation and its relation to western history. I owe thanks also to Professors Alexander M. Bickel and John M. Blum of Yale.

Two people helped me beyond the call of scholarly duty. R. Hal Williams read the manuscript several times, made countless valuable suggestions on style and substance, and laid aside his own research on several occasions to give me the benefit of his wise counsel on questions of interpretation.

Professor Howard R. Lamar has directed this project since it began as a dissertation in 1963. During that time, he has been a constant source of encouragement and guidance. Despite my incessant demands on his time, he never failed to supply patient and thoughtful advice which has improved every page of this study.

The dedication is an inadequate expression of my debt to my parents.

I am responsible for any errors of fact or interpretation that occur in this book.

CONTENTS

CHAPTER ONE. THE NEW TERRITORY

YOMING Territory was the child of the Union Pacific. The westward advance of the railroad brought General Grenville M. Dodge to the site of present-day Cheyenne in July 1867 for the purpose of locating a division point for the Union Pacific. Dodge was accompanied by Major General C. C. Augur who selected Cheyenne as the site for a military post. The arrival of the railroad several months later and the construction of Fort D. A. Russell at the same time assured Cheyenne of survival. More important, they symbolized the significance of the railroad and the federal government as factors contributing to the economic health of the new territory, a relationship which has persisted throughout Wyoming's history.[1]

Railroad men and soldiers were followed on July 9, 1867, by nine emigrants who quickly plunged into the lucrative business of selling railroad town lots. During the next two months, settlers continued to appear as the Union Pacific neared Cheyenne. An army doctor reported in October, "When I left here last July all the land was bare, and the only habitations were tents. Cheyenne has now a population of fifteen hundred, two papers, stores, warehouses, hotels, restaurants, gambling halls, etc., etc." A newspaper was started by a Colorado journalist, Nathan A. Baker, and the

1. Frances B. Beard, *Wyoming From Territorial Days to the Present* (3 vols. Chicago, 1933), *I*, 173.

Cheyenne Leader soon became a booster of the region's future and a strong voice for territorial organization.[2]

Other embryonic towns along the proposed line of the Union Pacific, including Laramie, Green River City, and Bear River City, appeared as the railroad proceeded west. Farther north, a small gold rush at South Pass City attracted a few enthusiasts, although the influx of population there did not reach sizable numbers until the summer of 1868. In the first months of its life, Wyoming found its destiny tied to the railroad, a predicament which produced no qualms but instead fostered euphoric dreams of commercial prosperity among the people.[3]

The denizens of Cheyenne, or the "Hell on Wheels" as it was known to the shocked but fascinated East, lost little time in starting the frenetic game of frontier politics. A rudimentary city government was formed in August 1867, and on September 27 a mass meeting of citizens chose a provisional board of county commissioners, who in turn arranged an election of county officers on October 8. The newly elected officials made Laramie County, created on paper by the Dakota legislature in January 1867, a reality. The voters also selected J. R. Whitehead, a salesman of Union Pacific town lots, as the county representative to the legislature in Yankton. At the same time, they picked a Union Pacific engineer, John S. Casement, as a provisional territorial delegate to go to Washington and lobby for organization of a new territory.[4]

2. Henry C. Parry, "Letters from the Frontier—1867," *Annals of Wyoming, 30* (1958), 142; Nolie Mumey, *Nathan Addison Baker* (Denver, 1965), p. 110.

3. T. A. Larson, *History of Wyoming* (Lincoln, Nebraska, 1965), pp. 36–63.

4. "History of Wyoming, Written by C. G. Coutant, Pioneer

As the railroad approached Cheyenne, the townspeople began to see drawbacks in their position as wards of Dakota Territory. Eight hundred miles separated Cheyenne from Yankton, and the populace believed that the new region, now called Wyoming by many of its inhabitants, was destined for a more affluent status than Indian-ridden, agricultural, and distant Dakota. Editor Baker set the tone of this unrest on October 22, 1867, when he called for the organization of a new territory: "Save the expense and difficulty of transacting business with a seat of government seven hundred miles distant, without roads and several months in the year almost without communication." To these arguments Baker added the clincher, "Dakota is a slow coach; we travel by steam."[5]

Steam arrived in Cheyenne on November 13, and the population celebrated the coming of the Union Pacific. The *Leader*, following the railroad festivities, renewed its call for immediate effort: "Let our citizens take steps at once and petition Congress in the matter, and let a few representatives and a few senators be entrusted with the bantling, and the matter will be attended too, and the object accomplished before bad blood is stirred up."[6]

The Union Pacific, laboring, as Wallace Farnham has shown, to overcome the effects of an enfeebled federal government, had every reason to encourage a territorial government as an aid to law and order. Since General Dodge represented Iowa in the House of Representatives, his political talents would be at the disposal of a Wyoming bill.

Historian, and Heretofore Unpublished," *Annals of Wyoming, 12* (1940), 323–27.

5. *Cheyenne Daily Leader,* Oct. 22, 1867.

6. *Leader,* Nov. 14, 1867.

His Union Pacific colleagues in Washington, especially Congressman Oakes Ames of Massachusetts, stood ready to give assistance. Delegate Casement, though denied a seat in Congress, remained in Washington to further the interests of his constituents as well as those of his employer.[7]

Dakota officials were as anxious to rid themselves of the dead weight of Laramie County as Wyoming people were eager to be jettisoned. Territorial Governor Andrew Jackson Faulk and Delegate Walter A. Burleigh, who looked with distaste on several thousand distant and uncontrollable voters, lent their support to the Wyoming campaign. Beset by problems of Indian supervision, railroad promotion, and political factionalism, Dakota officials could not waste time on a region with which they had only the most tenuous connection. In a message to the Dakota legislature in December 1867, Governor Faulk speculated whether his territory could provide sufficient protection for the residents of Laramie County. "We may render aid," he concluded, "to the extent of the authority given us under the organic law, but if this is not sufficient in their opinion I know of no good reason why they may not be clothed with all the blessings and protection of a separate organization."[8]

The legislature agreed with Faulk and drafted a memorial to Congress urging the creation of a new territory, "The present illy-proportioned and extensive area of Dakota," argued the memorial, "demonstrates that a division of this territory by Congress is inevitable, and only a question of

7. Wallace D. Farnham, " 'The Weakened Spring of Government': A Study in Nineteenth Century American History," *American Historical Review, 68* (1963), 670.

8. George W. Kingsbury, *History of Dakota Territory* (2 vols. Chicago, 1915), *1,* 468.

time, and sound policy would seem to dictate that all the guards of law and courts afforded by a separate territorial government should be extended to the already populous settlements of the proposed new Territory."[9]

Colorado politicians remained unenthusiastic. There, as Howard Lamar has shown, a statehood movement, led by ex-governor John Evans and the territorial delegate, Jerome B. Chaffee, had been foundering in the face of repeated presidential vetoes and local opposition. Chaffee seems to have decided that the addition of the new areas opened by the Union Pacific, specifically the land along the line of the railroad, to the territory of Colorado would ensure the success of the statehood campaign. As a result, Chaffee regarded with disfavor attempts to organize a new territory which would frustrate his plans.[10]

When General Dodge laid plans for a territorial bill, Chaffee began to throw obstacles in his path. On November 30, 1867, Chaffee boasted to Evans that he had "commenced long ago to prevent any new territory being organized north of us because I coveted a slice there." Chaffee added that he had won Representative James M. Ashley, an Ohio Republican and previously a friend of Wyoming Territory, to his side, and that Dodge and Casement would probably have to come around. "The general feeling is strong against any more new Territories & I am confident this can all be arranged to go as we want but we had better get pitching."[11]

At this point Henry M. Teller, Chaffee's political rival in

9. Marie H. Erwin, *Wyoming Historical Blue Book* (Denver, 1946), pp. 142–43.

10. Howard R. Lamar, *The Far Southwest, 1846–1912: A Territorial History* (New Haven, 1966), pp. 252–64.

11. Jerome B. Chaffee to John Evans, Nov. 30, 1867, Box 9, John Evans Collection, Colorado State Historical Society.

Colorado, undermined his strength in Congress. While the Colorado statehood bill lingered in the Senate Committee on Territories, Teller attacked the whole scheme as foolish and unpopular in Colorado. Teller also added some uncomfortable facts about Chaffee's failure to win local support for his plan to annex new territory to the proposed state of Colorado. Favorable resolutions had passed the lower house of the territorial legislature, Teller pointed out, but the Council, or upper house, had defeated the annexation proposal.[12]

The Colorado statehood bill became a casualty of this political infighting, but its eventual demise improved the prospects for a Wyoming territorial bill. On February 13, 1868, Senator Richard Yates of Illinois introduced a measure to organize the territory. Even with the Colorado obstruction gone, Wyoming Territory confronted several problems. The impeachment of President Andrew Johnson was slowing the legislative process; many congressmen were reluctant to add to the expenses of the national government by erecting another western territory; and most important, Radical Republican politicians disliked the possibility of Johnson's having another set of patronage positions to bestow on his friends.[13]

The lobbying tactics of Dodge, Burleigh, and their associates proved sufficient in the Senate, and the bill passed on June 3, 1868. Success in the House was another matter. Advocates of economy were stronger there, while the continued opposition of Congressman Ashley did not help the bill's chances. To counter these forces, General Casement

12. "Memorial of H. M. Teller," *Senate Miscellaneous Documents,* 40th Cong., 2d sess., No. 31, p. 4.
13. *Congressional Globe,* 40th Cong., 2d sess (Feb. 13, 1868), p. 1143.

induced Cheyenne leaders to send two lobbyists to Washington, John B. Wolff and Hiram Latham.[14]

Wolff has been correctly dismissed as a talkative bore, but Latham has received much of the credit for the final victory of the Wyoming bill. The quiet work of General Dodge and Walter Burleigh probably proved more effective. The Dakota delegate wrote Governor Faulk on June 17 that Dodge and other legislators were "aiding me most manfully," reported that "Six or eight Senators are going to their delegations in the House and press them to the mark," and concluded that "It now looks as though the 'Wyoming bill' would pass."[15]

Despite this optimistic forecast, the House Committee on Territories decided on July 14 to postpone favorable action on the Wyoming bill until the next session of Congress. During the ensuing week, friends of the bill intensified their efforts, and when the House considered the committee report on July 22, the lawmakers repudiated the committee's action and passed the Wyoming bill. Ashley made a strong attack on the measure as an attempt to increase the number of federal officeholders, but the House disregarded this argument and the bill sailed through by a vote of 106 to 50.[16]

President Johnson's signature on the Wyoming Organic Act on July 25, 1868, launched the territory. The President appointed territorial officers the same day, but while Congress was willing to organize the territory, it saw no reason to confirm Johnson's appointments. The nominations lan-

14. C. G. Coutant, *The History of Wyoming from the Earliest Known Discoveries* (Laramie, 1899), p. 623.

15. Walter A. Burleigh to Andrew Jackson Faulk, June 17, 1868, Andrew Jackson Faulk Papers, Yale Western Americana Collection.

16. *Chicago Tribune,* July 15, 1868; *New York Tribune,* July 23, 1868; *Congressional Globe,* 40th Cong., 2d sess (July 22, 1868), p. 4345.

guished in committee, were reported adversely, and were finally disapproved by the Senate.[17]

This dissension posed severe problems in Wyoming and Dakota. The Organic Act provided that Dakota laws be enforced until "the time when the executive and judicial officers herein provided for shall have been duly appointed and qualified." Congressional inaction thus perpetuated the disorganized state of affairs, and one Wyoming resident complained to the Secretary of State that "We are in a sad dilemma now—every thing here is confusion. We have no one to call our Election—the Judges of Dacotah refuse to hold Court here now & we are worse off than if we were not organized. We are suffering from want of some kind of government here."[18] Despite these pleas, the situation did not improve until Ulysses S. Grant took office in March 1869, and the feuding between Congress and the President ended.

Enthusiastic cheers greeted the arrival of the territorial officials in Cheyenne during a Wyoming rainstorm on May 7, 1869.[19] In the eyes of the populace, the coming of tangible federal authority meant the end of the unsettled conditions which had existed since 1867. This assessment was accurate to a degree, but it overlooked the physical, political, and economic realities of life in Wyoming which made effective

17. A. S. Paddock to F. W. Seward, July 30, 1868, O. T. B. Williams to Andrew Johnson, Aug. 31, 1868, Wyoming Series, State Department Territorial Papers, National Archives, Record Group 59.

18. Erwin, *Wyoming Historical Blue Book,* p. 156; E. P. Snow to William H. Seward, Aug. 8, 1868, Wyoming Series, State Department Territorial Papers, NA, RG59.

19. Francis E. Warren to Helen M. Smith, May 9, 1869, Francis E. Warren Papers, Western History Research Center, University of Wyoming.

government difficult. The optimism engendered by the advent of the territorial period also reflected certain basic assumptions by the people of Wyoming which, however understandable, had scant relationship to the facts of the Wyoming situation. For a decade Wyoming politics turned on the interactions of certain inflexible conditions with the confidence of Wyoming residents that their territory would within a few years become both an industrial center and the garden spot of the Far West.

During the 1870s, Wyoming was an impoverished territory in an underdeveloped West. Unlike its neighbors, Colorado and Montana, Wyoming had not been endowed with immediately available supplies of precious metals. The Union Pacific Railroad, to be sure, found much to admire in the coal deposits in the southwestern part of the territory, and in due time rich reserves of oil would be uncovered. America in the 1870s, however, felt no excitement over more coal, and the possibility of oil was of little interest. Gold, silver, and copper were the avenues to fame and prosperity, and despite recurrent bouts of fevered hysteria, Wyoming could not produce more than the justly neglected South Pass Gold Rush of 1868, which was over almost before it began.[20]

Farming, the other traditional outlet for pioneer enterprise, faced nearly insurmountable problems in the new territory. Walter P. Webb could not have found a more graphic illustration than Wyoming in the territorial period of the validity of his thesis about the effect of aridity on settlement of the Great Plains. The yearly rainfall amounted to much less than the necessary twenty inches, the growing season was short, and the soil proved inhospitable to the

20. Larson, *History of Wyoming*, pp. 112–14; Rodman W. Paul, *Mining Frontiers of the Far West, 1848–1880* (New York, 1963), p. 176.

plow. Settlers advanced a variety of answers to the unfavorable agricultural problem in Wyoming's first decade, but no solution had more than a brief vogue. Irrigation required capital which did not exist in the territory. Dry farming had not been perfected, and the technical devices described by Webb, which made agriculture practicable on the Great Plains in the 1880s, were still in their infancy. With less than two percent of its working force engaged in crop agriculture in 1870, Wyoming had the smallest percentage of its industrial structure devoted to farming of any western state or territory.[21]

While farming lagged, perceptive residents noticed that the territory possessed some of the best grazing land in the nation. Editor Baker of the *Leader* predicted as early as 1868 that "this country will make stock raising a specialty, since it is one of the most profitable branches of industry which it is possible for civilized man to engage in." Press agents and journalists spread the good word, but while the number of cattle gradually increased throughout the decade, several factors delayed the cattle boom until the 1880s. Eastern and foreign investors had not yet realized the possibilities in western cattle, while a hard winter in 1872–73 set back several fledgling enterprises. The most persistent difficulty, however, was the presence of Indians in the northern two-thirds of the territory, a problem which, as E. S. Osgood has noted, slowed the northern expansion of the Wyoming cattle industry.[22]

21. Walter P. Webb, *The Great Plains* (New York, 1931), pp. 321–33; Leonard J. Arrington, *The Changing Economic Structure of the Mountain West, 1850–1950* (Logan, Utah, 1963), p. 41.

22. *Leader*, May 8, 1868, quoted in Gene M. Gressley, *Bankers and Cattlemen* (New York, 1966), p. 40; Ernest S. Osgood, *The Day of the Cattleman* (Minneapolis, 1929), p. 58.

Lack of economic opportunity in agriculture or mining restricted settlement during Wyoming's first ten years to the line of towns along the route of the Union Pacific. Inevitably, the railroad became the dominant private economic force in the territory, employing the most workers and fostering a host of service industries in the towns it had created.[23] The railroad operated coal mines at Rock Springs, repair facilities in Cheyenne, and rolling mills at Laramie after 1875. These activities required the services of 848 people in 1870. The most graphic illustration of the territory's dependence on the UP was that thirteen percent of the Wyoming labor force worked for the railroad. With the exception of Colorado, where nearly six percent of the labor force did railroad work, no other Rocky Mountain state or territory had over three percent of its laboring population employed on steam railroads.[24]

Wyoming residents appreciated the railroad's economic power and were careful to make the proper obeisance to Union Pacific headquarters in Omaha, but living with the corporate giant did not always prove easy. In Cheyenne, for instance, the question of railroad town lots agitated local residents for several years as squatters on Union Pacific land attempted to formalize their holdings, while the railroad sought to retain control of its property. Settlement of the dispute by the Interior Department in favor of the Union Pacific did not end the rancor. The *Cheyenne Leader* complained in January 1875,[25]

The Union Pacific R. R. Co.'s Lot Department is not acting as well towards the towns of Laramie and Chey-

---

23. Arrington, *Changing Economic Structure,* p. 9.
24. Ibid., pp. 30, 41.
25. *Leader,* Jan. 29, 1875.

enne as it ought. Many persons in both places would buy lots and make permanent improvements on them if they could only purchase them. So far as this town is concerned the U. P. Railroad Company will make no improvements, nor permit any to be made if it can prevent them. The dog-in-the-manger policy may not prove the wisest for the Company in the long run.

Despite these occasional frictions, the inhabitants of Wyoming saw the railroad as the source of future prosperity, and through their business and political leaders they lobbied industriously for additional rail construction. The most popular notion looked toward the building of a line north from Cheyenne to Helena, Montana, but this railroad, often proposed and never begun, would be only the first link in a magnificent north-south line from Latin America to Canada. "When the great Rocky Mountain railroad from the Aetic [sic] cities of Mexico to the higher latitudes of British America and Alaska, crosses the Union Pacific at Cheyenne," trumpeted the *Leader* in 1870, "we shall begin to realize some of the marked advantages of our position. There's nothing like it. We expect to be the recognized *hub of the universe* in the course of time."[26]

A dominant economic position translated itself into political power for the Union Pacific. In the 1870s the railroad intervened more openly and consistently in Wyoming politics than it would a decade later. Railroad participation in politics resulted from non-ideological action by groups and individuals upset by a specific Union Pacific policy, and not by the fact of railroad power itself. Few wished the railroad to disappear; the question was how its blessings would be distributed.

26. *Leader,* Nov. 18, 1870.

The limited range of its economic attractions caused Wyoming's population, 10,000 at the first territorial census, to lag far behind the other western territories in the 1870s. Not until 1890 did Wyoming edge out of last place among western states and territories by passing Nevada in total population. Several territories surpassed Wyoming's area, 98,000 square miles, but the lack of residents combined with the great distances to hamper effective government. Economic underdevelopment narrowed the tax base, leaving the railroad as the primary contributor to county and city coffers and further restricting the sources of territorial revenue.[27]

Political struggle resulted over the distribution of what territorial and federal funds were available. The two largest towns, Cheyenne (seat of Laramie County) and Laramie (seat of Albany County), competed for the prize of the capital, which carried with it the operating expenses of the government. The eastern counties of Laramie and Albany vied with their western counterparts, Sweetwater, Carbon, and Uinta, for a piece of the biennial appropriations of the legislature. This rivalry fostered skills in the art of logrolling even if it did not bring ascendancy to any one county.[28]

This emerging sectionalism took its most virulent form in the battle between Cheyenne and Laramie. As the capital, Cheyenne fancied itself as "the Magic City of the Plains" which would one day be the "Altona" (sic) of the West. A Union Pacific promise to locate repair shop facilities in the city was not kept until the late 1880s, but the prospect kept Cheyenne perennially on edge. No matter where they

27. Erwin, *Wyoming Historical Blue Book,* p. 1408; Arrington, *Changing Economic Structure,* p. 30.

28. Lola M. Homsher, *The History of Albany County, Wyoming to 1880* (Lusk, Wyoming, 1965); Larson, *History of Wyoming,* pp. 195–99.

looked, Cheyenne settlers saw their future as assured. If the dream of being a railroad center faded, there would be the income as a cattle-raising junction, or, if that foundered, irrigation would ensure survival as a farming town. Nothing happened to dispel this confidence in the 1870s but little occurred to verify it, either.[29]

Forty miles to the west in Laramie, the "Gem City of the Plains," an aggressive rival to Cheyenne anticipated its eventual triumph as the preeminent town of the booming territory. The Laramie *Daily Sentinel* warned in 1871 that "if Cheyenne supposes her few dilapidated rum holes and large number of houses of ill-fame (the only thing she has left to boast of) constitute an attraction by which she can continue to govern, control and discommode the whole Territory for all time to come, she'll soon find out her mistake." Its acquisition of the rolling mill in 1875 was a victory over Cheyenne and over the Uinta County metropolis, Evanston, in the contest for economic supremacy. Despite these exertions, Laramie could barely keep pace with its eastern rival, and its failure to have the capital moved from Cheyenne in 1871 relegated it to a permanent second place position.[30]

The most noteworthy fact about Wyoming's economic position, symbolized in the feuding of its towns, was the territory's backwardness relative to the rest of the Rocky Mountain West. No other part of the arid region had such a glaring lack of an agricultural base; even the desert state of Nevada had five times as many people engaged in crop agriculture as Wyoming in 1870. Since a strong agricultural

29. *Leader*, June 10, 1870, Dec. 22, 1870, Apr. 28, 1871.

30. Laramie *Daily Sentinel*, Aug. 1, 1871; Larson, *History of Wyoming*, p. 111.

sector was necessary for a viable society or stable economy, the new territory began under crushing handicaps. Wyoming's dependence on the fortunes of the Union Pacific produced a similar imbalance in its economy which was avoided by its western neighbors. Most important, the territory in 1870 had little prospect of attaining an economic system not based on moderate returns from one or two extractive industries. Cattle and oil would, in the years ahead, each supply a portion of the diversity required to evoke a degree of stability; but Wyoming in the 1870s and afterward would never enjoy the heady effects of the bonanzas which would shape the political experiences of Nevada, California, Colorado, and Montana.[31]

Happily, Wyoming, like so much of the American West, did not have to rely solely on the personal resources of its citizens. The federal government stood ready, if solicited, to dispense its bounty through a variety of subsidizing devices. This process of federal support, a neglected feature of western economic development, kept Wyoming in a state of quasi-solvency during its first decade. Protection from hostile Indians, who used northern Wyoming as a hunting ground and battlefield, necessitated large numbers of troops who, in addition to their military duties, had the pleasant habit of spending pay day in the local town adjacent to their post. Fort D. A. Russell, on the outskirts of Cheyenne, drew on merchants for supplies and repairs, and this expenditure enabled army and civilians to resolve the periodic incidents of violence caused by bored soldiers on sprees. From 1870 to 1880, Wyoming gained from the presence of more than a thousand soldiers; they represented twenty-three percent of the territory's labor force, compared with a western average

31. Arrington, *Changing Economic Structure,* p. 41.

of four percent and a national figure of two-tenths of one percent.[32]

Less profitable than the army, the territorial government added twenty-five or thirty thousand dollars a year in salaries and allowances to the Wyoming economy. Its importance lay not so much in its direct monetary contributions to the financial health of the territory as in its ability to speed the allocation of government funds to the waiting settlers. From the territorial governor and delegate to the lowest postmaster in an obscure hamlet, federal officers could obtain appropriations and contracts for public buildings, bridges, and land surveys. The amount fluctuated, depending on the skill of the politicians involved, but their political survival depended on the continued existence and growth of federal spending. As the first Republican territorial platform asserted in 1869, "the Territory of Wyoming are entitled to liberal aid and appropriations from the general Government to assist in internal improvements, in building railroads and public buildings, and in establishing and supporting schools and other works of general public interest."[33]

The economic significance of federal money placed the Wyoming territorial government in a position of crucial importance. As the embodiment of the national government in the territory, the federal officers administered the flow of appropriations and, through reports to their superiors, defined the economic priorities of Wyoming. The process by which this was accomplished inevitably became involved with politics, if only because territorial officials operated within a system which had been conceived as an exercise in self-government, but which had been transformed over the

32. Ibid.

33. *Leader,* Aug. 18, 1869; Earl Pomeroy, *The Territories and the United States, 1861–1890* (Philadelphia, 1947), pp. 34–35.

years into a superb system of political reward and patronage.

When Wyoming was organized, the territorial system had slipped into a period of relative quiet and stability. The divisive issues of slavery and popular sovereignty, which at one time placed the territories at the center of national attention, had been settled by the Civil War. Where territorial policy had once prompted reflections on the nature and direction of American democracy, it now elicited calculations of the political effect of various appointments. Leaders in Congress and the White House viewed the West as a convenient dumping ground for obstreperous hacks or a suitable reward for deserving second-raters. As the Wyoming experience indicates, Congress in the 1860s drew the boundaries of western territories more in response to political ambitions and pressures than to the geographic and economic future of the region.[34]

This state of affairs, which persisted from 1861 to 1890, had not been the aim of the framers of the territorial system. The Northwest Ordinance of 1787 established a three-step process from congressional control to local sovereignty by which American colonial dependencies could attain full membership in the Union. Until the eve of the Civil War, the territories managed to achieve the proper level of population and economic development to qualify them for statehood with reasonable speed. The nine far western territories, however, labored under the difficulties of hostile Indians, aridity, distance, and economic deprivation which combined to lull an apathetic Congress into an acceptance of a prolonged territorial status for the West.[35]

Earl Pomeroy has shown that the territorial system in this

34. Pomeroy, *Territories,* pp. 62–79.
35. Ibid., pp. 1–5; Howard R. Lamar, *Dakota Territory, 1861–1889* (New Haven, 1956), pp. 1–27.

period blended administrative neglect, sporadic congressional supervision (which was no less absolute for being occasional), and an abiding concern for political consequences by all involved. To Wyoming residents, the apparatus of federal control consisted of a territorial governor, secretary, and three judges of the supreme court. Additional officers, including a surveyor general, land office receivers and registers, a United States marshal and district attorney, as well as a host of postmasters, completed the roster.[36]

Each post had its special attractions. With the approval of the territorial legislature, a governor could dispense a number of patronage plums, including territorial treasurer, auditor, and penitentiary commissioners. His annual report kept Washington aware of local conditions, he had to approve all acts of the legislature, and for the first two years of Wyoming's existence, he served as superintendent of Indian affairs. In general, the powers of the office were vague and could expand under forceful management, but most Wyoming governors found more prestige than substance in their responsibilities.[37]

The territorial secretary would have been no more than a glorified clerk if he had not had the federal printing to allocate. Even this could not, in most cases, make him anything other than a potential governor biding his time. Surveyor generals, registers, and receivers supervised the distribution and sale of public lands. If a land office appointee came West with the resolve to be honest and conscientious, his determination usually wilted in the face of an inadequate salary

36. Pomeroy, *Territories,* pp. 94–108.

37. Ibid., pp. 22–24; Kenneth Nelson Owens, "Frontier Governors: A Study of the Territorial Executives in the History of Washington, Idaho, Montana, Wyoming, and Dakota Territories," Ph.D. thesis, University of Minnesota, 1959.

and innumerable chances for private enrichment. Justice was the province of three judges who acted together as a supreme court and separately as district courts. They were aided, not always effectively, by a district attorney and a marshal. The amount of litigation varied, but the conditions under which the justices labored hardly inspired disinterested deliberation. Immense districts, petty cases, and the perennial lack of sufficient recompense limited the number of able jurists who ventured to the frontier.[38]

In any case, politics, not merit, determined who would hold offices in the West. Since the criteria for patronage fluctuated with the national administration in office or the benefactor seeking favors, it is impossible to establish hard and fast rules about the selection process. Defeated candidates for state offices made good territorial candidates, as did ambitious young men seeking a start in an area not crowded with influential politicians. By and large, however, easterners saw the West as an area to be exploited, either economically or politically, and they regarded their federal tenure as temporary—to be prolonged only if circumstances, usually political success, warranted it.

Westerners, on the other hand, saw the territorial system as the political means by which the economic development of their region could be hastened. Imbued with the American faith in the imminence of a bonanza in the West, settlers clamored for federal subsidies which would enable their economy to pass quickly from the primitive to the self-sustaining stage. This type of promotional activity, as Carter Goodrich has demonstrated, was a traditional function of national and state governments in the nineteenth century, and the West, in its quest for help, extended precedents

38. Pomeroy, *Territories,* pp. 51–61.

which had begun at least with the Whigs in the Jacksonian era.[39]

At no time, however, did the advocates of national promotion contemplate a permanent system of subsidy and incentive. Prolonged infusion of governmental monies would not be necessary; after a short period, the natural energies of private enterprise would produce a balanced and independent economy. The premises of this faith had not been severely tested in the East where an abundance of resources, a sizable population, and an efficient transportation network made economic self-sufficiency an attainable goal.

In the Wyoming context of scarcity and underdevelopment, federal funds could not long remain a temporary promotional expedient. They emerged as an essential part of the economic health of the territory. Political institutions developed to accommodate an ad hoc system of pump-priming now had to cope with the necessity of a perennial dependence on government money. In short, political behavior in Wyoming, as in other states of the arid West, had to be transformed into a system for the persistent and orderly acquisition of federal appropriations.

This shift in attitudes was not easily or quickly made, and it is scarcely surprising to see that Wyoming politics in the 1870s continued to operate on premises and assumptions more suited to the humid East. Settlers and federal officers contended over the traditional issues—capital location, sectionalism, and logrolling—because these seemed to be the indispensable preludes to the wealth and stability which would follow in the wake of the boom. The pervasive con-

39. Carter Goodrich, "American Development Policy: The Case of Internal Improvements," *Journal of Economic History, 16* (1956), 449–60; Robert A. Lively, "The American System: A Review Article," *Business History Review, 29* (1955), 81–96.

servatism of the westerner, expressed in his fidelity to eastern political patterns and institutions, was no more than the predictable response to a situation in which adherence to established norms would result in the readiest access to the federal largesse which could, so the westerners believed, spark the bonanza.

Earl Pomeroy's judgment that territorial politics "figured as a channel in the large process of acculturation, transporting American ways from East to West,"[40] is perfectly correct, but it does not reveal why westerners chose so readily to be imitative and repetitive. The Wyoming experience suggests that this policy arose from a recognition that western economic needs dictated an allegiance to eastern political patterns. Inevitably, this imitation defeated the very goals it was intended to serve. On the one hand, the requirement of maintaining good relations with the national party degenerated into a politics of personality in which ambitious and sometimes unscrupulous men worked to blacken the reputations of their rivals and to glorify their own actions. At the same time, economic conditions called forth a network of shifting temporary alliances among politicians and businessmen to secure specific federal appropriations for the promotion of railroads, mining companies, irrigation works, and other local enterprises. The two major parties in Wyoming, especially the Republicans, were beset in the 1870s by a constant and relentless struggle for supremacy among internal factions bent on achieving a share of the limited economic bounty of the territory.

This instability made an orderly manipulation of the appropriation machinery impossible; unity, cohesion, and

40. Earl Pomeroy, "Toward a Reorientation of Western History: Continuity and Environment," *Mississippi Valley Historical Review,* *41* (1955), 583.

strength were not present in Wyoming politics, and the territory suffered accordingly in its relations with the federal government. Strong leadership or economic growth could have broken this vicious circle, but Wyoming, in its formative era, had to contend with the twin burdens of having the products of the territorial system as its political masters and the drab reality of backwardness as its economic heritage.

CHAPTER TWO. THE CAMPBELL ERA, 1869–1875

 Wyoming historian has asserted that "there can be no question about the superior competence" of the first group of territorial officers "as a whole."[1] Certainly, their records in private life and the Civil War qualified some of them for the positions to which President Grant appointed them. An assessment of the quality of the federal officials sent to Wyoming is, to a large degree, beside the point. As average products of the American political system, they faced unique problems which the traditional techniques of partisan behavior complicated rather than solved. In the context of Wyoming's economic backwardness, political supremacy came to depend on the maintenance of close ties with the appointing power in Washington. Yet from 1869 to 1875 President Grant exercised his patronage power whimsically and indecisively. This policy created an atmosphere of uncertainty which encouraged devious intrigues and treachery.

The first territorial governor of Wyoming, John A. Campbell, took office at the age of thirty-three, after a brief career as a printer and journalist in Cleveland and distinguished service in the Union Army. As a member of the staff of General J. M. Schofield, he had taken part in the Reconstruction of Virginia and had been assistant secretary of war in 1868–69. His work brought him to President Grant's attention, and he was given the Wyoming appointment on April 3, 1869, A short, handsome man with a long beard, Campbell had a well-developed sense of his own importance. He

1. Larson, *History of Wyoming*, p. 70.

labored conscientiously at his duties, was a confirmed Republican partisan, and sought to produce the kind of territorial administration that would endear him to Washington. Unhappily, the governor also possessed an endless capacity for making or finding enemies, and Campbell became the object of acrimonious controversy among Wyoming politicians and officeholders within a year of his arrival in the territory.[2]

The new secretary, Edward M. Lee, and the United States marshal, Church Howe, were less able than the governor. Lee was a professional Republican orator and temperance lecturer from Connecticut. Once he settled in Wyoming, he developed ambitions to become a territorial delegate and a taste for Cheyenne low life. Howe, a Nebraska politician, was, according to William W. Corlett, "the most indefatigable intriguer that I ever knew in my life." The three judges, William T. Jones, John H. Howe, and John W. Kingman, as well as the U.S. attorney, Joseph M. Carey, had been recommended to Grant because of youthful eagerness or experience in the Union Army.[3]

Complete organization of Wyoming Territory required the election of a delegate and legislature in the fall of 1869. In a series of proclamations, Governor Campbell drew up judicial districts on May 19, apportioned the legislature on August 3, and set September 2, 1869, as election day. This

2. Erwin, *Wyoming Historical Blue Book*, p. 166; John A. Campbell, "Diary, 1869–1875," *Annals of Wyoming, 10* (1938), 5–11, 59–78, 120–43, 155–85; J. Thomas Gregory to Andrew Jackson Faulk, Apr. 4, 1869, Faulk Papers.

3. Erwin, *Wyoming Historical Blue Book*, pp. 171, 190, 1311; Edward M. Lee to Hamilton Fish, Mar. 27, 1869, Appointment Files, Department of State, NA, RG59; William W. Corlett Dictation, Bancroft Library, University of California.

flurry of public action was matched by private machinations of territorial officers intent on creating political careers for themselves in Wyoming. Marshal Howe sought to win Republican support for his delegate candidacy by purchasing newspapers and making expansive promises of future investments in the event of his election. Governor Campbell reacted angrily to this maneuver; the executive had lost patience with the marshal when Howe's late arrival in Wyoming delayed the taking of the territorial census. The governor also vetoed the office-seeking plans of Secretary Lee and territorial Judge John Howe. "Told them," Campbell remarked in his diary on June 9, 1869, "that I was in favor of Jack Casement, and after him of some of the men from the territory."[4]

As the summer progressed, two local candidates joined the marshal in the race for the Republican delegate nomination. Three ballots at the territorial convention on August 12, 1869, ended Marshal Howe's hopes and resulted in the selection of William W. Corlett of Cheyenne as the party's standard-bearer. A resident of Wyoming since 1867, Corlett had gone West for his health and had built up a flourishing law practice during his stay. The Democrats countered two days later in their convention at Rawlins Springs by picking Stephen F. Nuckolls, a Cheyenne merchant, as their choice.[5]

A bitter campaign ensued in which the Republicans waved the bloody shirt and reminded voters that a radical Congress would hardly be willing to give appropriations to a Democrat. Charges of slaveholding were also raised against Nuckolls. Democratic speakers concentrated on the large German population in Cheyenne among the railroad work-

4. Erwin, *Wyoming Historical Blue Book*, pp. 160–61; *Leader,* July 24 and 29, 1869; Campbell, "Diary," p. 11.
5. *Leader,* July 29, 1869, Aug. 14 and 17, 1869.

ers and warned of the dangers of temperance and Negro suffrage. Wyoming legend has also credited the Democratic Party with vote buying and bribery. These tactics caused the Republicans to be "beaten at election," as Campbell noted in his diary. Nuckolls carried every county, trounced Corlett by 3,301 votes to 1,963, and swept in a unanimously Democratic legislature. Wyoming had fallen into the pattern noticed two years earlier by a western traveler: "Our new Territories in their early history show wonderful uniformity. At its first election each invariably votes the democratic ticket."[6]

The legislative assembly began its session on Oct. 12, 1869, and enacted a number of useful laws, including mining regulations, designation of the capital at Cheyenne, and selection of Laramie as the site for a penitentiary. The solons demonstrated their independence of the governor by passing, over the executive's veto, laws which licensed gambling and forbade miscegenation. Several acts attacked the interest of the Union Pacific, but Congress repealed them at the railroad's behest in the spring of 1870. The legislature also sought to whittle down the governor's power by appointing fifty-seven county officials, but a court test upheld Campbell's sole prerogative in the selection of officers.[7]

Wyoming's first legislature, even with its challenge to the governor and railroad, would have won scant attention if it had not passed a woman suffrage act. This bill, as Professor T. A. Larson has shown, was the creation of William H. Bright, president of the upper house, a Union Army veteran

6. *Leader,* Aug. 23, 1869; Campbell, "Diary," p. 64; Albert D. Richardson, *Beyond the Mississippi* (Hartford, 1867), p. 502, quoted in Pomeroy, "Toward a Reorientation of Western History," p. 587, n. 20.
7. Larson, *History of Wyoming,* pp. 74–77; Territorial Papers, Wyoming, United States Senate, NA, RG46.

and saloon owner. While historians have ascribed a multitude of motives to the legislators in enacting the bill, three factors persuaded the lawmakers to act. Woman suffrage would help to publicize the territory in the East, the grateful ladies might be induced to back the Democrats at the polls, and the Republican Party, the political champion of Negro suffrage, would be embarrassed by the absurdity of giving the vote to women. The first objective was achieved in the publicity following the selection of female justices of the peace and jurors, but political effects at the time and later were relatively slight.[8]

For Governor Campbell, the effect of this burst of legislative independence compounded the setback he had suffered in the election. Sent by Grant to make Wyoming a staunchly Republican territory, Campbell had to live with a Democratic delegate to Congress and an anti-Negro and seemingly anti-railroad legislature. His troubles had hardly begun, and Wyoming Territory soon impressed itself on the Grant administration as a persistent and annoying minor problem.

Secretary Lee and Marshal Howe now turned their formidable political ambitions to the delegate election in the fall of 1870. Howe effected an alliance with the editor of the *Cheyenne Leader* and Lee, to advance his own cause, decided to start a rival paper in Cheyenne. The secretary imported his brother-in-law, S. Allan Bristol, from Colorado to edit the *Wyoming Tribune*, and to keep it afloat, he awarded the paper the territorial printing. The outraged Howe decided that Lee must pay for his deception. Soon letters deluged the State Department attacking Lee as a drunkard and a consort of prostitutes, including one "Circassian Girl." The missives described his Wyoming career

8. Larson, *History of Wyoming,* pp. 78–94.

27

as "a series of continued drunken revelries and licentious and shameful debaucheries, in open and unblushing companionship with the lowest creatures of both sexes."[9]

Lee counterattacked vigorously and denied all the charges; his statement declared "that he does not frequent saloons or houses of evil repute of any class whatever and that he does not associate with persons of bad reputation." His replies did not satisfy President Grant, and he was removed. Lee's friends sought to have Howe suffer the same fate, and they informed the Justice Department that the marshal had practiced law while in office and that he had misused federal monies. Howe acknowledged his law business but quickly dropped it and, by speedy disavowals of other wrongdoings managed to retain his job. The skirmish divided the territorial Republicans into two camps, each determined to have one of its members elected as delegate; the Lee forces found themselves labeled as pro-Campbell, and the Howe adherents stood against the executive.[10]

Governor Campbell's administration did not gain luster from the fight, and other events in the spring of 1870 hurt its standing even more. In late 1869, an enterprising band of adventurers had begun to organize an expedition to settle

9. W. A. Buckingham to Hamilton Fish, Dec. 8, 1869, Church Howe to U. S. Grant, Jan. 20, 1870, Nathan A. Baker to U. S. Grant, Jan. 29, 1870, Appointment Files, Department of State, NA, RG59; *Leader,* Nov. 23, 1869, Feb. 19, 1870.

10. Statement of E. M. Lee, Feb. 18, 1870, Appointment Files, Department of State, NA, RG59; Lee et al. to Ebenezer R. Hoar, Feb., 26, 1870, E. P. Johnson to Hoar, Apr. 12, 1870, Church Howe to Benjamin F. Butler, Apr. 12, 1870, Wyoming Appointment Papers, Justice Department, NA, RG60; Howe to U. S. Grant, Mar. 10, 1870, Letters Received, Attorney General, Justice Department, NA, RG60; Hoar to Howe, Apr. 4, 1870, Attorney General's Instruction Book, A–2, Justice Department, NA, RG60.

and exploit the Big Horn country of the territory. Intrigued by the stories of gold and heedless of the Indian menace, the Big Horn expedition confidently expected government support for its venture. President Grant, beset with the vexing Sioux problem, did not regard with favor the prospects of a war started by white incursions into Indian land. A long, complex, and arid controversy finally produced the collapse and disbanding of the Big Horn Association after it had been allowed to go north but had found no gold. Wyoming Territory and, by implication, its governor had blundered into a delicate area of federal policy, risked an Indian conflict for private gain, and embarrassed the Grant administration. The obscure territory was beginning to acquire a reputation.[11]

Matters did not improve in May 1870 when a suit against the Union Pacific came before Judge John H. Howe in Cheyenne. The case, brought by a contractor, James W. Davis, asked an award of $600,000 from the trustees of the UP as the amount due him for work on the transcontinental line. Judge Howe required the railroad to put up security for the Davis claim in case a judgment was rendered in his favor. To the astonishment of the railroad attorneys, the judge refused to accept the bond signed by the Union Pacific directors and financiers because they did not live in Wyoming or own property there. The judge proposed, instead, to appoint a receiver.[12]

11. Charles Lindsay, *The Big Horn Basin* (Lincoln, Nebraska, 1930), pp. 74–88; James C. Olson, *Red Cloud and the Sioux Problem* (Lincoln, Nebraska, 1965), pp. 91–95; Gilbert A. Stelter, "The City and Westward Expansion: Cheyenne's Big Horn Expedition of 1870," paper delivered at 1966 meeting of Western History Association.

12. Oakes Ames to Grenville M. Dodge, Apr. 13, 1870, A. J. Poppleton to Dodge, Apr. 14 and May 3, 1870, Box 160, Grenville M. Dodge

The Union Pacific management, from Oakes Ames to Grenville M. Dodge, reacted with irate protests. Ames called Howe's action "an outrage that ought not to be submitted to." The Davis claim was spurious, the line had more than enough assets, and the appointment of a receiver would only encourage other suits by even less scrupulous men than Davis. "If this is submitted to," Ames continued, "any thief or Swindler that swears the Co. owe him anything or that says we have or are wasting our property can have a receiver appointed and charge a commission on the value of the road."[13]

Behind these complaints one can detect apprehension about an examination by a receiver of the Union Pacific's financing and operation. Whatever the cause of railroad outrage, it soon expressed itself in a concentrated offensive against Judge Howe and his ruling. The judge, perhaps zealous, perhaps bought by Davis, learned, in the words of a UP spokesman, that "There is a very short & swift retribution here for men who deviate from the paths of rectitude." Railroad attorneys descended on Cheyenne, the Justice Department outlined to other Wyoming judges the government's desire to see the road kept running, and Howe himself found his own removal imminent.[14]

Within two weeks, Howe allowed the Davis case to proceed without benefit of a receiver, and Oakes Ames was

Papers, Iowa State Department of History and Archives; Robert W. Fogel, *The Union Pacific Railroad: A Case in Premature Enterprise* (Baltimore, 1960), pp. 61–62.

13. Oakes Ames to Dodge, May 4, and 8, 1870, Box 160, Dodge Papers.

14. William E. Chandler to Dodge, May 18, 1870, U. H. Painter to Dodge, May 18 and 24, 1870, Oakes Ames to Dodge, May 21, 1870, Box 160, Dodge Papers.

"gratified that the Wyoming Courts have come to their senses." The railroad now believed that maintenance of this sanity required direct intervention in the 1870 delegate election. The unhappy actions of the legislature and the Davis imbroglio had been the result of lax supervision by the Union Pacific. Circumstances demanded a docile delegate. When informed of the railroad's intention to "assist us in our election for delegate to Congress provided the Republicans will nominate a man selected by the officers of the RR," Governor Campbell told General Dodge of his disbelief that "such can be the case, and trust we can look to you for support for our nominee no matter who he may be— provided he is otherwise a good man and no enemy of the RR."[15]

Church Howe did not place any such qualifications on his loyalty to the railroad, and Union Pacific spokesmen soon told leading Republicans that the line "had determined to support Church Howe for delegate to Congress." Howe distributed railroad passes as evidence for his boast that his election had "all been fixed in Boston." Nevertheless, Governor Campbell fired off a vigorous protest to Dodge. "It is useless for us to nominate a man we cannot elect," he pointed out, adding that "The nomination of Church Howe would I believe result in splitting our party."[16] Three days later, the governor set forth the consequences of blatant UP interference:

The influence of the RR to be effective in our behalf should be used seemly and with the greatest discretion.

15. Oakes Ames to J. F. Wilson, May 26, 1870, John A. Campbell to Dodge, July 13, 1870, Box 160, Dodge Papers.
16. Joseph M. Carey to John A. Campbell, Aug. 29, 1870, Box 161, Campbell to Dodge, July 17, 1870, Box 17, Dodge Papers.

Any open display of passes and boasting of what the Co. is going to do will do us more harm than good. It will unite all who have any real or fancied grievance against the RR.

In William T. Jones, judge of the territorial supreme court, Campbell saw the ideal Republican candidate for delegate. An Indiana native and Union Army veteran, Jones had been an inconspicuous Campbell supporter and had avoided incidents like Judge Howe's involvement in the Davis case. The railroad, cool to all Wyoming judges, might have preferred the marshal as a nominee, but Campbell's persistent queries to General Dodge finally drove the UP into a position of grudging neutrality. This was all Campbell required. At the territorial convention at Laramie in August, the governor secured a telegram from the railroad which released all delegates from any previous obligations. The wire prompted Howe's withdrawal, and Jones won the nomination by acclamation.[17]

The clumsy action of the Union Pacific agents and their failure to disguise their support of Howe led General Dodge to complain to his superiors that "It is necessary for us sometimes to interfere in matters where we have great interests at stake, but it should be done in such a manner that our action should never be known."[18] That precept was followed so well in the future that few traces of similar railroad intrigues can be found over the course of the next two decades.

Campbell's efforts on behalf of Jones produced a united

17. Campbell to Dodge, July 20 and Aug. 20, 1870, Box 17, Campbell to Dodge, Sept. 3, 1870, Box 161, Dodge Papers; *Leader,* Aug. 26 and 27, 1870.

18. Dodge to Oakes Ames, July 27, 1870, Box 161, Dodge Papers.

Republican Party which looked forward with anticipation to the election. Democratic prospects were less bright. Their convention in Evanston selected John Wanless, a Colorado politician and sometime Wyoming resident, to oppose Jones. Cheyenne newspapers remarked that Wanless was the tool of schemers hoping to annex Wyoming and make Colorado a state. Dissident party members picked a Cheyenne saloonkeeper, T. D. (Luke) Murrin, to represent the territorial Democratic Party. With his opponents in disarray, Jones squeaked into office by a vote of 1,669 to Wanless' total of 1,440.[19]

The governor exulted at the "glorious news" of Jones's success, especially when eastern Republicans assured him that "if you have any Federal Office Holders out there who don't help you, we can hitch teams and send them kiting."[20] Campbell later received a similar endorsement from Dodge, to which the Wyoming executive replied that "if we are properly supported we can maintain the ascendancy we have gained with the honest kind of fighting."[21] The sweetness of Jones's election was, however, one of the few moments of political "ascendancy" that Campbell enjoyed during his residence in Wyoming. His attempts to remove his opponents and the ineptness of his supporters combined to fracture the Republican Party and initiate four years of intraparty bickering.

By the end of 1870 the two contending factions had taken on recognizable shapes. The delegate, the governor, the

19. *Leader,* Aug. 30, 1870; Erwin, *Wyoming Historical Blue Book,* p. 362.

20. Campbell, "Diary," p. 121; J. H. Platt to John A. Campbell, Sept. 15, 1870, John A. Campbell Papers, Wyoming State Historical Society.

21. Campbell to Dodge, Nov. 5, 1870, Box 17, Dodge Papers.

register and receiver of the Cheyenne land office, the editor of the Laramie *Daily Sentinel,* J. H. Hayford, and Judge Joseph M. Carey formed the nucleus of the Campbell Ring. On the other side were the editor of the *Cheyenne Leader,* the marshal, the new territorial secretary, Herman Glafcke, and Silas Reed, the surveyor general. Unlike the rings of New Mexico, Arizona, and Dakota, these groups do not seem to have included members from the Democratic Party, and their perennial feuding prevented each from successfully carrying on, in Howard Lamar's phrase, the "politics of development"[22] so typical of other territories. Instead, each faction regarded itself as the sole repository of Republican honesty and disinterested virtue and viewed its opponents as greedy, corrupt, ruthless, and traitorous.

The Campbell group had the upper hand in the winter of 1870–71, and they moved to eliminate the enemy leader, Marshal Howe. Petitions, charges, and protests poured into the Justice Department charging the marshal with opposition to incumbent federal officers, abuse of his trust, and betrayal of President Grant.[23] On May 15, 1871, Grant ordered Howe's ouster and, at Senator O. P. Morton's request, appointed a successor from Indiana. The new man arrived in Wyoming, looked over the feuding politicians and the economic prospects, and, Campbell reported, "left Cheyenne in the night on a cattle train." Howe wrote the President to ask for reinstatement, and Grant agreed: "Notify Church Howe that he is to continue as Marshall of Wyoming. If necessary reappoint him." The bewildered

22. Howard R. Lamar, "Carpetbaggers Full of Dreams: A Functional View of the Arizona Pioneer Politician," *Arizona and the West,* 7 (1965), 206.

23. William T. Jones to A. T. Akerman, Apr. 6, 1871, Wyoming Appointment Papers, Justice Department, NA, RG60.

Campbell could only respond with a hasty note which declared that Howe's retention "would be the greatest blow that could be given to the Republican party of the Territory."[24]

Howe, surprised and pleased at his good fortune, promised General Dodge that he would keep the peace and solicited help from the UP to silence the governor. "Rest assured General," he told Dodge, "*I shall stand squarely on the defensive* & do all in my power to prevent any further quarreling," but added his thought that "if Campbell was given to understand that this quarrel *must stop* he would pursue a different course." [25] Campbell did win one patronage victory when Grant endorsed two of his judicial appointments in October 1871. In other areas, however, the governor suffered reverses and defeats which wounded the Republicans and hurt his own prestige.[26]

The second territorial legislature numbered some Republicans among its members for the first time, but the Democrats still controlled both houses when the body convened at the Rollins House on 16th Street in November 1871. Democratic strategists, who blamed the ladies for the Republican victory in 1870, were intent on repeal of woman suffrage. A bill passed both houses, but its one-vote margin in the Coun-

24. Horace Porter to A. T. Akerman, May 15, 1871, U. S. Grant to Akerman, July 11, 1871, President's Chronological Files, Justice Department, NA, RG60; O. P. Morton to Akerman, May 16, 1871, Robert M. Milroy to U. S. Grant, July 1, 1871, John A. Campbell to O. E. Babcock, July 4, 1871, Wyoming Appointment Papers, Justice Department, NA, RG60; Horace Porter to G. M. Dodge, July 12, 1871, Box 18, Dodge Papers.

25. Church Howe to Dodge, July 21, 1871, Box 18, Dodge Papers.

26. Campbell to B. H. Bristow, Sept. 23, 1871, Wyoming Appointment Papers, Justice Department, NA, RG60; Campbell to Dodge, Dec. 4, 1871, John A. Campbell Papers.

cil meant that a gubernatorial veto could kill the repeal movement. Since the governor had endorsed the experiment of woman suffrage in his message to the lawmakers, the Democrats knew that Campbell could not reverse himself but hoped he would let the bill become law without his signature. In return, the Democrats hinted at a private conference with Campbell, the governor's contingent fund would be set at $1,000. After some haggling, Campbell told his Democratic visitor that "my answer to his propositions would be indicated by my action on the woman suffrage bill." The governor vetoed the measure and thereby beat back the last important challenge to women's voting in the territorial period.[27]

Other issues took on a more regional and sectional tone. Throughout the summer, the Laramie *Daily Sentinel* boasted that the capital would be moved from Cheyenne; it doubted that Wyoming people were willing that "the Capital of the Territory should be kept in that dilapidated nest of deserted shanties away in the extreme corner of the Territory." Unfortunately, Evanston in Uinta County shared this goal, and the conflicting ambitions of the two aspiring towns produced a stalemate in the legislature which preserved the status quo. To add insult to defeat, Laramie County managed to shift its boundaries westward at the expense of Albany County. Laramie and Evanston retired to nurse their hurt feelings and plan for the next session.[28]

Campbell's regime received renewed assaults in November and December 1871 as the Howe forces concentrated their fire on Frank Wolcott, receiver of public monies in the land office in Cheyenne. Iron Mountain, a peak in the range

27. *Leader,* Nov. 18, 1871; "Memorandum," Nov. 30, 1871, Campbell Papers.
28. *Sentinel,* Aug. 1, and Dec. 11 and 21, 1871.

outside Laramie, seemed to offer rich supplies of ore which, to the expectant entrepreneurs of the 1870s, appeared a sound opportunity to realize Wyoming's industrial destiny. Governor Campbell, Surveyor General Reed, and other politician capitalists put aside their personal differences to organize the Cheyenne, Iron Mountain, and Pacific Railroad and introduced legislation in Congress to obtain federal land grants for the proposed road.[29]

Acting on the assumption that construction of the line would increase the value of the previously unoccupied Iron Mountain area, Wolcott and his associates went to the mountain, made unauthorized surveys, and then used land warrants in the form of "Sioux Indian scrip" to obtain title to the land. Marshal Howe informed Washington of this claim jumping and noted that Wolcott had done all this while a federal officer. The receiver did not help his own cause when he was fined ten dollars for disturbing the peace, using indecent language, and committing assault and battery at a Christmas party in Cheyenne. His opponents lost no time in transmitting news of this performance to Washington, where the charges convinced the Department of the Interior that Wolcott would have to be dismissed. Bureaucratic delay, however, kept Wolcott in office through the spring of 1872.[30]

A possible scandal in the award of contracts for the territorial penitentiary at Laramie began to emerge in the fall of

29. Osgood, *The Day of the Cattleman,* p. 69.

30. J. R. Whitehead to Columbus Delano, Nov. 29, 1871, J. W. Kingman to Silas Reed, Dec. 20, 1871, statement by Frank Wolcott, Apr. 9, 1872, Appointment Papers, Cheyenne Land Office, Interior Department, NA, RG48; *Leader,* Dec. 22, 1871; Columbus Delano to U. S. Grant, May 28, 1872, Wyoming Appointment Papers, Justice Department, NA, RG60.

1871. On the recommendation of the Campbell group, a Laramie man had been chosen to oversee the construction of the structure, and he in turn had bestowed the contracts on John W. Donnellan, the territorial treasurer and a confederate of Wolcott's in the Iron Mountain scandal. Howe sent charges of fraud and collusion to Washington, and in March 1872 a government inspector concluded that the contracts should be voided. The inspector added that neither the superintendent nor the contractor had the necessary experience to build the prison.[31]

By the spring of 1872, therefore, Governor Campbell's position had deteriorated. Delegate Jones had not been able to obtain any meaningful legislation from Congress, and it was becoming apparent that he lacked the qualities necessary for successful tapping of the pork barrel. The Wolcott and penitentiary affairs had crippled the Republican cause, while the legislature had been indecisive. In spite of the scars from the abortive attempt to remove Marshal Howe, the Campbell forces now decided that his dismissal was imperative if Jones were to have any hope of victory in the 1872 delegate canvass.

The marshal traveled east in April 1872, leaving his office and accounts in disarray. This lapse supplied his enemies with the opportunity they sought. Delegate Jones wrote the attorney general that Howe had overstayed his leave of absence, had mismanaged his accounts, and had made no provision for the operation of the office while he was away. As a result, the legal business of Wyoming had come to a halt. The marshal was removed, and in a startling action, Frank

31. *Leader*, Nov. 6, 1871; Report of Q. A. Pearson, Apr. 19, 1872, Wyoming Territorial Papers, Interior Department, NA, RG48; George Thomson, "The History of Penal Institutions in the Rocky Mountain West, 1846–1900," Ph.D. thesis, University of Colorado, 1965.

Wolcott, the discredited receiver, was named to take his place. Anti-Campbell Republicans reacted with "surprise" and "amazement" to this "sad blow to our party organization."[32]

The dismissal of Howe, who returned to his native Nebraska, set in motion a series of events which cost the Republicans the election in 1872. The forces opposing the governor began an effort to win bipartisan support for a replacement for Jones as delegate. Their "people's movement" had only local application, but it immersed the Wyoming politicians in the developing struggle within the national Republican Party. Both groups pledged their loyalty to the Grant administration and endorsed his renomination. Yet the choice of the title "people's movement" gave the Campbell faction the chance to claim that their enemies were followers of Horace Greeley and the Liberal Republican reformers. This tactic eventually forced the anti-Campbell men back into the Republican ranks, but not before the party was subjected to severe strains.[33]

A rally in Cheyenne on June 10, 1872, found the pro-Howe forces in control, and they adopted resolutions attacking Wolcott's appointment. Campbell's newspaper voice, the Laramie *Sentinel*, struck back, but the "people's" men continued their program of meetings. They even had a potential candidate for delegate in Surveyor General Silas Reed, whose efficient promotional activities had won him popular acclaim. Reed told his wife that his electoral attractions had induced the Democrats to approach him about

32. W. T. Jones to George H. Williams, May 18, 1872, Silas Reed to Columbus Delano, May 28, 1872, Herman Glafcke to Delano, May 28, 1872, Wyoming Appointment Papers, Justice Department, NA, RG60.
33. Silas Reed to Columbus Delano, June 13, 1872, Wyoming Appointment Papers, Justice Department, NA, RG60.

arranging a fusion ticket for the fall canvass. Democratic sources, on the other hand, attributed the initiative to the surveyor general; their rejection of Reed's overture, they claimed, stemmed from their confidence that they could defeat Jones, and no matter whom they selected from their ranks, he could not "do less than Jones has done for the Territory." Whatever the cause, the attempt to put together a bipartisan ticket collapsed.[34]

The surveyor general seems to have been satisfied with this result. A fervent Grant supporter, Reed was not prepared to repudiate the national administration to achieve the defeat of Campbell. The "people's movement" ultimately disintegrated over the question of how to hurt Campbell without offending the President. Increasing bitterness between Grant and Greeley, coupled with the prospect of the President's reelection, made it advisable for all Republicans to maintain party regularity. By July 24, the *Leader* warned Republicans against the "people's movement" and pointed out that fusion with the Democrats would mean a victory for them and ruin for the Republican Party. Renewed harmony, at least on the surface, enabled Jones to win renomination over weak opposition in a relatively placid convention at Green River on August 14.[35]

As the threat of Republican dissension receded, Governor Campbell once again found evidence of railroad interference in Wyoming politics. On July 21, 1872, he wrote a com-

34. *Leader*, June 11, 1872; Silas Reed to Henrietta Reed, June 8, 10, 11, and 13, 1872, Silas Reed Papers, Yale Western Americana Collection; Gibson Clark to John Hunton, June 9, 1872, Gibson Clark Letters, Wyoming State Historical Society.

35. *Leader*, July 24 and 31, 1872. In the spring of 1872, Herman Glafcke, the territorial secretary, became the owner of the *Leader*, and operated it in the interest of the anti-Campbell group.

pany official to complain that railroad agents were being used on behalf of the line's Wyoming attorney, W. R. Steele, a Democrat who was a former law partner of Marshal Howe and a Civil War veteran. Campbell conceded that the Union Pacific did not have to support the Republicans on every occasion, "but I do demand as a right that the Republicans of this Territory be permitted to manage their own affairs without this absurd interference on the part of Railroad officials who know nothing whatever concerning the political issues in this Territory and are using the influence of their positions to destroy the power which gave them any position whatever."[36]

Despite Campbell's charges, the railroad experienced difficulty in making Steele the Democratic nominee. The scent of victory had intoxicated the Democrats and produced two rivals to Steele. The resulting deadlock was not broken until the one hundred and seventh ballot, when Steele finally triumphed.[37] Steele's connection with the Union Pacific seemed to offer an inviting issue for the Republicans, but orators and editors quickly perceived the dangers in the tactic and drew back. The Democrat's position was further enhanced when the delegate candidate of the remnants of the "people's movement" withdrew in favor of Steele. Party campaigners capitalized on Jones's lack of legislative achievement and this, with railroad help, was enough. On September 3, 1872, Steele beat Jones by 1,933 to 1,662 votes. The Campbell camp ascribed the defeat to a persistent Democratic majority in Wyoming, railroad assistance for Steele, and

36. John A. Campbell to George Pullman, July 21, 1872, T. E. Sickels to Campbell, July 31, 1872, Campbell Papers; *Leader,* Aug. 13, 17, and 18, 1872.

37. *Leader,* Aug. 17, and 18, 1872.

the treason of the dissident wing of the party, led by Howe and Reed.[38]

The Union Pacific's intervention in the 1872 election underscores the difficulties which the line faced in translating its economic power into political effectiveness in Wyoming. Despite the railroad's endorsement of Steele, the one hundred and seven ballots required to secure his nomination and his narrow margin of victory in the general election indicated the political dangers of the railroad's staking its prestige on the fate of one faction in the territory's personality-oriented public life. Since neither party threatened any vital interest of the Union Pacific, it seems plausible to conclude that the company decided to keep its participation to a minimum in the absence of challenges to its favored position.

Elimination of the Howe-Reed element became the leading aim of Governor Campbell and his supporters over the next six months. Finally, in March 1873, President Grant removed the territorial secretary, Herman Glafcke, and Reed. The charges were based on an alleged participation in the anti-Grant "people's movement" and relied on newspaper clippings of campaign meetings at which Glafcke and Reed had supposedly been present. Reed, a friend of the Grant family, countered with denials and told the President that he had "cut down an old & *true* friend without a *real* cause." Glafcke made similar pleas and informed the chief executive that his loyalty was demonstrated by his son who, "born on the day of election in November 1868, carries the name of 'Grant' Glafcke."[39]

38. Erwin, *Wyoming Historical Blue Book,* p. 362.

39. G. W. Corey to U. S. Grant, Mar. 8, 1873, W. T. Jones to Grant, Mar. 15, 1873, Silas Reed to Grant, Mar. 19, 1873, Appointment Papers, Wyoming Surveyor General, Interior Department, NA, RG48; Her-

Reed's task, as his son-in-law remarked, was to find a way to "penetrate [Grant's] stolid brain which seems to have been aroused at the word Greeleyism and deaf to anything else." The surveyor general hurried to Washington and, after some difficulty in obtaining an appointment, managed to convince the President of his honesty and devotion. By June 1873, Reed was reinstated and vowed unrelenting warfare against the governor in language that Grant would surely find congenial. "I have therefore come here to take issue with this universally hated clique (in Wyoming)—and those who know me best and longest know that *I will fight it out on this line, even if it should take more than all summer.*"[40]

Reed's reappointment was symptomatic of President Grant's spasmodic response to political affairs in Wyoming. Impressed by the letters and petitions of one faction, Grant would remove their enemies from office and then, when the ousted group protested, he would return them to government service. His capriciousness encouraged perpetual confusion and uncertainty; the resulting tendency of all Wyoming politicians to keep their fences mended in Washington effectively diverted energies which might have been better spent governing the territory. Absence of a clear presidential policy toward western patronage helped to promote the conditions of disorder and drift which held back Wyoming in the Campbell era.

The first opportunity to strike at the Campbell clique

man Glafcke to Grant, Mar. 20, 1873, Appointment Papers, Wyoming Secretary, Interior Department, NA, RG48.

40. Nathan Anthony to Silas Reed, May 1, 1873, Reed Papers; Reed to U. S. Grant, May 28, 1873, Appointment Papers, Wyoming Surveyor General, Interior Department, NA, RG48.

came at the legislative elections in September. Reed argued that the governor's forces wanted to sit out the election in Cheyenne in order to produce a Democratic victory which could be blamed on the restoration of the surveyor general and the appointment of Glafcke as Cheyenne postmaster. To counter this, the Reed group nominated "our most popular anti-Campbell, anti-Ring Repub [licans] and began the Contest."[41] The Republicans eked out control of both houses by single votes, and the *Leader,* charging that Campbell had collaborated with the Democrats, said that "The late election may, therefore, be fairly claimed, throughout the Territory, as a triumph over this miserable, political clique, by the independent, manly voters of both parties." Silas Reed reported to the Secretary of the Interior that "With one or two exceptions the *whole* legislature was elected as anti-Campbell & the people are looking to it to pass a respectful resolution requesting the President to send them a Govr of more force & character."[42]

Reed tempered this forecast with the observation that the plan might be thwarted by the Campbell group. This gloomy prediction was borne out by the 1873 legislature which brought solace to neither the governor nor his foes. Campbell's adversaries hoped to force the ouster of the territorial auditor and editor of the Laramie *Sentinel,* J. H. Hayford, by investigating the conduct of his office. Hayford's reputation survived the inquiry, and when a successor declined to take the auditorship, Governor Campbell allowed Hayford to retain his post. The *Leader* swallowed this bitter pill reluctantly and chided "our very *smart*

41. Silas Reed to Columbus Delano, Sept. 6, 1873, Reed Papers.
42. *Leader,* Sept. 6, 1873; Silas Reed to Columbus Delano, Nov. 19, 1873, Appointment Papers, Wyoming Governor, Interior Department, NA, RG48.

young friends who have muddled things so beautifully in the last legislature."[43]

The remainder of the legislative session was marked by the passage of a bill creating a territorial militia and a commissioner of immigration to publicize Wyoming. These accomplishments were overshadowed by the comic opera spectacle of the "Rump" legislature of 1873. On the last day of the session, the Cheyenne representatives adjourned the Council before the other legislators had a chance to arrive and vote on a bill, passed by the House, shifting the capital from Cheyenne to Laramie. When the tardy lawmakers appeared, they declared themselves to be the legal council, deposed the elected officials of their body, and passed the capital bill. In the sarcastic words of the *Leader*, "the 'Rump' ... proceeded to business, and passed various 'rump' bills in a rump like manner; and *rump-ed* things through at a rumpid rate. They rump-ed the Territorial capital out of Cheyenne, 'over the hills and far away' to Laramie city; and then rumped the existence out of the 'Rump.' "[44] To the chagrin of the "Rump" members, Governor Campbell decided to avoid a nasty legal controversy and did not sign the bill.

Campbell's opponents renewed their offensive against him in early 1874 with petitions asking for the executive's dismissal "because he is odious to our people and does no good among us."[45] Confirmation of the governor's reappointment had been delayed until December 1873, when Congress met, but he had then succeeded in gaining another four-year term. During the spring of 1874, Campbell

43. *Leader*, Dec. 13 and 29, 1873.

44. *Leader*, Dec. 15 and 17, 1873.

45. Petition for the removal of Campbell, n.d., Appointment Papers, Wyoming Governor, Interior Department, NA, RG48.

strengthened his Wyoming ties by investing in a Laramie ranch and building a Cheyenne home. Full success as a territorial officer still eluded him; as long as a Democratic delegate served in Washington, Wyoming and its officers would not justify President Grant's faith in them.[46]

The delegate election of 1874 soon loomed as the crucial test for the governor and his enemies. If Campbell could secure a Republican candidate who could unseat Steele, he would win an unqualified claim on the President's favor. Failure, on the other hand, would be the signal for another round of partisan warfare within Republican ranks. More important, an electoral defeat would give the Reed-Glafcke faction potent evidence for their contention that Campbell had placed personal interests ahead of party concerns.

Delegate Steele would not be easily beaten. He had labored hard during his two years in office and in June 1874 capped his legislative career with the announcement of a $15,000 appropriation for a bridge across the Platte River. The Republicans did not have many candidates eager to oppose the Democratic railroad attorney; editor Glafcke of the *Leader* withdrew his name from consideration with the plea that his party select "an able, upright and consistent gentleman as a candidate." Governor Campbell believed he had just the man to meet these criteria and wrote in his diary on July 20, 1874, "Judge Carey returns from the West and agrees to run for Congress." Ten days later the Republican territorial convention ratified Campbell's choice but, to avoid opening old wounds, did not issue a formal platform.[47]

Joseph M. Carey had served as district attorney and terri-

46. Campbell to Orville E. Babcock, Nov. 26, 1873, Babcock to Campbell, Dec. 4, 1873, B. R. Cowen to Campbell, Dec. 25, 1873, Campbell Papers; Campbell "Diary," pp. 165–177.

47. Campbell, "Diary," p. 177; *Leader*, July 10 and 31, 1874; John

torial judge from 1869 to 1873 and had been identified with the Campbell group in the intrigues which marked those years. The Laramie *Sentinel* hailed Carey's nomination and, when the Democrats chose Steele to run again, complained of the delegate's railroad connections. The *Leader,* for its part, gave only the most belated endorsement to Carey's candidacy, and on election day Surveyor General Reed "Rec'd joyful news of Carey's Defeat." Steele had indeed triumphed with a doubled majority and carried every county.[48]

The *Leader* attributed the disaster to the usual cause—the Campbell Ring. But in the wake of Democratic success the Republican factions recessed their feuding during the rest of 1874.[49] Early the next year, a major source of political discord was removed from the Wyoming scene when on January 27, 1875, Governor Campbell received a letter from Secretary of State Hamilton Fish offering him a position as third assistant secretary of the State Department. Campbell put off immediate acceptance pending a trip to Washington, but when he arrived a chat with Grant persuaded him to accept the office. The news evoked anguish from the *Sentinel,* which wailed, "We shall lose our Governor, the best Governor any territory ever had." Judge Carey reviewed the executive's achievements in the Cheyenne *Daily News* on February 15, 1875, and remarked that "the people of the Territory regardless of politics sincerely regret that he finds it to his interest to leave Wyoming."[50]

D. McDermott, "Fort Laramie's Iron Bridge," *Annals of Wyoming, 34* (1962), 138–39.

48. Laramie *Daily Sentinel,* Aug. 7, 1874; Diary entry, Sept. 4, 1874, Reed Papers; Erwin, *Wyoming Historical Blue Book,* p. 363.

49. *Leader,* Sept. 5, 1874.

50. Campbell, "Diary," p. 184; *Sentinel,* Feb. 11, 1875; Cheyenne *Daily News,* Feb. 15, 1875.

47

Firm evidence for Campbell's motives in leaving Wyoming is not available, but it is hard to avoid the conclusion that repeated failures to achieve Republican electoral success, coupled with the vicious infighting among the territorial officers, made a State Department post attractive. Historians have suggested that Campbell was promoted to get him out of Wyoming, and it may well be that his successor, John M. Thayer of Nebraska, pushed Campbell's elevation to gain the governorship for himself.[51]

The Byzantine feuding of Campbell's administration abated over the next decade, although it did not disappear. Some legacies persisted from the Campbell years. Personalities ruled in place of parties, and factions formed around men, not issues. The major drawback of this situation was that it prevented the orderly acquisition of the federal subsidies so important to the economic health of Wyoming. Division at home meant failure in Washington, and Wyoming politicians began to appreciate the virtues of unity.

More important, the departure of Campbell coincided with an improvement in Wyoming's economic prospects. Gold in the Black Hills of Dakota and cattle on the prairies lifted the territory out of the doldrums and laid the basis for a more viable, if not self-supporting, economy. An era of relative political tranquillity, interrupted by an occasional partisan episode, began in 1875, to be ended only a decade later with the accession of Grover Cleveland to the presidency. In the meantime, modern Wyoming, the domain of the cattleman, the arena of the cowboy, began to emerge.

51. *News*, Feb. 16, 1875; *New York Tribune*, Feb. 10, 1875; Owens, "Frontier Governors," p. 135.

CHAPTER THREE. A DECADE OF TRANSITION, 1875-1885

HE political turbulence of the Campbell years precluded any sustained effort to deal with the unfavorable economic conditions which had hobbled Wyoming Territory since its organization. In many ways, however, the territory's prospects depended on events and circumstances which were beyond the control of any territorial government or group of federal officials. During the decade from 1875 to 1885, external forces removed most of the immediate impediments to progress. The Black Hills Gold Rush spurred the growth of the territorial economy, and the subsequent elimination of the Indian menace, the most important result of the gold rush for Wyoming, fostered the expansion of the range cattle industry. In neither case, unfortunately, did the bright hopes of an economic bonanza materialize. Wyoming benefited from the Black Hills rush only in its early stages, while the bonanza aspects of the cattle business disappeared after a few years of frenzied development.

The other ingredient of future prosperity, effective political leadership, also emerged during the ten years following Campbell's departure. In Joseph M. Carey and Francis E. Warren, the two most prominent resident politicians, Wyoming could claim two public-spirited citizens of recognized ability and impressive skill. Drawn from the ranks of old territorial settlers, Carey and Warren commanded an allegiance from Wyoming residents that was denied to transitory federal officers. By 1880 the shifting balance of power toward the local leaders, added to Wyoming's gains in economic stability, helped to give the movement for state-hood its initial impetus.

Until 1880, however, Wyoming continued to suffer from the effects of the appointment of territorial officers from the East. Governor John M. Thayer's administration was marred by the legacy of the Campbell-Glafcke feud, while his tenure ended because of a federal judge whose rulings outraged the residents of western Wyoming. Finally an unscrupulous territorial secretary in 1879–80 sought to use his office for illicit ends, and his ouster sparked another factional upheaval. Relatively insignificant in themselves, and connected by chronology only, these events combined to perpetuate a condition of political discord and to produce a pervasive distrust of federal officials.

John Milton Thayer took up the duties of the territorial governorship on March 1, 1875, determined to end the quarreling which Campbell had bequeathed to him. His western background made Thayer more receptive to the desire for the rapid development of the territory, and his vigorous espousal of the aims of settlers seeking removal of the Indians from northern Wyoming gave him wide popularity. More politically adept than Campbell, Thayer used his Washington connections, acquired while he was a senator from Nebraska in the late 1860s, and his negotiating talents to good advantage during his first year in Wyoming.[1]

On the political front Thayer indicated where his loyalties lay by staying with Glafcke during his first visit to Cheyenne. The optimism of Glafcke and Surveyor General Reed was soon dissipated when rumors began to circulate that Reed had been a party to a scandal involving the son

1. Earl G. Curtis, "John Milton Thayer," *Nebraska History*, 29 (1948), 55–68.

of Secretary of the Interior Columbus Delano. Accused of funneling the proceeds from surveying contracts to the young man, who had not done any work, Reed resigned under fire in the summer of 1875, and this revelation, when linked to other disclosures, prompted the secretary's own retirement in the autumn.[2]

The Thayer forces did win some victories, but they were short-lived. Marshal Wolcott was removed, but his replacement proved to be dishonest and clumsy, and Grant reinstated Wolcott over the protests of his enemies. The bitterness that followed sabotaged the Republican legislative tickets in September 1875, and the Democrats emerged with firm control of both houses. Thayer turned out to be a more deft executive than Campbell in his relations with the legislature, and the session passed with little excitement. An attempt to shift the capital to Evanston failed, and two new counties, Pease, later named Johnson, and Crook, were added.[3]

The final spasm of the feud between dissident Republican factions occurred early in 1876. Thayer and his friends sought a clean sweep of the judicial offices and the replacement of Carey and the two other justices by new men. They also wanted to obtain the ouster of Wolcott and the United

2. "Surveys in the Territory of Wyoming," *House Report*, No. 794, 44th Cong., 1st sess.; Allan Nevins, *Hamilton Fish* (New York, 1936), pp. 774–75; Silas Reed to Ulysses S. Grant, July 30, 1875, Appointment Papers, Wyoming Surveyor General, Interior Department, NA, RG48.

3. B. M. Brice to Edwards Pierrepont, June 2, 1875, Wyoming Appointment Papers, Justice Department, NA, RG60; U. S. Grant to Pierrepont, July 3, 1875, President's Chronological File, Justice Department, NA, RG60; Frank Wolcott to Pierrepont, Nov. 3, 1875, Wyoming Chronological File, Justice Department, NA, RG60; Larson, *History of Wyoming*, p. 129.

States Attorney. According to Thayer, these changes would bring peace to Wyoming. As he told the President, "You have been annoyed with the quarrels and squabbles here in Wyoming for years. I want to relieve you of them, and I am glad to be able to say that they are dying out. If the administration will take my advice in regard to appointments here, I am willing to be held responsible."[4]

Carey and the others counterattacked resolutely, and a standoff ensued. Wolcott and Carey lost their jobs, but the remaining officers escaped unscathed. A general relaxation of political tension followed this mixed result, caused in part by the exhaustion among the factions but also by the emergence of new concerns—the Indian question, the 1876 presidential election, and general territorial improvement. This amicable turn of events bore fruit in the 1876 delegate election when the Republicans turned W. R. Steele out of office. The Democrat's quest for a third term, his alleged connection with Indian frauds, and charges of collusion with Mormon settlers in western Wyoming joined to diminish Steele's once formidable appeal. At first it seemed as though the Republicans would squander their opportunity; their territorial convention at Rawlins in September pressed the nomination first on Stephen W. Downey of Laramie and then on William W. Corlett of Cheyenne, but both declined. A month of newspaper pressure convinced Corlett to accept the honor, and in October a second convention named him to oppose Steele. On November 7, 1876, Corlett unseated Steele by a vote of 3,864 to 2,760 and informed

4. Joseph M. Carey to Edwards Pierrepont, June 28, 1875, T. D. Abbot to Pierrepont, July 29, 1875, J. W. Kingman to Pierrepont, July 30, 1875, J. M. Thayer to U. S. Grant, Dec. 4, 1875 (the quotation is from this letter), J. M. Thayer and W. R. Steele to Grant, Jan. 18, 1876, Wyoming Appointment Papers, Justice Department, NA, RG6o.

his friends, "The result was a surprise to everybody and to no one more than myself."[5]

The political calm within Republican ranks which this victory produced lasted for nearly a year. Like the rest of the nation, Wyoming followed the Hayes-Tilden contest with fascination; the inauguration of the Republican in March 1877 left the customary order of things undisturbed. Hayes's appointment of Carl Schurz as secretary of the interior indicated that the practices of the Grant era would no longer be followed, but most Wyoming politicians looked for no drastic changes.

In July 1877 President Hayes decided to appoint a successor to Judge E. A. Thomas, whose term had expired in March. The fortunate candidate was William Ware Peck, a New York City lawyer and reportedly an old schoolmate of the President. Peck was assigned to the third judicial district, embracing the western counties of Uinta and Sweetwater, and he took up his duties in the month of his nomination. In a short time Judge Peck had the residents of Evanston demanding his removal. He administered his court with scrupulous care for the rules of law, required full records made for each case, and consumed large amounts of time in gathering relevant details in any trial. All this concern for procedure raised court costs, borne by the county, from $3,800 to $11,000. To one "Taxpayer," Peck was a judge whose "predilections" were "utterly in variance with our ideas of a pure, impartial administration of justice."[6]

5. W. W. Corlett to J. K. Moore, Nov. 16, 1876, J. K. Moore Collection, Wyoming State Historical Society; *Leader,* Sept. 17 and 20 and Oct. 1 and 15, 1876.

6. John M. Thayer to W. W. Corlett, Jan. 3, 1878, Wyoming

Peck's foes had two possible avenues of attack. His nomination had to be confirmed by the Senate in December, and Delegate Corlett, more responsive to his constituents than fearful of the President, could be counted on to use such influence as he possessed with the Judiciary Committee. At the same time, the 1877 legislature could help the cause with resolutions and memorials against the judge. Accordingly, the western Wyoming lawmakers drafted and passed a memorial opposing Peck's confirmation. Corlett sent the memorial on to George F. Edmunds with his opinion that "As the legislature thus speaks without a dissenting voice it seems to me the authorities here ought to hesitate before sending Judge Peck to Wyoming as a Judge, when he must necessarily be without usefulness to our people."⁷

The Senate disregarded the legislature's plea, and Peck was confirmed on December 14, 1877. In retaliation, the territorial assembly passed a redistricting bill which relegated Peck to the unorganized counties of Pease and Crook. This "sagebrushing" to an uninhabited area effectively exiled Peck from Uinta and Sweetwater and accomplished the goal of the irate citizens. Governor Thayer vetoed the bill as first passed, but a redrawn act won his approval. Thayer asserted to Corlett that there was no other course for him to take. "Before so decided and all but unanimous expression of the Legislature I did not feel called upon to express a dissent and signed the bill. If I had vetoed it, it was

---

Appointment Papers, Justice Department, NA, RG60; "Taxpayer," *Rocky Mountain Courier,* Nov. 29, 1877, William Ware Peck Nomination File, United States Senate, NA, RG46; T. A. Larson, "Exiling a Wyoming Judge," *Wyoming Law Journal, 10* (1956), 171–79.

7. W. W. Corlett to George F. Edmunds, Dec. 11, 1877, Peck Nomination File, United States Senate, NA, RG46.

evident it would have passed over my head by the same vote."[8]

Cheyenne businessman Francis E. Warren was skeptical of this defense of Thayer's action. He believed that the governor had been anxious to have a bill passed allowing the executive to sit on the board of penitentiary commissioners. Warren charged that the Democrats had held up action on this measure and threatened the governor with ouster if he did not sign the anti-Peck bill. The combination of these two actions, Warren maintained, caused Thayer to approve the "sagebrushing" bill. In any case, its passage constituted a direct rebuke to the Senate and the President, and Washington's reaction soon followed.[9]

Led by members of the Judiciary Committee, the Senate passed a measure which voided the Wyoming act. In debate, eastern senators attacked the Wyoming legislature for its defiance of Congress. "It is simply the question, presented in the bill before us," said Henry L. Dawes of Massachusetts, "whether Congress shall surrender to the Territory or whether the Territory shall conform, as in times past, and as in all other Territories they have, to the administration of the law according to its forms enacted here." Henry M. Teller of Colorado defended Wyoming by arguing that the opposition to Peck was based on an accurate evaluation of Peck's incompetency as a judge. This support for the western position brought Teller grateful notes of thanks from Wyoming citizens.[10]

8. J. M. Thayer to Corlett, Jan. 3, 1878, Wyoming Appointment Papers, Justice Department, NA, RG60.

9. Francis E. Warren to W. W. Corlett, Mar. 25, 1878, Francis E. Warren Papers, Western History Research Center, University of Wyoming.

10. *Congressional Record,* 45th Cong., 1st sess. (Feb. 20, 1878),

After the Peck bill passed the Senate, Corlett managed to block action on it in the House. As a result, Peck spent the four years of his term writing opinions for the territorial supreme court and agitating for an appointment to another federal job. The success of the anti-Peck campaign cost Governor Thayer his post in May 1878, however. David Davis of Illinois had observed during the Senate debate, "I am amazed at the governor of the Territory for signing the act, and were I President of the United States I would very soon settle that question with him."[11]

President Hayes indicated his agreement with Davis in April when he offered the governorship to John Wesley Hoyt, a Wisconsin educator, politician, and agricultural reformer. Many years later, Hoyt recalled that he had not wanted and had even declined the governorship but had "at length acquiesced" because of Hayes's "settled purpose to remove the offending incumbent (ex-Senator Thayer) and his confidence in my easy confirmation."[12]

Hoyt began a tour of the territory shortly after his confirmation in May 1878, but the new governor's fact-finding junket did not interrupt the political ramifications of the Peck episode.[13] Ex-governor Thayer began to take sound-

---

pp. 1203, 1206; Orlando North to Henry M. Teller, Feb. 25, 1878, E. P. Johnson to Teller, Mar. 2, 1878, John M. Thayer to Teller, Mar. 5, 1878, Henry M. Teller Letters, Denver Public Library.

11. *Congressional Record,* 45th Cong., 1st sess. (Feb. 20, 1878), p. 1201.

12. John Wesley Hoyt to Benjamin Harrison, June 27, 1892, Benjamin Harrison Papers, Manuscripts Division, Library of Congress; *New York Times,* Mar. 18, 1878.

13. "Report of the Governor of Wyoming Territory," *Annual Report of the Secretary of the Interior, 1878* (Washington, 1878), p. 1177.

ings about running for delegate in the fall election. Francis E. Warren wrote Corlett, "Thayer is evidently angling around for the nomination and is I think being encouraged a good deal by democrats (as to dem vote in election etc.) with a view on their side of having an easy man to beat."[14] By the autumn, Warren was desperately seeking an alternative to Thayer. Corlett did not want to run again, and Warren eyed Territorial Supreme Court Justice James B. Sener or cattleman A. H. Swan as possible choices. Thayer, Warren argued, would run several hundred votes behind any other Republican candidate in Laramie County.[15]

Thayer's hopes were frustrated at the territorial convention on October 12, 1878, when a deal between Laramie and Albany counties produced a majority of votes for the territorial auditor and Laramie attorney, Stephen W. Downey. A former territorial treasurer, Downey had been tendered the nomination in 1876 but had declined. To oppose Downey, the Democrats picked E. L. Pease, a leader in Uinta County's fight against Peck. On election day, however, Downey triumphed by nearly the same margin as Corlett in 1876, 3,862 to 2,821.[16]

The Republican victory in 1878 and his stalwart boosting of Wyoming's prospects made Governor Hoyt's administration a success in the first half of 1879. Ambitious federal officers, however, continued to plague the territory, and by the end of the year another unseemly feud erupted in

14. Warren to Corlett, June 3, 1878, Warren Papers.

15. Warren to M. C. Brown, Oct. 3, 1878, to J. B. Adams, Oct. 3, 1878, to W. W. St. Clair, Oct. 3, 1878, Warren Papers.

16. Warren to Orlando North, Nov. 29, 1878, Warren Papers; J. H. Hayford to John W. Hoyt, Nov. 19, 1878, Wyoming State Treasurer's Records, Wyoming State Archives, Cheyenne; Erwin, *Wyoming Historical Blue Book,* p. 363.

Cheyenne. Hayes had appointed A. Worth Spates, a Maryland politician, as secretary on January 7, 1879. Spates had large goals and few scruples. He came west determined to construct a political career and displace Governor Hoyt. By the autumn of 1879, tension between the two top officials of Wyoming Territory became evident. Hoyt wrote Secretary Schurz in October that Spates was, "by want of common sense, dignity, and respect for the Gov't, wholly unfit for any responsible position under it."[17]

Spates used his position for more than political advancement. His Maryland associates set up the Great Western Distribution Company, a lottery which, according to Francis E. Warren, did not conduct drawings or distribute prizes. To facilitate his friends' schemes, Spates awarded the public printing as well as the printing business for the lottery to Herman Glafcke and the *Leader*. Spates recognized that public opinion was turning against the use of Wyoming as a haven for these operations and that the forthcoming session of the legislature would pass anti-lottery legislation if the interests of the Great Western Company were not safeguarded.[18]

Herman Glafcke seemed to be the man for the job. The difficulty was that the Laramie County Republicans and Democrats had agreed on a fusion ticket of legislative candidates, none of whom were friends of the lottery. A few days before the election, Glafcke sponsored a convention of

17. John W. Hoyt to Carl Schurz, n.d. [Oct. 1879], Carl Schurz Papers, Manuscripts Division, Library of Congress.
18. John S. Ezell, *Fortune's Merry Wheel: The Lottery in America* (Cambridge, 1960), p. 240; Philip G. Nordell, "Pattee, the Lottery King: The Omaha and Wyoming Lotteries," *Annals of Wyoming, 34* (1962), 193–211; Francis E. Warren to Joseph M. Carey, Dec. 24, 1879, Warren Papers.

the Workingmen's and People's Party, which named a slate of legislative hopefuls, among whom was Glafcke himself. Because of support from laborers in Cheyenne as well as those partisans upset by the fusion tactics of the major parties, the Workingmen's party triumphed and elected Glafcke.[19]

Governor Hoyt added to the political unrest when, shortly before the convening of the legislature, he mishandled a reception for General Grant who was on his way east from the Pacific Coast. By keeping the details of his own plans secret and by missing the reception altogether, Hoyt produced a fiasco. The affair went off clumsily, Grant was angered, and the people of Cheyenne were irritated at the governor. The most important effect, however, may have been to convince Spates and Glafcke that Hoyt could be successfully challenged. Certainly their subsequent actions in the legislature reflected either an excess of confidence or a lack of judgment.[20]

The events of the legislature resulted in the ruin of Spates and Glafcke. When the editor opposed the anti-lottery bill, the other members of the upper house, or Council, became suspicious of his fidelity to the Great Western Company's interests. Glafcke's downfall came, however, when he contested the confirmation of Francis E. Warren as territorial treasurer. Hoyt had appointed the Cheyenne

19. *Leader,* Aug. 21, 23, and 30, 1879; Cheyenne *Sun,* Aug. 21, 22, 29, and 30 and Sept. 2 and 4, 1879. Herman Glafcke continued to operate the *Leader* on behalf of his brand of Republicanism, while E. A. Slack, editor of the *Sun* and former Laramie journalist, had also upheld the principles of the G.O.P. in Cheyenne since his arrival in 1876. The rivalry between the two papers found a natural outlet in the lottery question.

20. *Leader,* Nov. 1, 1879.

merchant, and the selection was quickly assailed from several quarters. Warren's former business partner, Amasa R. Converse, angry at alleged mistreatment by Warren, marshaled the Laramie County delegation against the nominee. The other Democrats in the Council hoped to induce the governor to name a member of their party to the vacant auditorship. By blocking Warren, they sought to force the governor to trade his confirmation for a Democratic auditor.[21]

Glafcke's motives in opposing Warren were more mercenary: Converse simply purchased his services. A lengthy struggle took place, but Warren finally prevailed by one vote. Glafcke had made a powerful enemy, one who would not stop until he achieved the ruin of those who stood in his way. Since Glafcke was the postmaster of Cheyenne and Warren was a cosigner of his official bond, Glafcke had placed himself in a most vulnerable position.[22]

Meanwhile Secretary Spates did not distinguish himself, either. At the close of the legislature, his carelessness resulted in the theft of the copy of a bill from his office, a clumsy mistake which Spates unsuccessfully tried to hide. This blunder, together with other indiscretions by the secretary, caused the governor's attacks on Spates to mount in November and December. The secretary was, Hoyt informed Secretary Schurz, "constitutionally base," in the "habit of frequenting low places of resort for drinkers, games, and lewd characters," and appeared "to have *not one redeeming quality.*" Schurz assured Hoyt on November 30, 1879, that "The case of the Secretary is also under consideration," and Spates's ouster came in mid-December.

21. Francis E. Warren to J. B. Adams, Dec. 10, 1879, to Matthew Smith, Mar. 4, 1880, Warren Papers; *Sun,* Dec. 10, 1879.
22. Warren to Smith, Mar. 4, 1880, Warren Papers.

The secretary was "astounded at my contemplated removal" and hurried to Washington to seek vindication.[23]

Opposing documents showered down on the Department of the Interior during December and January. The *Leader* came to Spates's defense and attacked Hoyt as immoral, corrupt, and adulterous. On the other side, W. W. Corlett wrote, "The pretense that Spates has any following or support here among respectable people is absolutely ridiculous."[24] The final blow, however, came from Francis E. Warren. In late December he wrote Joseph M. Carey of his intention to withdraw as a signer of Glafcke's bond. "I cannot afford morally or financially to leave my name affixed to the bond of an officer, who will disgrace himself so far as to become the valiant supporter of, and *a partner in,* a lottery of any kind, much less the 'clean steal' that this institution is, never having made a drawing or distribution since its organization." Warren sent enough evidence to persuade the Post Office Department to send an inspector to Cheyenne in February 1880. Despite Glafcke's attempts to explain away his misconduct, the whole story of his connection with Spates came to light, and he was dismissed from the postmastership. As a result Spates's Washington venture failed, and his successor was confirmed on March 15, 1880.[25]

23. Carl Schurz to John W. Hoyt, Nov. 30, 1879, Hoyt to Schurz, Dec. 7, 1879, Carl Schurz Papers; A. Worth Spates to Rutherford B. Hayes, Dec. 26, 1879, W. W. Corlett to Joseph M. Carey, Dec. 30, 1879, Appointment Papers, Wyoming Secretary, Interior Department, NA, RG48.

24. *Leader,* Dec. 30, 1879; *Chicago Tribune,* Feb. 16, 25, and 27, 1880; Corlett to Carey, Dec. 30, 1879, Appointment Papers, Wyoming Secretary, Interior Department, NA, RG48.

25. Warren to Carey, Dec. 24 and 28, 1879, and Jan. 22 and Feb. 4, 1880, to S. W. Downey, Feb. 6, 1880, to H. F. Loutee, Feb. 7, 1880, to G. W. French, Mar. 13, 1880, Warren Papers; Hoyt to Schurz, Feb. 5,

This sordid episode is noteworthy not so much for its immediate effects but for what it represented about the change in Wyoming's politics since 1875. In the Spates case, a group of federal officers were vanquished for the first time by a set of local residents intent on preserving what they conceived to be the good name and future of the territory. A lottery, they believed, could not develop the economic prospects of Wyoming, and its overt illegality went beyond even the flexible limits of territorial practice. To be sure, Hoyt's connection with Secretary Schurz helped destroy Spates, but the effective leadership came from Joseph M. Carey, Francis E. Warren, and William W. Corlett. The future of Wyoming politics belonged to these men, and their participation in the Spates incident marked the emergence of a small group of native leaders who were to dominate territorial affairs until the achievement of statehood.

The delegate election in the autumn of 1880 offered additional proof of the dramatic changes that had affected Wyoming in the five years since the departure of Governor Campbell. Morton E. Post, the Democratic candidate, defeated Alexander H. Swan, the Republican hopeful, by a vote of 3,907 to 3,760, and this electoral victory after two decisive defeats cheered the Wyoming Democrats. Nevertheless, the significance of the election lay more in the respective candidates themselves than in the result. Both Post and Swan were identified with the booming Wyoming cattle industry, which since 1875 had developed from a negligible factor in the territorial economy into a rival to the

---

1880, Appointment Papers, Wyoming Secretary, Interior Department, NA, RG48; Hoyt to Schurz, Jan. 19 and Feb. 14 and 28, 1880, Schurz Papers.

Union Pacific for supremacy as a source of commercial livelihood.[26]

The major obstacle to the rapid growth of the cattle business in the early 1870s had been the presence of hostile Indians on the plains of northern and central Wyoming. This barrier between the eager settlers and excellent grazing lands began to give way before the pressure of gold seekers in the summer of 1874. Colonel George A. Custer's Yellowstone expedition brought news of gold deposits in the Black Hills to a waiting public and "almost singlehandedly" Custer started "a gold rush." From August 1874 through the spring of 1875 prospectors and expectant miners gathered at likely approach points for the assault on the gold country. In Cheyenne all was anticipation. "The vast tide of immigration which is destined to pour into the gold fields of Northern Wyoming at no distant day," said the *Leader* on February 11, 1875, "will concentrate in this town to complete outfitting, preparatory to a final start for the Eldorado."[27]

Over the next two years, Cheyenne grew more prosperous as the Black Hills rush flourished to the northeast of the Magic City. Emigrants rested and outfitted themselves in the bustling shops where "the jewelers, merchants and bankers of Cheyenne, with smiling countenances" could "be seen with their little gold scales, weighing the precious metals and giving equivalents in provisions, arms, ammunition, &c." After a weary day, a Black Hills hopeful could

26. Erwin, *Wyoming Historical Blue Book,* p. 364; for Swan, see John Clay, *My Life on the Range* (Norman, Oklahoma, 1963), p. 50; for Post, see Gressley, *Bankers and Cattlemen,* pp. 77–78.

27. *Leader,* Feb. 11, 1875; William H. Goetzmann, *Exploration and Empire* (New York, 1966), pp. 419–21; Paul, *Mining Frontiers of the Far West,* pp. 177–78.

relax at J. Greer's Saloon, "the place for a guest card party as everything here is neat and orderly." If liquid refreshment seemed in order, the traveler was directed to McDaniel's Saloon, which boasted "two eminent professors of mixology."[28]

The bounty which Wyoming obtained from its services to the Black Hills rush enabled the territory to avoid many of the ill effects of the depression of the 1870s. Governor Thayer told the 1877 legislature that the economic downturn "has not been felt by our people," and he reported that "business has enlarged; branches of industry have increased, and additional capital has found investment in different sections." Despite this improvement over the early years, the major significance of the Black Hills interlude was its effect on the Wyoming Indian population. The campaigns which followed Custer's defeat freed the territory from the menace of savage raids, and by early 1878 "adventurous pioneers" looked to northern Wyoming as a grazing area for their herds.[29]

The subsequent cattle boom, which lasted until the mid-1880s, is one of the most celebrated episodes in the history of the American West. Drawn by the lure of adventure and easy profits, eastern and foreign investors came to Wyoming and in their wake left a legacy of opulence and extravagance which invested the cattle business with an aura of romance it has never lost. Yet its limited duration is the most important single fact about the Wyoming cattle boom. Begun

28. "Cheyenne Illustrated: The Gateway to the Land of Gold," *Omaha Daily Bee*, 1876, Yale Western Americana Collection.

29. *Message of Governor Thayer to the Fifth Legislative Assembly of Wyoming Territory* (Cheyenne, 1877), p. 3; "Report of the Governor of Wyoming Territory," *Annual Report of the Secretary of the Interior, 1878* (Washington, 1878), p. 1164.

in 1878 or 1879, it ran its course by 1883 or 1884, with the hard winter of 1887 acting as the final curtain for the bonanza hopes of even the most optimistic ranchers. In its brief career of unabated prosperity, the cattle business did show itself uniquely suited to the Wyoming environment and became the characteristic economic pursuit of the territory. Pervasiveness did not, however, necessarily equal profit, and by the end of the 1880s it was clear to the most perceptive observers that Wyoming could not rely on range cattle for economic stability. To be sure, the business helped Wyoming progress from backwardness to a lesser degree of underdevelopment, but dependence on federal money still remained the primary fact of political life.

Such considerations seemed far away in the frenzied days of the boom. At the end of the 1870s, all looked promising for the Wyoming cattle grower. English herds had dwindled over the course of the decade because of disease and a growing population, and annual imports of beef increased to meet the rising demand. In 1876, England imported 1,732 tons of fresh beef, but by 1878–80 the average annual import exceeded thirty thousand tons, eighty to ninety percent of which came from the United States. As Wyoming residents realized the appeal of their limitless grazing lands and huge herds for the foreign and American investor, advertising brochures hawked the virtues of the territory in New York, London, and Edinburgh. A Royal Commission on Agriculture concluded, "With regard to cattle, for the present the American stockman in the West is possessed of singular advantages; land for nothing, and abundance of it."[30]

30. Osgood, *The Day of the Cattleman*, p. 83; W. T. Jackson, "British Interests in the Range Cattle Industry," in Maurice Frink, W. T. Jackson, Agnes Wright Spring, *When Grass Was King* (Boulder, Colorado, 1956), pp. 135–330; Clare Read and Albert Pell, "Further

In the next eight years English, Scottish, and American investors plunged heavily into Wyoming cattle. As Gene Gressley has shown, between 1882 and 1886 ninety-three cattle companies, with a capitalization of more than $51,000,000, incorporated in Wyoming. John Clay reported that in Edinburgh, "drawing rooms buzzed with the stories of this last of bonanzas; staid old gentlemen who scarcely knew the difference betwixt a steer and a heifer discussed it over their port and nuts." As their stake in Wyoming society grew, the wealthy denizens of British clubs and eastern society sought to recreate their accustomed environment in Cheyenne. For a brief moment, Cheyenne shook off its dusty air and blossomed as a center for the genteel society of the 1880s.[31]

The Cheyenne Club became the focus of opulence. In its ornate building, rich stockmen gambled, drank, and concluded business deals over brandy, cigars, and billiards. "Entertained at dinner in the Club," wrote Horace Plunkett, "I never saw such a cordial drunk. Everyone was drunk. No one beastly drunk. The singing and speaking were humorous and good." Yet the heyday of the Club ended almost before it began. Ostentatious wealth, the offspring of the boom, disappeared when the speculative bub-

---

Reports of Assistant Commissioners, Ministry of Agriculture and Fisheries," *Royal Commission on Agriculture, 1879–1882*, pp. 7–16, quoted in ibid., p. 142. The literature on the range cattle industry is immense, but the two best guides are Lewis Atherton, *The Cattle Kings* (Bloomington, Indiana, 1961), and Gressley, *Bankers and Cattlemen*.

31. Gressley, *Bankers and Cattlemen*, p. 109; Clay, *My Life on the Range*, p. 128; Moreton Frewen, *Melton Mowbray and Other Memories* (London, 1924); Margaret Digby, *Horace Plunkett: An Anglo-American Irishman* (Oxford, 1949), pp. 21–38.

ble burst. In 1884, Moreton Frewen discussed the problems of an overstocked range and declining cattle prices with Thomas Sturgis, president of the Wyoming Stock Growers Association, and such "an exchange of views was at once the leading topic at our pleasant Cheyenne Club." Wyoming cattlemen had reason to be concerned; steers which had sold for "an average of $54.17 in 1884 . . . brought only $46.58 in 1885."[32]

From the first the rush of investment into the cattle business in Wyoming had overlooked the difficulties of absentee ownership: "Inflicted with the optimism of the boom years, and enjoying the luxury of spending the un-audited funds of a group of investors a thousand or more miles distant, too many Western managers let the day-to-day managerial chores slide." Manifold abuses appeared. Careless handling, inattention, theft, and waste combined to eat away profits. In addition, the sheer number of firms caused the number of cattle to increase with the attendant evils of overstocking and overgrazing. Finally, with the large numbers of cattle available, prices sagged. "By 1885 two things are clear to the student of the cattle range industry; first, the business was ceasing to be a frontier industry, and second, it was falling a victim to over-expansion."[33]

The crisis came in 1886. The decline in cattle prices began to threaten the foreign investments; companies capitalized in the heady days of 1881–83 found themselves

32. The Cheyenne Club has yet to find its historian. Maurice Frink, *Cow Country Cavalcade* (Denver, 1954), p. 109, is useful for flavor, but Clay, *My Life on the Range*, pp. 72–78, is better; Digby, *Plunkett*, p. 27; Frewen, *Melton Mowbray*, p. 213; Jackson, "British Interests in the Range Cattle Industry," *When Grass Was King*, p. 245.

33. Gressley, *Bankers and Cattlemen*, pp. 248–49; Frewen, *Melton Mowbray*, p. 211; Osgood, *Day of the Cattleman*, pp. 112, 216–42.

unable to meet dividends and, finally, with worthless herds on their hands. After a hot dry summer, the hard winter of 1886–87 "brought Wyoming stockmen back to earth." Substantial losses of cattle rendered any hopes of total salvaging of investments futile, and in the spring of 1887 the dramatic failure of the Swan Brothers company signalled the end of the open range in Wyoming: "There was still a place for large-scale cattle operations in Wyoming, but large and small operators alike had to employ more scientific methods, and had to give up hopes of huge profits."[34]

The passing of this romantic era did not mean the end of eastern investment in Wyoming cattle. "Although the entrepreneurs might diversify their investments in the nineties, they left the gold-edged stock with the embossed popeyed steers in their portfolios."[35] Nevertheless, the cattle business had lost its expansive character, and no longer could Wyoming residents expect to rely primarily on steers as the basis for prosperity. Failure of grandiose ventures like the American Cattle Trust, an ambitious attempt to control the sale of western beef in the way Standard Oil governed the sale of petroleum products, only underlined the point.[36] Range cattle could not be dislodged from the Wyoming economy, but neither could they support it unaided.

As Wyoming cattlemen grew in importance within their territory, they created a formal institution to safeguard their interests, and the subsequent entrance of this body into politics has, for some historians, provided the key to territorial history in the late 1870s and 1880s.[37] In 1885 the

34. T. A. Larson, "The Winter of 1886–87 in Wyoming," *Annals of Wyoming, 14* (1942), 17.

35. Gressley, *Bankers and Cattlemen,* p. 247.

36. Ibid., pp. 259–66.

37. W. Turrentine Jackson, "The Wyoming Stock Growers Associa-

Wyoming Stock Growers Association had three hundred and sixty-three members who owned two million head of cattle, and their power enabled the organization to become a quasi-legal arm of the territory on matters directly affecting the administration of the range. The Maverick Law, passed in 1884, made the WSGA the official agent for the operation of the yearly roundups in Wyoming. Any cattle running loose in the territory were regarded as "mavericks," and the foremen of the roundups were required to brand the cattle and sell them at auction. The cattlemen used the bulk of the money realized from such sales to finance the continued operation of the system, which included a far-ranging network of inspectors and stock detectives. Enemies of the WSGA charged, with some justice, that "mavericks" were defined as any steer not belonging to a member.[38]

After 1886 the decline of the cattle business lowered proceeds, and in 1888 the Association asked the territorial government to assume the burden; but no satisfactory arrangement was worked out until Wyoming became a state. Meanwhile the stock growers had to cope with competition, rustling, and encroaching groups of small farmers. Lumping all these problems under the label of cattle stealing, the WSGA sought, first in the courts and later by indiscriminate use of the rope, to rid itself of these annoyances. The arrogance symbolized by such tactics embittered Wyoming politics from the late 1880s onward.[39]

----

tion: Political Power in Wyoming Territory, 1873–1890," *Mississippi Valley Historical Review, 33* (1947), 571–72, 594.

38. Helena Huntington Smith, *The War on Powder River* (New York, 1966), pp. 57–63.

39. W. Turrentine Jackson, "The Wyoming Stock Growers Associa-

The scope of WSGA influence, however, was less wide than historians have claimed. In the larger context of territorial politics, many of the alleged cases of WSGA interference were of minor importance. The Association's papers are nearly empty of letters dealing with elections, appointments of territorial officers, or federal policy toward Wyoming. It is not enough to cite lists of WSGA members in the Wyoming legislature; the historian must show that these men acted as a cohesive unit in passing and enacting territorial laws. This can be easily done when only cattle legislation is considered, but an attempt to establish a similar pattern on other kinds of bills breaks down. The Association was a powerful pressure group in Wyoming in the later territorial period, but it was not the real governing body of the territory. Moreover, if the historian concentrates on its activities to the neglect of traditional struggles between the two major political parties, he will be unable to understand the development and significance of Wyoming politics between 1880 and 1896.

The relative calm in Wyoming politics in the four years before 1884 may have helped to mislead historians about the precise role of the WSGA. As political discord ebbed, attention naturally turned to the more exciting cattle boom. In the 1882 delegate election, Morton Post won a second term easily by defeating John W. Meldrum, a Republican stalwart. John W. Hoyt was replaced as governor earlier in the year by William Hale of Iowa, despite the endorsements he obtained from the territorial legislature in favor of another term. Hale, an Iowa lawyer and politician, prevailed because of the support of Senator William Boyd Allison, but

---

tion, Its Years of Temporary Decline, 1886–1890," *Agricultural History*, 22 (1948), 260–70.

his poor health made him no more than a shadow executive. From 1882 to 1884, the problems of territorial politics seemed far away to the majority of Wyoming residents.[40]

While not in itself a departure from this pattern, the territorial election of 1884 set in motion events which opened more than a decade of virulent and vicious political contention. The election of Joseph M. Carey as delegate, followed by the appointment of Francis E. Warren as territorial governor, combined with the elevation of Grover Cleveland to the presidency to produce dramatic changes in the Wyoming scene. For the next twelve years the political landscape of the territory underwent periodic shifts, and both parties saw their fortunes rise and fall.

The approach of the 1884 campaign confronted Wyoming Republicans with the problem of finding a candidate to oppose the still popular Morton E. Post. Party leaders contended that only Francis E. Warren had a chance to beat the Democratic incumbent, and their appeals temporarily swayed Warren from his reluctance to serve as delegate. Late in September, however, Warren was *"credibly informed"* that Post would *"not* accept nomination under any circumstances."* Other Democratic possibilities were so few and so feeble that Warren concluded his business interests could safely take precedence over his obligations to his party.[41]

40. Erwin, *Wyoming Historical Blue Book,* p. 364; A. H. Swan to Chester A. Arthur, n.d. [Mar. 1882], F. J. Stanton to J. A. Logan, Apr. 3, 1882, Appointment Papers, Wyoming Governor, Interior Department, NA, RG48; Warren to M. E. Post, Mar. 8 and 10, 1882, Warren Papers; William Hale to William Boyd Allison, July 14, 1882, to Allison and J. W. McDill, July 14, 1882, Box 116, William Boyd Allison Papers, Iowa State Department of History and Archives.

41. Francis E. Warren to H. V. S. Groesbeck, Sept. 27, 1884, Warren Papers.

Territorial Republicans did not agree. Warren received a unanimous nomination from the convention in October, and a notification committee hurried to obtain his official acceptance. To the disappointment of the faithful, Warren declined unequivocally because of the pressures of his private affairs.[42] Republicans turned to Joseph M. Carey at once and induced him to become the party's choice. "The acceptance of the nomination by Judge Carey," wrote E. A. Slack in the Cheyenne *Sun,* "was the consummation devoutly wished for and earnestly sought after by all the prominent republicans of the city and territory, and every influence possible to exert has been brought to bear upon him during the past few days."[43]

William H. Holliday, a colorless Laramie merchant, emerged as the Democratic challenger to Carey. Unlike Post, Holliday could not match Carey's standing and popularity throughout the territory. Backed by a united Republican Party, Carey gained most from the solid support of Warren. At an election eve rally in Cheyenne, Warren ended a speech for Carey by asking the throng "what they were going to do today. Were they going to vote for Judge Carey[?]" The *Sun,* understandably partisan, reported that "a tremendous response of yes answered the question."[44] The vote confirmed the *Sun's* journalistic judgment. Carey triumphed by a vote of 7,225 to 5,586; his majority of sixteen hundred votes was the largest ever recorded by a delegate aspirant in Wyoming, and only a narrow Holliday victory in Uinta County prevented a Republican sweep.[45]

42. *Sun,* Oct. 21, 1884.

43. *Sun,* Oct. 22, 1884.

44. *Sun,* Nov. 4, 1884; Warren to J. H. Conrad, Oct. 24, 1884, to William Maxwell, Oct. 25, 1884, Warren Papers.

45. Erwin, *Wyoming Historical Blue Book,* p. 364.

The new delegate hastened to Washington in December for the opening of Congress to help Post in promoting Wyoming's interests. Meanwhile the election of Grover Cleveland seemed to augur a shift from Republican dominance after March 1885. Wyoming Democrats anticipated the appointment of a territorial governor from their party, and candidates began angling for a favorable position. If Cleveland did remove Governor Hale, it was believed that Post would be the inevitable choice. Concern for his own gubernatorial future explains why Post lingered in Washington during the waning days of his term.[46]

On January 13, 1885, Governor Hale's chronic illness finally ended in death. The vacancy immediately presented Wyoming Republicans with an unexpected opportunity. If President Chester A. Arthur could be persuaded to appoint a territorial resident to fill out Hale's term, it would take away much of the advantage the Democrats hoped to gain from Cleveland's selection of a Democratic governor from Wyoming. Delegate Carey decided that Warren was the logical man for the job: his candidacy could draw backing from all sections of the territory, and as Carey wrote Arthur, "should you appoint him, but little effort would be made in this Territory to encompass his removal, under the next administration."[47]

For Post this surge of support for Warren was bitter news. He had expected to assume the duties of governor as soon as Cleveland took office. On February 18, 1885, friends of Post held a meeting in Cheyenne and adopted resolutions which purported to prove widespread enthusiasm for the Democrat's selection. In fact the meeting, like Post's cam-

46. *Leader,* Jan. 4 and 7, 1885.
47. Joseph M. Carey to Chester A. Arthur, Jan. 26, 1885, Appointment Papers, Wyoming Governor, Interior Department, NA, RG48.

paign, was small, local, and ineffective. Carey meanwhile bombarded President Arthur and Secretary of the Interior Henry M. Teller with petitions, telegrams, personal appeals, and letters urging the elevation of Warren. Teller, a former leader of the western bloc in the Senate, responded sympathetically to the Wyoming desire for a resident governor, and his advice, when linked with Carey's efforts, convinced President Arthur to send Warren's name to the Senate on February 25.[48]

Warren had anxiously followed the course of events from Cheyenne. He coveted the governorship far more than the honor of being delegate. His duties would keep him in Cheyenne, close to his business, and his influence on the legislature would enable him to advance his plans for the economic development of Wyoming. With customary guile and politeness, he wired Carey his congratulations: "Please express thanks and heartfelt gratitude to the President, Secretary Teller and friends—Will it be necessary for us here to reach different Senators?" Two days later the Senate confirmed Warren's appointment, and when the report reached Cheyenne the new governor told Carey that "you are a 'North American success.' "[49]

All segments of the territorial press applauded Warren's good fortune. His long residence in Wyoming, his many economic connections within the territory, and his personal popularity joined to produce a wave of approval. The Demo-

48. Warren to Carey, Feb. 19, 24, and 25, 1885, Warren Papers; Joseph M. Carey to Henry M. Teller, Jan. 26, 1885, Carey to Benjamin Harrison, Jan. 26, 1885, Appointment Papers, Wyoming Governor, Interior Department, NA, RG48; W. T. Jackson, "The Governorship of Wyoming, 1885–1889: A Study in Territorial Politics," *Pacific Historical Review, 13* (1944), 1–11.

49. Warren to Carey, Feb. 25 and 27, 1885, Warren Papers.

crats, chagrined at being outmaneuvered, could only add their voices to the chorus of cheers and promise that when Cleveland removed Warren, he would also appoint a Wyoming resident. "This appointment . . . is a good beginning in the right direction," commented the *Leader,* a Democratic paper since Glafcke's ouster as postmaster in 1880, "and we trust that the incoming government may adhere to the principle, and give to the people of Wyoming home rule through all its several departments."[50]

Carey's election and Warren's appointment made them the two most influential politicians in Wyoming. Both wealthy, both talented, both ambitious, both Republican, and both from Cheyenne, they were natural contestants for supremacy within the territory. From 1884 to 1890 they cooperated successfully, and their union brought statehood to Wyoming and electoral victories to their party. After 1890 they drifted apart, and their quarrels, struggles, and mutual antipathy enfeebled the Republicans and allowed the Democrats to compete on even terms through the election of 1896. Warren's victory over Carey for control of the party in that year did not end the feud, which continued for two more decades. The shape of Wyoming history cannot be understood without an examination of their characters and abilities.

Joseph M. Carey remains a shadowy figure for the historian. He did not, like Warren, preserve his personal papers, and detailed insight into his life and personality is consequently impossible. Nevertheless, the broad outlines of his career are clear. Joseph Maull Carey was born in 1845 at Milton, Delaware, attended Union College, and was graduated from the University of Pennsylvania Law School

50. *Leader,* Feb. 26, 1885.

in 1867. While studying law, Carey stumped Pennsylvania on behalf of Republican candidates and campaigned for Grant in 1868. After Grant's inauguration, the young lawyer wrote the President to ask for an appointment as district attorney for the territory of Wyoming. Supported by members of the Philadelphia bar, Carey triumphed over aspirants from Michigan and Wyoming.[51]

Upon his arrival in Wyoming, Carey plunged into his official tasks. Several months later he wrote his brother about the prospects in Wyoming cattle. "A man with some capital that will stick to the business for five years, with but ordinary luck can be worth a hundred thousand dollars. I believe it to be a sure road to a fortune." For the moment, however, Carey confined himself to law and politics. His allegiance to Governor Campbell and his performance as district attorney led to his appointment to the Wyoming supreme court in 1871. He made his unsuccessful race for delegate against W. R. Steele three years later.[52]

Although political pressures prevented Carey's reappointment as judge in 1876, he was named national committeeman for the territory at the Republican convention in that year, a post he was to hold for two decades. Assessments of Carey's performance at the bar and on the bench vary. Opponents accused him of incompetence, but his friends described him as dedicated and diligent. In any case, by

51. George W. Paulson, "The Congressional Career of Joseph M. Carey," *Annals of Wyoming, 35* (1963), 21–23; Henry M. Flanders to W. M. Evarts, Mar. 25, 1869, Joseph M. Carey to U. S. Grant, Mar. 29, 1869, Leonard Myers to Grant, Mar. 30, 1869, Wyoming Appointment Papers, Justice Department, NA, RG60.

52. Joseph M. Carey to R. Davis Carey, Oct. 24, 1869, in *Collected Writings and Addresses of William Chapin Deming*, ed. Agnes Wright Spring (4 vols. Glendale, California, 1947), *4, 20.*

1878 Carey's energies had turned to other areas, and a politician noted that he was "still wholly absorbed in the cattle business to such an extent that he can do and does little to help his friends in the political or any other field."[53]

Carey's business interests included the firm of J. M. Carey & Brother, which raised cattle under the famous CY brand, did some construction work in Cheyenne, and promoted irrigation projects outside the city. The Judge, as he was known, participated in the affairs of the Wyoming Stock Growers Association, including a term as president. John Clay recalled that Carey "was fluent, fair, patient, and in every way an ideal presiding officer."[54] When the University of Wyoming was founded, he "had a custom of traveling from Cheyenne to Laramie every spring to present funds for anonymous scholarships to the president."[55] Popularity and influence, the natural result of this public service, led to his election as mayor of Cheyenne from 1881 to 1885.

This is a distinguished record which fully entitles Carey to a prominent niche in Wyoming history. In his private life, Carey well merited the accolades of such a perceptive observer as Agnes Wright Spring, who describes him as "most understanding, generous, [and] fair-minded."[56] Yet as a politician his liabilities were as noteworthy as his assets. Carey looked the very picture of a western statesman—his ample bulk, tidy beard, and balding pate gave an impression of intelligence and effectiveness. Beneath this facade other forces operated. Carey's constituents found him aloof, cold, and forbidding. He lacked the common touch and smooth-

53. E. P. Johnson to John A. Campbell, Oct. 23, 1878, Campbell Papers.
54. Clay, *My Life on the Range*, p. 114.
55. Gressley, *Bankers and Cattlemen*, p. 75.
56. Agnes Wright Spring to author, Nov. 6, 1966.

ness which Warren possessed. He regarded office and prefer-
ment as his just due and paid little attention to the neces-
sities of political life. A cattle king and an old Wyoming
resident, Carey saw no need to develop a personal following
or a political organization.

Carey's willingness to accept political defeat rather than
compromise his views on the silver issue in 1894 won for him
the acclaim of his friends and the praise of historians. The
nobility acquired in this struggle has invested Carey with a
reputation for rectitude which, in the absence of his personal papers, may be impenetrable. A different picture
emerges from the writings of Francis E. Warren, and even
with an allowance for bias, some weight must be given to the
opinion of a political strategist who rarely misunderstood
the nature of his opposition. In Warren's eyes, Carey was
an irresolute intriguer who concocted grand schemes to be
executed by others, but who was personally unreliable and
vacillating in a crisis. In 1912, at the climax of their feud,
Warren wrote:

> If I hadn't known Carey from the time he stepped off
> the train in 1869, a green boy, up to the present, and
> hadn't figured inside of the inner circles so much with
> him in political affairs, he might possibly fool me once
> in a while, for he surely is the most monumental
> hypocrite, the most seductive and successful hypocrite,
> and the most infernal liar—when 'necessary'—that God
> ever permitted to live whom I have been permitted to
> meet.[57]

Warren's own involvement in the political and economic
life of Wyoming began in May 1868 when he took a job as a

57. Warren to C. W. Burdick, Apr. 8, 1912, Warren Papers.

clerk in the store of Amasa R. Converse. The twenty-four-year-old Warren had enlisted in the Union Army from Hinsdale, Massachusetts his birthplace, and had achieved a distinguished record as a member of the 49th Massachusetts Regiment, receiving the Congressional Medal of Honor for his bravery at Port Hudson. After his discharge, he held a variety of jobs before coming to Cheyenne. Within a few months he reported to his future wife, "I love Cheyenne because primarily I am doing very well here and the time I shall remain here will depend upon future circumstances of which at present I am totally ignorant."[58]

From the beginning of his life in Wyoming, Warren showed those qualities which were to mark his rise to power. " 'The Root hog or die' system of training up young men is I'll admit a very good one to learn them the ways of the world," he told his fiancée in 1869, and his indefatigable energy soon won him Converse's trust and confidence. "Mr. Converse went east last Mon. Eve. so I am now left at the helm," noted Warren in July 1869, and two years later he became a full partner in the firm of Converse & Warren.[59]

Over the next six years Warren expanded his interest in the company until he bought Converse out and became the sole owner in 1877. Using the store, now called the Warren Mercantile Company, as a base, Warren extended his commitments into every phase of the territorial economy. The Warren Land and Livestock Company was his most important venture, but he owned or had investments in public utilities, banks, and railroads. Matching an obsession for detail with an eager lust for profit, by 1885 Warren had

58. Warren to Helen M. Smith, July 26, 1868, Feb. 1, 1869, Warren Papers.
59. Warren to Helen M. Smith, Feb. 21 and July 1, 1869, Warren Papers.

amassed a sizable fortune and was constantly alert for ways to increase it.[60]

To his correspondents Warren maintained that politics bored him, yet he practiced the art with a zest and ability unmatched by any of his colleagues. After a term as city trustee in 1871, he advanced as a member of the legislature, territorial treasurer, mayor of Cheyenne, and finally territorial governor. Warren brought to politics a passion for order which was revolted by disunity in the Republican Party. From 1885 on he devoted himself to bringing peace and strength to the contending factions. For Carey and others, accustomed to a politics of personality and friendship, Warren's insistence on discipline and loyalty seemed ludicrous. But Warren realized that friendship was an unnecessary luxury when patronage and graft were more dependable and lasting.[61]

Warren built his political organization to further the two objectives of his political creed, his own enrichment and the development of Wyoming. In his mind, and often in fact, the two aims were identical. During a career undistinguished by national achievement, Warren campaigned ceaselessly for more forts, buildings, and appropriations for his territory and state. As a senator after 1890, he badgered presidents and cabinet members to appoint deserving Wyoming Republicans to every imaginable federal office. No position was too small, no constituent, if of the true faith, too inconsequential to escape his omnivorous attention.[62]

60. Anne Carolyn Hansen, "The Congressional Career of Senator Francis E. Warren from 1890 to 1902," *Annals of Wyoming, 20* (1948), 4–12; *Leader,* Jan. 5, 1878, discusses Converse's withdrawal from the firm.

61. Hansen, "Congressional Career of Warren," pp. 12–16.

62. For examples of Warren's aims and methods, see Warren to

Warren was forty-one in 1885, and years of hard work and success had rubbed off the rough edges of his personality. A large, handsome man, he sported a flowing white mustache and exuded a sense of physical vitality. His stature, coupled with his incisive mind, made him an individual of power and influence over his contemporaries. An adept orator, Warren sprinkled his speeches with statistics, added a few literary allusions, and wound up with a vituperative denunciation of his partisan opponents. On the stump, before a legislative body, or in a smoke-filled room, Warren bent men to his will by the force of his presence.

Preservation of his lengthy and massively detailed correspondence has assured Warren of attention from students of Wyoming history and has also guaranteed that his side of every controversial incident will be available in convenient form. Though they must be used with due caution, the Warren papers do reveal a matchless artist of the pork barrel process, an adept and gifted master of intrigue, and an outstandingly successful political leader. Ruthless, direct, and imperious, Warren was always in command of his fortunes, even in moments of adversity. Accustomed to a life of hard work and exertion, he defeated his enemies by the simple expedient of demonstrating to the voters that his methods produced the greatest economic gain for Wyoming. "You know my motto is 'Never hunt ducks with a brass band,'" Warren told an associate, and the results of his quiet labors were the best advertisement for his effectiveness.[63]

What distinguished Warren from other Wyoming leaders, and what enabled him to emerge by 1896 as the dom-

---

W. A. Richards, Dec. 7, 1898, to E. A. Slack, Mar. 1, 1899, to A. J. Parshall, Dec. 18, 1899, Warren Papers.

63. Warren to E. A. Slack, Mar. 30, 1897, Warren Papers.

inant figure in state politics, was his practicality and clear sense of how to secure tangible achievements for his constituents. In 1897 he remarked to a Cheyenne banker:

> The fact is, ideal politics and practical politics seldom if ever clasp hands as to *all* of the appointments, all of the work of the legislature, or all of the accomplishments of any one party. Our ideals are what we should strive for but there are always so many obstructions; side issues; so many influences, and in fact the power of the party so much divided on the one hand, and so surely made up on all hands, of people of all classes and degrees and opinions, that the motto "always do the best you can under the circumstances" has to suffice.[64]

In the spring of 1885, both Warren and Carey, or "Me and F. E." as the Democratic newspapers derisively labeled the team, believed that their temporary victory would be of short duration. Cleveland, they felt sure, would soon act to give the governorship to a deserving resident of his party. Meanwhile Warren resolved "to attend to the duties of the office while I do hold it concientiously & well—working for the advancement & good of the Territory—Endeavoring to be just to all." The new governor hoped that the incoming administration would "bring about such a state of affairs that a public officer can attend strictly to his business; let partizanship alone & be judged & measured by his capacity honesty & industry."[65] This was a noble vision even for Warren, but the differing ideas of Wyoming's needs held by the territorial Republicans and the Cleveland administration quickly brought "partizanship" back to the center of territorial politics after 1885.

64. Warren to Henry G. Hay, Mar. 7, 1897, Warren Papers.
65. Warren to W. W. Corlett, Mar. 25, 1885, Warren Papers.

CHAPTER FOUR. WYOMING AND LAND POLICY, 1885-1889

OVERNOR Warren's plans for the economic development of Wyoming included the standard promotional devices which were to mark his political career. He sought to encourage a north-south railroad through Cheyenne by offering financial inducements to the Union Pacific management and at the same time reopened the question of the location of repair shops in the capital city. Through the action of the territorial legislature and the Congress, he proposed to spur the growth of Wyoming's urban economy by a program of public building construction, with special emphasis on the erection of a capitol building in Cheyenne. Finally, he began to explore the related problems of land policy and irrigation with a view to discovering the political means for the creation of an agricultural base for the territory.

The achievement of these ends depended on a commitment by the federal government to the idea that positive action could promote the economic expansion of the nation. Unfortunately for Warren, the accession of Grover Cleveland to the presidency brought to power an administration devoted to the concept of limited government, strict economy in the appropriation process, and honesty in the disposition of the public domain. For the dominant wing of the Democrats, the kind of economic assistance which Warren sought was anathema; the Bourbon leaders of the party preferred to trust the natural laws of economic activity to produce prosperity without the stifling interference of the federal government. In his inaugural address President Cleveland asserted, "It is the duty of those serving the people in public place closely to limit public expenditures to the actual needs of the government economically administered, because this bounds the right of the government to exact tribute from the earnings of labor or the property of the citizen, and because public extravagance begets extravagance among the people."[1] Such sentiments did not bode well for the Warren program.

Land reform represented a natural offshoot of the Cleveland administration's attitude toward government intervention in the economy. Conscious of the widespread fraud in the land system, the President and his advisers believed that "Care for the property of the nation, and for the needs of future settlers, requires that the public domain should be protected from purloining schemes and unlawful occupation."[2] Consequently, Cleveland brought to the administration of the public lands a reforming zeal which expressed itself in every phase of the problem. As the historian of the land laws in this period, Harold H. Dunham, has written, "If it was difficult to change the land laws the Democrats nevertheless checked cattlemen in their abuses and violations of laws and the domain; railroad grants were supervised with greater care than ever before; timber depredations were halted and prosecution for past offenses was pushed; surveying and private land claims frauds were un-

1. Albert E. Bergh, *Grover Cleveland: Addresses, State Papers and Letters* (New York, 1909), p. 62. The principles of the Cleveland Democratic Party have been set forth by Horace S. Merrill in *William Freeman Vilas: Doctrinaire Democrat* (Madison, Wisconsin, 1954), and *Bourbon Leader: Grover Cleveland and the Democratic Party* (Boston, 1957).
2. Bergh, *Cleveland,* p. 63.

covered and prosecuted; manipulation of settlement entries was discouraged; and successful efforts were made to reclaim large areas for general use."[3]

The chief agent of the Cleveland administration's impulse for change was its commissioner of the General Land Office, the headstrong and dedicated former congressman from Illinois, William Andrew Jackson Sparks. A divided Congress made the enactment of land reform legislation impossible, and Sparks's administrative rulings became the principal means of regulating the disposition of the public domain. Appointed in late March 1885, Sparks lost little time in opening his offensive on land grabbers. On April 3, 1885, he suspended final action on most homestead, desert land, and Timber and Stone Act entries in the West. Sparks's action drew a volley of criticism from those who profited, honestly or dishonestly, from the sale of public lands, and in December 1885 the commissioner drew back from his April edict and created a Board of Review to speed action on legitimate entries. The pressure from the West did not abate until the Secretary of the Interior, L. Q. C. Lamar, rescinded the order on April 9, 1886.[4]

Sparks's ruling provoked much discontent in Wyoming, but other action by the President upset the cattlemen in the territory even more. On August 10, 1885, Cleveland issued a proclamation which demanded the immediate removal

3. Harold H. Dunham, *Government Handout: A Study in the Administration of the Public Lands, 1875–1891* (New York, 1941), p. 169.

4. Dunham, *Government Handout*, pp. 186, 187–211; Roy M. Robbins, *Our Landed Heritage, The Public Domain, 1776–1936* (Lincoln, Nebraska, 1962), pp. 291–95; John B. Rae, "Commissioner Sparks and the Railroad Land Grants," *Mississippi Valley Historical Review*, 25 (1938), 211–30.

of all fences on the public domain.[5] This order struck at the efforts of Wyoming ranchers to obtain large holdings at low cost by enclosing sizable sections of government land. When the Justice Department began suits to block further illegal fencing, the organ of the Republican Party and the stockmen, the Cheyenne *Daily Sun,* complained that Cleveland's policy was, "Thou shalt have no other gods than William Andrew Jackson Sparks, and none other shalt thou worship. Thou shalt not raise cattle upon the land, neither sheep or asses nor any living thing, but only corn the same as in the State of Illinois."[6]

The policy of Sparks and Cleveland has generally received a favorable assessment from historians of the period. Allan Nevins, the President's foremost biographer, concluded in 1932 that "Nothing in the first Administration was more creditable than Cleveland's jealous regard for Federal property and settlers' rights in the West."[7] According to Roy M. Robbins, Sparks "wanted more than reform; he wanted to revolutionize the land system."[8] For the West, and Wyoming in particular, however, the Sparks policy appeared to be an attempt by the eastern bureaucracy to choke off the development of the territory. Residents were willing to

5. Dunham, *Government Handout,* pp. 179–83.

6. *Sun,* Feb. 27, 1887, quoted in Osgood, *The Day of the Cattleman,* p. 207.

7. Allan Nevins, *Grover Cleveland: A Study in Courage* (New York, 1932), p. 360.

8. Robbins, *Our Landed Heritage,* p. 295. For the workings of the Sparks policy in other western states and territories, see George L. Anderson, "The Administration of Federal Land Laws in Western Kansas, 1880–1890: A Factor in Adjustment to a New Environment," *The Kansas Historical Quarterly, 20* (1952), 233–51, and R. Hal Williams, "George W. Julian and Land Reform in New Mexico, 1885–1889," *Agricultural History, 41* (1967), 71–84.

tolerate fraud in the land system in exchange for the ability to acquire their own holdings as quickly as possible. They remained skeptical of federal officials who sought to compel adherence to the letter of land laws which had little relevance to western conditions.

In addition to the discontent caused by his official actions, Sparks irritated western politicians when he tried to carry out his policies by more traditional means. At the height of his anger with Sparks, Warren relayed to Carey the news that the Cheyenne land office employees had "instructions to insert land notices only in such papers as support Sparks, notwithstanding settlers *pay* for notices and have right to select paper. This practice through all land offices accounts for Sparks support in Western papers." Another device favored by Sparks was the dispatching of special agents and inspectors to ferret out land frauds and illegal practices.[9]

To ensure that his policies were loyally followed, Sparks also intervened in the selection of territorial officials, an action which had severe political repercussions in Wyoming. The Democratic national platform in 1884 had promised the appointment of residents to the vacant offices in the territory, and the Wyoming Democrats confidently expected to receive the blessing of patronage which would help to achieve political dominance in the event of statehood. Factionalism within the party worked, in part, to frustrate this goal from 1885 to 1889; but the main obstacle to an abolition of nonresident appointments was the necessity of finding men willing to execute the Sparks orders. Most of the leading candidates were involved, to one degree or another, in the condemned practices of fencing and

9. Francis E. Warren to Joseph M. Carey, Jan. 24, 1887, Warren Papers.

illegal acquisition of land, which inevitably meant that Cleveland would have to go outside Wyoming for an acceptable choice. However necessary from a national standpoint, this condition carried with it the enfeeblement of the territorial Democratic Party. From 1885 to 1888, Cleveland played into the hands of the Republicans by appointing, without exception, nonresidents to major territorial offices. Out of the thirty-four nonresidents named in Cleveland's first administration, Wyoming had five.[10]

Irritated by the Republican coup of Warren's appointment as governor, the Wyoming Democrats began an immediate campaign for the ouster of the territorial executive in March 1885. Events combined to frustrate their ambitions and prolong Warren's tenure. First the party was unable to agree on a candidate in the summer of 1885; M. E. Post could not win party endorsement because of his Cheyenne residence. Later, Warren's adept handling of the Rock Springs riot threw the powerful influence of the Union Pacific behind the incumbent.[11]

Rioting erupted at Rock Springs on September 2, 1885, when the white miners in the Union Pacific coal camp attacked Chinese laborers there, killing twenty-eight, wounding fifteen, and causing extensive property damage. The disturbance grew out of the agitation by the Knights of Labor, who were strongly entrenched in Rock Springs, against Chinese workingmen in the 1880s, the hard times in the middle of the decade, and the Union Pacific's willingness to use docile Orientals in place of undependable union men. Warren, who urged the railroad not to "recede in the slightest degree from the stand taken, that Chinese shall

10. Pomeroy, *Territories*, p. 73.
11. Jackson, "Governorship of Wyoming," p. 4.

work and that criminals shall not," reacted quickly to the news of the uprising, and his requests for military assistance won him national acclaim.[12]

After the disorder was put down, the railroad management came to Warren's aid with the Cleveland administration. Charles Francis Adams, the company president, wrote the Secretary of War that "these Rock Springs murderers" were "behind the whole movement" to have Warren replaced. Adams added that failure to retain Warren *"would mean complete immunity to anti-Chinese rioters and murderers, and encouragement to do it again."*[13] Such statements convinced the President that Warren should not be removed for the time being.

As governor, Warren had originally anticipated an early ouster. He was only "anxious to hold the place a few months, or at least until others in similar positions had been removed so that I might not be first." When it became apparent after the riot that he could expect to stay in office, Warren started to prepare an ambitious program for the session of the Ninth Territorial Assembly. With an eye to the elections in 1886, Warren's legislative goals represented a coherent effort to promote Cheyenne, the Republican Party, and his own fortunes. The Democrats, fearful of Warren's political effectiveness, tried to convince Cleveland that "the interests of the Democratic party of the territory imperatively demand the immediate appointment of a Democratic Governor";

12. Francis E. Warren to S. R. Gallaway, Sept. 18, 1885, Wyoming Territorial Papers, Interior Department, NA, RG48; Paul Crane and T. A. Larson, "The Chinese Massacre," *Annals of Wyoming, 12* (1940), 47–56.

13. Charles Francis Adams to W. C. Endicott, Oct. 17, 1885, Warren Papers.

but the President, influenced by the Union Pacific and his brief commitment to civil service reform, refused to act.[14]

There was one problem to be met before the legislative agenda could be tackled. The Eighth Legislative Assembly had failed to reapportion the Council and House districts as the law required, and the Republicans either had to hold an expensive special election or persuade Congress to pass a law validating the 1884 election. Choosing the latter course, Delegate Carey managed to have the bill passed by the middle of January 1886, and Warren reported, "the achievement seems to meet with the approval of nearly *everybody* of both parties. It is an excellent 'starter' for you, and you can deservedly take great credit." Despite Warren's claims of Democratic support, the opposition intended to challenge the legality of the legislature if its accomplishments brought too much credit to the Republicans.[15]

Warren's legislative program consisted of two parts. The most important was a bill to promote the building of a railroad north from Cheyenne with the cooperation of the Union Pacific. Aware that the Chicago and Northwestern Railroad was laying track into Lusk and Douglas in Converse County, Warren bombarded the Union Pacific with pleas for help in the construction of a northern road. He warned the railroad officials that failure to act would cost them the lucrative business which would be available when the new region was opened: "Make no effort for this, or come in at a later time; and you will have left to the U.P. a strip across the southern line of Wyoming 50 to 75 miles, and

14. Warren to Miss Kate E. Thomas, Aug. 12, 1886, Warren Papers; R. C. Mayor and J. C. Friend to Grover Cleveland, Jan. 10, 1886, Daniel S. Lamont Papers, Manuscripts Division, Library of Congress.

15. Warren to Carey, Jan. 17, 1886, Warren Papers; *Leader,* Jan. 12, 1886.

that is *all you will have.*"[16] Responding to these entreaties, the railroad gave its blessing to Warren's sponsorship of a bill which authorized the Laramie County Commissioners to call a Bond election on behalf of a northern railroad.[17] Since the project meant increased expenditures and new jobs, little opposition developed and the measure passed easily. The bonds were voted by the Cheyenne electorate and construction began the next year. Warren had won the first notable victory of his executive career.[18]

Of secondary economic importance, but politically more significant, was the attempt to secure the erection of public buildings in Cheyenne. When finished, they would guarantee the retention of the capital, a prize which carried with it the revenue and the patronage attendant to the functioning of government. Drawing on the unhappy experience of other western territories and his memory of the capital removal fights of the 1870s, Warren hoped to spare Wyoming subsequent disputes over the capital location, quarrels which could only threaten Warren's personal fortunes.[19]

Alert on all fronts, Warren supported Carey's efforts to gain a federal appropriation for public buildings, but the main avenue was to be the territorial legislature. The campaign opened late in the session, for on January 22, 1886, Warren told Carey, "I scarcely think Legislature will act on public building matter." On February 24, however, Nick O'Brien, a Warren agent, introduced a bill to "provide for the erection of a capitol building at the capitol of the Terri-

16. Warren to S. R. Gallaway, Jan. 5, 1886, Warren Papers.
17. Warren to Gallaway, Feb. 1, 1886, Warren Papers.
18. Larson, *History of Wyoming,* p. 159.
19. "Annual Report of the Governor of Wyoming," *Annual Report of the Secretary of the Interior, 1885* (Washington, 1885), 2, 1213; Warren to Carey, Mar. 8, 1886, Warren Papers.

tory and for other purposes."[20] Willis Van Devanter, a Cheyenne lawyer who was soon to become Warren's most trusted lieutenant, had drafted the measure several days before, and it was artfully constructed to achieve passage. If Laramie County, Albany County, and Uinta County could combine, the bill would pass easily. As a sweetener for Albany, Van Devanter's legislation provided for a university at Laramie, and as the Laramie *Daily Boomerang* noted, "Whoever drafted the bill must have copied entire the charter of some eastern university, as it covered every conceivable point."[21] In order to bring Uinta County into line, the Cheyenne and Laramie representatives acted favorably on legislation to supply an insane asylum at Evanston. In return, Uinta County delegates kept the log rolling by voting for the capitol building bill.[22]

The success of Warren's program in the legislative session added to the already numerous Democratic woes. Cleveland's western policies, combined with his dilatory approach to the patronage, first tried the patience of Wyoming Democrats and finally drove them into outright opposition to the President. The *Cheyenne Daily Leader,* by now the most important Democratic paper in the territory, complained in April 1886 that "The mills of the powers at Washington grind out exceedingly small news items of interest to Wyoming people. Were it not for Secretary [L. Q. C.] Lamar, who now and then causes rejoicing among our people by revok-

20. Warren to Carey, Jan. 22, 1886, Warren Papers; *House Journal of the Ninth Legislative Assembly of the Territory of Wyoming* (Cheyenne, 1886), p. 176.

21. Laramie *Daily Boomerang,* Feb. 26, 1886; Wilson O. Clough, *A History of the University of Wyoming, 1887–1937* (Laramie, 1937), pp. 13–18.

22. Warren to Carey, Mar. 4, 1886, Warren Papers.

ing one of Sparks' orders, the Democrats of this territory would despair of getting recognition from the present administration."[23]

To offset the damage caused by the Cleveland program, Wyoming Democrats resolved to mount a determined attack on Warren's position. Shortly after the legislature adjourned, prominent Democrats sought an injunction from the territory's chief justice, asking that Warren be restrained from using the money appropriated for the contingent expenses of the governor's office. Basing their claims on the alleged illegality of the legislature, the Democrats hoped to embarrass Warren sufficiently to induce Cleveland to appoint a Democratic successor.[24]

The judge denied the request which, as Warren remarked, "originated in the brain of one of our crazy, pettifogging lawyers," but the loss of the case in Wyoming did not alter the overall strategy of the anti-Warren forces. In a lengthy set of charges sent to Cleveland, they attacked Warren's actions as governor and pleaded for his removal. Several candidates came forward to fill the anticipated vacancy. The perennial Post was still in the field, but he had been joined by George T. Beck, the son of a Kentucky senator, W. H. Holliday, Carey's opponent in 1884, and George W. Baxter, an army officer turned cattleman. During the summer of 1886, letters of recommendation for each man piled up in Washington, but President Cleveland took no action on the protest or the hopeful candidates.[25]

23. *Leader,* Apr. 8, 1886.

24. *Leader,* Mar. 14, Apr. 1, 1886.

25. William Ware Peck and A. C. Campbell to L. Q. C. Lamar, Apr. 30, 1886, Francis E. Warren Charges File, Interior Department, NA, RG48; Warren to Rollins & Young, Mar. 18, 1886, Warren Papers.

By September, preparations got under way for the 1886 territorial election. The Republicans hoped to capitalize on the discontent with Sparks and Cleveland, but Warren sought to achieve this end in a way that would entice as many Democrats as possible to vote for the Republican ticket. On September 1, 1886, Secretary of the Interior Lamar overruled Sparks's rigid interpretation of the Desert Land Act, and this action won praise for Lamar in Wyoming newspapers. In drawing up the plank on land policy, Warren suggested to Van Devanter, his agent at the Republican territorial convention, that the gathering applaud Lamar's leniency and criticize the harsh interpretations of his subordinates. "Also ask Administration for laws liberal to poor settlers on public domain; that frauds be prevented by special agents examining land before proof instead of after and patent immediately issue after final proof. This must be advisedly done if put in at all."[26]

At the convention, held in Rawlins, the platform precisely reflected Warren's suggestions; adoption of the land plank enhanced the already favorable position of the Republicans in the races for delegate and territorial legislature.[27] They renominated Carey for another term, and his popularity drove all the Democratic candidates from the race. The convention of the Wyoming Democratic Party tendered its nomination to M. E. Post, who declined immediately, and then to a Laramie banker and rancher, H. G. Balch, who also refused the dubious honor. After this rebuff the Democrats gave up, and Carey ran without opposition. At the same

26. *Decisions of the Department of the Interior and General Land Office in Cases Relating to the Public Lands, 1886–1887* (Washington, 1887), pp. 120–123; Warren to Willis Van Devanter, Oct. 4, 1886, Warren Papers.

27. *Sun,* Oct. 8, 1886.

94

time, the Democratic convention, as angry as the Republicans over land policy and Sparks, declined to pass the standard resolution endorsing the presidential administration. As a result, the party faced electoral defeat in Wyoming and Cleveland's displeasure in Washington.[28]

Cleveland and Sparks had decided to make a change in the Wyoming governorship even before Carey's victory on November 6, 1886. Warren had irked the commissioner by noting, in his annual report to the secretary of the interior, that "Efforts of the General Land Office to protect the United States and the public domain for actual settlers and to prevent frauds are commendable, but if an overzealous course is pursued and the acquirement of land by bona fide entrymen is made so difficult as to amount almost to proscription, very great injury is done the class sought to be benefited by such efforts."[29]

This report, and the information he had obtained from his special agents, drove the commissioner to write the President on October 23,

I am fully impressed with the conviction that F. E. Warren Gov. of Wyoming Territory should be removed—I am satisfied that he has been engaged in personally in very doubtful if not absolutely fraudulent entries of the Pub. Lands, and he has certainly been used as an efficient *official* agent of men engaged in fraudulent and speculative appropriations of Pub. Lands to thwart and defeat me in my effort to reform Land abuses in that Territory. My opinion is that Morell [sic] E. Post

28. *Sun,* Oct. 16, 1886; Warren to Miss Kate Thomas, Oct. 11, 1886, Warren Papers.

29. "Annual Report of the Governor of Wyoming," *Annual Report of the Secretary of the Interior, 1886* (Washington, 1886), 2, 1007.

95

of said Territory is 'tarred with the same brush.' I
should regard his appt as equally fatal to Land reform
in that Territory.[30]

Following Sparks's advice Cleveland, on November 5,
1886, named the wealthy cattleman George W. Baxter to
replace Warren, but this resident appointment backfired
when Republicans revealed that Baxter had illegally fenced
government lands. Baxter described the charges as "unquali-
fiedly and absolutely false" but his protests were fruitless.
Disgusted with the Wyoming Democrats, on January 5,
1887, Cleveland turned to Thomas Moonlight, the recently
defeated Democratic candidate for governor of Kansas.
Happy to be rid of Baxter, whom he described as "an unmiti-
gated liar and a treacherous, tricky, indolent, incapable,
pusillanimous little wart besides," Warren saw a political
advantage in Moonlight's appointment: "With B[axter] we
would have to admit he was a home Gov. while he has nothing in common with us and would serve us in no way—with
an outsider, we can at least have the satisfaction of kicking
because he is an outsider and have the Administration and
the Dems on the 'hip' accordingly."[31]

As Warren recognized, the Cleveland administration, because of its ignorance of western conditions and lack of
sensitivity to the intimate relationship between federal
action and territorial politics, had managed to create the
worst possible result in Wyoming. The President had de-

30. William A. J. Sparks to Grover Cleveland, Oct. 23, 1886,
Grover Cleveland Papers, Manuscripts Division, Library of Congress.
31. George W. Baxter to L. Q. C. Lamar, Nov. 9, 1886, Appointment
Papers, Wyoming Governor, Interior Department, NA, RG48; G. W.
Glick to Grover Cleveland, Dec. 8, 1886, Cleveland Papers; Warren to
Carey, Jan. 24, 1887, Warren Papers; Jackson, "Governorship of
Wyoming," pp. 6–7.

layed his appointment of a successor to Warren until local Democrats had become confused and frustrated, and when he finally acted, the choice of Baxter had embarrassed his administration, strengthened the Republicans, and forced the selection of a nonresident governor. By his indecisive and ineffective actions, the President had advanced neither the cause of land reform nor the prospects of his party in a crucial western territory.

Governor Moonlight arrived in Cheyenne in January 1887 when the effects of the hard winter were ending the bonanza years in the Wyoming cattle industry. Faced with problems of political adjustment to the new economic situation, Wyoming politicians speculated about the attitude and policies of the new appointee. "I hear every kind of reports concerning him," Warren told Carey, "ranking him all the way from twin brother to J--- C--- down to a degenerate specimen of S--- of a B---. I notice the Administration are boosting him magnificently." This confusion about Moonlight's position on the significant economic and political questions was soon to be dispelled.[32]

A granger with a reverence for the small homestead, Moonlight believed that the territory must abandon large-scale cattle ranching and adopt forms of agriculture more suited to a growing population: "The first great important demand, then, in the way of population is farmers, practical, every-day farmers, who will put their hands to the plow and not look back." He further noted, in his annual report for 1887, that the residents of Wyoming had been unsympathetic to an increase of settlers while the cattle business prospered, but now, "The bars are down; the land is open; and where it is not open, those holding it are willing and anxious

32. Warren to Carey, Jan. 24, 1887, Warren Papers.

to sell, and will afford every facility for purchasing at a low price and on long time."[33]

This attitude placed Moonlight in direct opposition to the prevailing economic order in Wyoming, and he compounded his error, in Republican eyes, by his insistence on economy in government. A dogmatic advocate of lower spending, Moonlight had a highly developed sense of his prerogatives as governor and proved quick to challenge any inroads, real or imagined, on his authority. Rigid and self-righteous, Governor Moonlight brought the Cleveland policies to Wyoming with an immediacy which convinced the Wyoming populace that statehood, whatever its risks, could not be worse than a continuation of their territorial status.

The session of the Tenth Legislative Assembly, which opened in January 1888, brought the conflict between Moonlight and Wyoming to the surface. Although the Republicans had a large majority in the upper house, the Democrats controlled the House of Representatives. During the first month of the gathering, the legislators settled down to work, and by the middle of February had, according to Warren, "got in about the usual number of vicious and mischievous bills and show the usual reluctance about getting in really good bills."[34]

The placid quality of the early part of the session disappeared when the lawmakers reached the serious bills which affected the territory. The Stock Growers Association, seeking a substitute for the Maverick Law, passed an act creating a territorial agency to administer roundups. Moon-

33. "Annual Report of the Governor of Wyoming," *Annual Report of the Secretary of the Interior, 1887* (Washington, 1887), *1,* 1009, 1011.

34. *Sun,* Jan. 26, 1888; Warren to Carey, Feb. 15, 1888, Warren Papers.

light, convinced that the act would erode his appointing power, vetoed it and held out until a substitute measure was redrawn and passed. Because of the involvement of the WSGA, this bill has been given much attention by historians; but it was not, like the capitol building controversy, the major issue of the 1888 legislature, and the eagerness of all sides, even the governor, to work out a compromise is apparent in the contemporary accounts.[35]

Creation of new counties gave Moonlight his first real chance to joust with the legislature. Residents of the northern portions of Laramie and Albany counties, chafing under the domination of Cheyenne and Laramie, sought to form new counties, an aim which received Warren's blessing. "We certainly don't 'want to hold the children in after they are large enough to support themselves.' " Moonlight found the county of Converse, formed from Laramie and Albany, objectionable and vetoed the legislation; it was attached as a rider to an appropriation bill, and when the governor vetoed the money bill, the legislature passed the measure over his veto.[36]

Moonlight's action on these proposals evoked mild irritation from both parties during the session, but the governor alienated all factions by his disapproval of the bill appro-

35. T. B. Adams to Frank Canton, Feb. 24 and Mar. 7, 1888, Wyoming Stock Growers Association Papers, Western History Research Center, University of Wyoming; *Leader,* Jan. 15 and Feb. 8, 14, 22, and 23, 1888; W. T. Jackson, "The Administration of Thomas Moonlight," *Annals of Wyoming, 18* (1946), 155.

36. Thomas Moonlight to John Lobban, Mar. 5, 1888, to Henry A. Coffeen, Feb. 6, 1888, to William Springer, Feb. 27, 1888, Thomas Moonlight Letterbooks, Wyoming State Historical Society; Charles A. Guernsey, *Wyoming Cowboy Days* (New York, 1936), p. 41; Warren to F. S. Lusk, Jan. 21, 1888, Warren Papers.

priating money to finish the public buildings begun in 1886. Anxious to have the capitol completed and fixed at Cheyenne, Warren rallied the Republicans behind the measure, but his plans were upset when "Albany County 'fell out of bed with us' on the building proposition." A new combination was arranged with Carbon, Uinta, and Fremont County representatives, whose counties each received a share of the monies allocated for public buildings.[37]

Public opinion solidly supported the bill, and both Cheyenne newspapers urged Moonlight not to veto it. The governor remained dedicated to economy, believing that in vetoing the bill he "was performing my whole duty to the people of Wyoming and not in the interest of some locality." In his message, Moonlight warned the legislators, "The passage of this act, then, is enlarging the foundation for biennial attacks upon the Treasury of the Territory, and which all good citizens will condemn when public opinion has had time to ripen and mature." But to some Wyoming citizens, Moonlight's action proved that "M. is against about everything and everybody."[38]

The appropriation bill secured the necessary two-thirds for passage over Moonlight's veto, and the session dragged to a close with a squabble between the governor and the Council over the executive's nominations for territorial offices. The bitter taste of the legislature's troubles with Moonlight intensified Republican zeal for statehood. The

37. Warren to Thomas Sturgis, Feb. 23, 1888, to Carey, Mar. 17, 1888, to Sturgis, Mar. 27, 1888, Warren Papers.
38. *Sun*, Mar. 1, 1888; *Leader*, Mar. 1, 1888; Moonlight to John Lobban, Mar. 5, 1888, Moonlight Letterbooks; Warren to Carey, Mar. 17, 1888, Warren Papers; *House Journal of the Tenth Legislative Assembly of the Territory of Wyoming* (Cheyenne, 1888), p. 245.

first order of business was Moonlight's removal. "We ought to bounce this fellow," Warren told Carey, "and take the chances on getting worse. I know of nothing worse we could get unless it might be Baxter and he would probably have no show." Moonlight's ouster depended on a change in national administrations, and Wyoming Republicans prayed for Benjamin Harrison's victory in 1888.[39]

In the territorial election, the Republicans planned to renominate Carey and seek a repetition of his success in 1886. As a campaign tactic, the party decided to stress Wyoming's readiness for statehood and to claim that the Republicans could most easily achieve that goal. Late in August the Cheyenne *Sun* argued, "it is time to commence the agitation for statehood. Wyoming has stronger claims in that direction than is usually conceded, and as it seems to take several years of hard knocking at the door of the Union before the attention of Congress can be obtained, Wyoming ought to commence rapping on the door."[40]

Benjamin Harrison gave the Wyoming Republicans another push along the road to statehood when he noted in his letter of acceptance on September 11, 1888, that "Several Territories are well able to bear the burdens and discharge the duties of free Commonwealths in the American Union." The *Sun* responded with a renewed call for speedy admission, and Republican county conventions passed resolutions endorsing statehood. At the territorial convention on October 9, 1888, the platform asserted, "We now have the taxable wealth and the population necessary to support a state government, and, being therefore entitled to admission into the Union, we earnestly favor such congressional legislation

39. Warren to Carey, Mar. 17, 1888, Warren Papers.
40. *Sun,* Aug. 23, 1888.

as will enable us to adopt a constitution and secure the rights of statehood."[41]

The Republicans strengthened their appeal when they picked Carey as their standard-bearer once again. Running as the champion of statehood and the protective tariff, Carey began a spirited canvass of the territory. Meanwhile Warren turned his unique talents to Carey's cause. He wrote an Omaha hotel operator that "All the 'boys' and the 'good fellows' up in this country want to see Judge Carey returned to Congress and I am sure we can reckon on you as belonging to one of the 'gangs' above mentioned. I hope you will see your way clear to persuade all the voters at the Pacific Hotels in Wyoming to agree with us!"[42]

Against the formidable array of the statehood issue, Carey's candidacy, and Warren's tactics, the Democrats could only marshal a drab candidate and an equivocal platform. "On the question of statehood," said the party convention, "the Democrats, when the proper time arrives, will be found working enthusiastically in the front of the battle, but we do not believe in indulging in any spread eagle blatherskitism." Democratic newspapers continued this tone during the rest of the campaign; *"A vote for Carey,"* the *Leader* remarked on October 19, 1888, *"is a vote for statehood and ruinous taxation."* Having taken the unpopular side of the admission issue, the Democrats burdened their campaign by choosing Caleb Perry Organ as their delegate candidate. A Cheyenne storekeeper, cattleman, and relative unknown, Organ lacked speaking ability, a territorial reputation, and political skill.[43]

41. *Official Proceedings of the Republican National Convention, 1888* (Minneapolis, 1903), p. 248; *Sun,* Oct. 10, 1888.
42. Warren to Thomas Swobe, Oct. 30, 1888, Warren Papers.
43. *Leader,* Oct. 6 and 19, 1888.

Carey won easily, 10,461 to 7,557. His total was swelled by illegal votes in the western counties where some of the miners in Carbon and Sweetwater "voted two to four times apiece." Despite those illegal actions, Carey's victory did represent a repudiation of the Cleveland policies and was a mandate for statehood. The *Leader's* contention that the election had "not hinged on statehood. That was a subsidiary issue that cut scarcely any figure,"[44] sounded hollow to most Wyoming residents. By electing to oppose admission, rather than arguing that they could achieve it more readily than their opponents, the Democrats had placed themselves in a difficult and awkward position. Their situation did not improve as Republican moves for statehood began to bear fruit.

Governor Moonlight further crippled the Democratic cause when he wrote Secretary of the Interior William F. Vilas that Wyoming's population totaled only 55,500, far below his 1887 and 1888 estimates of 85,000. Since Moonlight was a lame duck executive and would be replaced when Harrison took office, this reappraisal appeared to Wyoming citizens as a calculated attempt to injure their statehood hopes. The *Leader* called Moonlight's attitude toward his associates "harsh, domineering and arbitrary. Instead of a simple governor, the chief executive official of a free people, he seemed to regard himself more in the light of a subordinate sent out by a Turkish sultan to rule one of his provinces with an iron hand."[45]

Public opinion started to coalesce around Warren as a successor to Moonlight in the three months before Harrison's inauguration. Warren's reputation for constructive

44. *Leader,* Nov. 9, 1888; Warren to W. C. Irvine, Sept. 20, 1890, Warren Papers.
45. Larson, *History of Wyoming,* pp. 242–43; *Leader,* Dec. 23, 1888.

action was enhanced by his participation in negotiations between Cheyenne and the Union Pacific for repair shops and a supply depot, which ended successfully in January 1889. Warren was elated by this success, but he had even greater plans for his city's economic development. As he reported to a friend later in the year, "poor old Cheyenne has had so many kicks and cuffs in the last four years, that she is now like a dog with tail between its legs, courage nearly gone; and it will take quite a little attention, good food and success to enable her to erect her caudal appendage in the fashion formerly worn."[46]

Warren's second gubernatorial campaign refined and elaborated the techniques which had worked so well four years earlier. More important, it showed how far his gift for marshaling support and creating the appearance of an overwhelming consensus had matured. During January and February 1889, there was little need for more than a perfunctory effort. Except for some desultory bickering about Cheyenne's claims on the governorship, little overt opposition to Warren surfaced. Meanwhile Warren stressed to his friends that he was not seeking the office but was responding to a popular tide: "I think perhaps it is just as well for me not to get too 'hot on the trail' and let them all have a chance to try for it, that want it, and let our 'constituency' understand, that I do not have to have this in order to live, and that it is a question that I have to have it at all."[47]

As long as he was unopposed, Warren found no difficulty in adhering to this policy. Early in March, however, a former territorial secretary, E. S. N. Morgan, opened a campaign against Warren by soliciting support in Cheyenne

46. Warren to Carey, Jan. 12, 1889, to Thomas Sturgis, Dec. 14, 1889, Warren Papers.
47. Warren to W. C. Irvine, Jan. 26, 1889, Warren Papers.

and Laramie. Basing his canvass on the supposed resentment toward the capital city, Morgan threw a momentary scare into Warren, who began writing daily, detailed letters to Carey with copious suggestions for counter-strategy. "I suppose you are tired of hearing about Morgan," he remarked on March 9, "and I apologize for it, but the stand he is taking this way and the extraordinary claims he makes, together with the vehemence with which he is pursuing the subject creates quite a little commotion, and I take it you would like to be fully advised, as I would want to be under similar circumstances."[48]

Morgan's candidacy was simply overwhelmed. Warren received endorsements from seventeen out of twenty members of the territorial Republican committee, the solid backing of party newspapers, and numerous petitions from businessmen, legislators, and local officials in his favor. On March 12, 1889, Warren could inform a Laramie colleague, "I have private advices from Washington, dated from there to-day (not from Carey) which are very assuring. You can bet the last dollar you have got, that Mr. Morgan will not get there, and draw on me for all damages."[49]

Harrison appointed Warren to the governorship on March 27, 1889, and Carey wired the Secretary of the Interior two days later that "the people greatly elated over appointment of Warren, Governor. They desire to have some ceremonies to celebrate inauguration of home rule for territories." The *Sun* described Warren's selection as "a blessing to the territory as well as a fitting recognition of the man and an exemplification of President Harrison's home rule policy." In accord with Carey's suggestion,

48. Warren to Carey, Mar. 9, 1889, Warren Papers.
49. Warren to Homer Merrell, Mar. 12, 1889, Warren Papers.

preparations quickly went forward for a formal ceremony of inauguration when Warren was confirmed. Everyone in the territory anticipated that Warren would deliver a call for a concerted statehood campaign.[50]

Warren's return to the governorship marked the end of the most frustrating period in Wyoming's territorial history. The policies of Cleveland, Sparks, and Moonlight had been inappropriate, ill-conceived, and irrelevant to the economic needs of Wyoming. The territory was beset with the same problems of underdevelopment which had retarded it since 1869; the cattle industry had receded from its boom heights to a level of activity which brought only moderate returns to its practitioners. Further expansion of the economy depended on the discovery of new resources, an unlikely event, or an increased amount of federal expenditures to promote irrigation, settlement, and agricultural growth. For Cleveland and his administration, dogmatic parsimony and rigid allegiance to the letter of the homestead system were the answers to western problems. This attitude brought defeat to the Wyoming Democrats from 1885 to 1888 and enabled the Republicans to seize the initiative in the statehood movement.

The first Cleveland administration made clear to Warren and Carey the need for added political power, a condition which only statehood could provide. Warren also realized that successful implementation of his ideas for Wyoming's economic development would require not only supremacy over the Democrats but also mastery of the Republicans. During the four years of Harrison's term, Warren collaborated eagerly in the statehood quest. In this he was no

50. Carey to John W. Noble, Mar. 29, 1889, quoted in Jackson, "Governorship of Wyoming," p. 11; *Sun,* Mar. 27, 1889.

different from Carey and other politicians. What set Warren apart was his perception that the prerequisite for economic improvement, federal aid, could be obtained only in the absence of political strife. A continual turnover in the congressional delegation from Wyoming would make control of the appropriation process impossible. Thus the significance of the period from 1889 to 1892 lies as much in Warren's enhanced understanding of the need for a strong political organization as in the more celebrated achievement of statehood.

CHAPTER FIVE. STATEHOOD AND AFTER, 1889-1892

RANCIS E. WARREN'S inauguration day, April 9, 1889, began in "a drizzling rain" which "continued the entire morning, leaving the streets in frightful condition." As the three thousand spectators gathered before the Wyoming capitol, the rain stopped and a cold breeze made everyone "chilly."[1] The "raw atmosphere and lowering clouds" did not affect the enthusiasm of the crowd as it waved banners reading "Home Rule, Francis E. Warren" and "Vox Populi, Vox Dei; Warren." I. S. Bartlett, a sometime journalist and poet, caught the mood of the throng in verses published by the *Sun* in its account of the ceremonies:

> And so this hour, our new career begun,
> We celebrate our independence day,
> And welcome him, Wyoming's favorite son,
> To weild [sic] our sceptre and our fortunes sway.[2]

At three o'clock Warren stepped forward, heard the invocation, took the oath of office, and bent to kiss the Bible. "If I understand the genius of this meeting and demonstration," he began, "you have assembled less to honor the individual, and more to pay tribute to a principle, and celebrate our material progress—to show our appreciation of home rule, and to hail coming statehood."[3] He quickly

1. *Leader,* Apr. 10, 1889.
2. *Sun,* Apr. 10, 1889.
3. Erwin, *Wyoming Historical Blue Book,* p. 582.

reviewed the background of the statehood agitation in the West and turned to Wyoming's qualifications for admission:

> It being granted then that the law which admits us to statehood will fully provide in revenue for all deficiencies, occasioned by the change, there can be no objection on the score of economy. . . .
>
> Wyoming will be in area the eighth state in the union. Her broad acres contain the most extensive oil, coal and iron fields of which we have knowledge. Her grazing and farming lands are extensive and her other resources are great and diversified. Excellent educational, charitable, penal and other buildings have been constructed. The moral and financial condition of the territory is good, and there is less illiteracy than in any other political division of the union . . . and as state government will not increase, but rather decrease taxation, there remains no possible objection to statehood. This being true, and there being many advantages in local government, *let us have statehood!*[4]

Political opposition blocked an immediate start on the statehood effort. Five days after Warren's inauguration, an unsigned article appeared in the *New York Times* attacking the governor for partisanship, sympathy with the cattlemen, and involvement in the strikebreaking tactics of the Union Pacific. At first Warren shrugged off the charges; but in June three more letters appeared in the *Times,* and this time the author, former judge William Ware Peck, revealed himself and made his charges more specific. Peck's indictment, which was to plague Warren for years, included allegations that Warren had enclosed government land il-

4. Ibid., p. 584.

legally through his livestock company and had committed fraud in acquiring his large holdings in Wyoming.[5]

Peck described the "mammoth inclosures" of the Warren Live Stock Company as "mammoth evils" and charged that the firm's "appetite for territory" was "absolutely insatiable. . . . The chief and head and front of this offending, of this stupendous, system and practice of oppressiveness and wrong is the Governor of Wyoming, sworn to obey an act of Congress, which he audaciously defies."[6] Warren reacted angrily to these political attacks and told Carey, "you will agree with me that this dirt is being systematically sent out from here by an organized clique to each & every democratic paper they can reach, the determination being to break me up here politically." Peck, who had been made an assistant United States attorney by the Democrats, suffered the usual penalty of rebellious western politicians and was removed by the President in response to Carey's appeals.[7]

Despite his ouster, Peck managed to plague the Republicans once again during the summer. Warren and Carey had decided that William W. Corlett should be the home rule candidate for chief justice of the territory. Unfortunately, Corlett had openly supported Grover Cleveland in 1884, and Peck reported this to Harrison. Corlett's strictures

5. *New York Times,* Apr. 14 and June 9, 22, and 24, 1889. For the way the charge pursued Warren, see Theodore Roosevelt to E. A. Hitchcock, Jan. 24, 1907, in *The Letters of Theodore Roosevelt,* ed. Elting Morison (8 vols. Cambridge, 1952), 5, 564–65.

6. *New York Times,* June 22, 1889.

7. Warren to Carey, July 6, 1889, Warren Papers; Carey to W. H. H. Miller, July 12, 1889, Wyoming Appointment Papers, Justice Department, NA, RG60. Warren received support from eastern sources as well; see H. K. Thurber to Benjamin Harrison, June 26, 1889, Benjamin Harrison Papers, Manuscripts Division, Library of Congress.

against James G. Blaine were harsh enough to convince the administration to veto his appointment. Harrison's attorney general, William H. H. Miller, broke the news to Carey who was, understandably, "somewhat embarrassed." When it became evident that Corlett would not be appointed under any circumstances, Carey fell back on his second choice, Willis Van Devanter. This appointment began Van Devanter's judicial career which eventually led him to the United States Supreme Court.[8]

Peck's assaults delayed but did not stop the Republican statehood drive. In May Carey persuaded several boards of county commissioners to adopt resolutions asking Governor Warren to summon a convention to write a constitution, and on June 3, 1889, Warren responded with a proclamation calling for the election of delegates. Since a bill to admit Wyoming as a state had failed in the Fiftieth Congress, the Republicans, following the advice of Senate leaders, hoped that if Wyoming fulfilled the provisions of the defeated admission bill, the territory's chances for admission in the Fifty-First Congress would be enhanced.[9]

To avoid arousing political opposition in Congress, the Republicans tried to cover the proceedings with a bipartisan veil. As Carey later assured Attorney General Miller, "it has been the earnest endeavor of our best men to pass from the

8. William Ware Peck to Benjamin Harrison, June 25, 1889, Carey to W. H. H. Miller, Aug. 1, 1889, Wyoming Appointment Papers, Justice Department, NA, RG60; Willis Van Devanter to Isaac Van Devanter, July 22, 1889, to William Lawrence, Aug. 3 and 16, 1889, Willis Van Devanter Papers, Manuscripts Division, Library of Congress.

9. Erwin, *Wyoming Historical Blue Book*, pp. 561–710, summarizes with relevant documents the events which led to Wyoming statehood.

Territorial condition to that of a State without complications." To accomplish this, the constitutional convention's delegates had to be chosen from both parties with as little turmoil as possible.[10]

In a few counties the Democrats did oppose the Republicans or balk at fusion tickets, but their usual tactic was to keep the vote down to embarrass the Republicans in Congress, where the question of the size of Wyoming's population was sure to arise. Warren, ever cautious, sent agents to distant counties to make sure that a substantial vote was obtained. "It was too late, when I came home, to do effective work in the northern line of counties, but I have had some sharp telegraphing done." Warren also told Carey that he had "arranged, that a perfect understanding was had regarding funds necessary, it being that they [other Republicans] could call on me for what was needed, if they got into hot water anywhere." These exertions by the G.O.P. demonstrate the political character which, however subdued, marked the statehood campaign in Wyoming.[11]

The Republican tactics succeeded, and the convention met in September 1889. In its month of deliberations the convention showed little originality, taking most of the Wyoming constitution from the documents in effect in North Dakota, Montana, and Idaho. As John D. Hicks has pointed out, Wyoming followed the precedent of other western states in doing this. The delegates did break new ground in the section on water rights where, following the

10. Carey to W. H. H. Miller, Sept. 25, 1890, Wyoming Appointment Papers, Justice Department, NA, RG60; Warren to Carey, July 5, 1889, Warren Papers.

11. Warren to Carey, July 5, 1889, Warren Papers; William M. Neil, "The American Territorial System Since the Civil War: A Summary Analysis," *Indiana Magazine of History, 60* (1964), 239.

advice of territorial engineer Elwood Mead, they wrote a provision for state control of Wyoming's waters that based the right of prior appropriation on the criteria of beneficial use. They also provided the governmental structure to administer the principle.[12]

Analyzing the political implications of the convention, Warren believed that the lawmakers had shown too much regard for the rights of miners, settlers, and the less fortunate. In addition, he argued, the legislative apportionment drawn by the convention discriminated against Laramie County in favor of the northern counties and would have to be changed by the first state legislature. Because the political leaders, Warren and Carey, remained aloof from the convention's proceedings, the gathering could exercise considerable independence; this led Warren in later years to characterize the body as the "fool Constitutional Convention."[13]

With the constitution signed and an "Address to the People of Wyoming" issued, it remained for the people of Wyoming to approve the document. On November 5, 1889, they voted 6,272 to 1,923 to accept the constitution; the low vote did not help the statehood cause, but Wyoming residents claimed that the turnout had been small because everyone felt sure the constitution would be ratified. With the election over, Delegate Carey returned to Washington

12. *Journals and Debates of the Constitutional Convention of the State of Wyoming* (Cheyenne, 1893), pp. 497–512, 534–37; John D. Hicks, *The Constitutions of the Northwest States* (Lincoln, Nebraska, 1923); Henry J. Peterson, "The Constitutional Convention of Wyoming," *University of Wyoming Publications,* 7 (1940), 101–30; Larson, *History of Wyoming,* pp. 243–56.

13. Warren to Carey, Feb. 26, 1890, Warren Papers; Warren to Willis Van Devanter, Nov. 13, 1890, Van Devanter Papers.

to begin agitation when the Fifty-First Congress convened in December.[14]

Since both parties in Wyoming had their own reasons to avoid any political excitement, the progress of the admission was followed with little concern by the populace. While the lack of outward enthusiasm served the Republicans well, it forced Carey to wage the struggle in Congress alone, and in a series of letters he complained to Willis Van Devanter of political inaction and begged territorial officials for help. On January 24, 1890, he moaned that he was "receiving but little assistance from the people of Wyoming in this fight," and believed he was "entitled to the assistance of the press and of the Wyoming legislature." In response to Carey's request for a memorial from the lawmakers asking Congress to admit Wyoming, Warren summoned reliable legislators together to produce the desired document.[15]

By early March Carey had arranged with the leadership in the House of Representatives for the speedy consideration of the admission bill, and on March 15 he told Van Devanter that the "State matter, up to this point is in the best possible shape." On March 26, 1890, following an eloquent speech by Carey, the House approved the Wyoming bill by a party vote of 139–127 and sent the measure to the Senate. Since action by the upper chamber was sure to be favorable, Wyoming politicians turned to the question of the state election which would follow Senate ratification.[16]

14. Erwin, *Wyoming Historical Blue Book,* pp. 648–51.

15. Carey to Van Devanter, Jan. 24, 1890, Van Devanter Papers; Warren to Carey, Jan. 29, 1890, Warren Papers; Lewis L. Gould, "Joseph M. Carey and Wyoming Statehood," *Annals of Wyoming,* 37 (1965), 157–69.

16. Carey to Van Devanter, Mar. 15, 1890, Van Devanter Papers;

Several factors contributed to the relatively easy achievement of Wyoming statehood. Given the Republican majorities in Congress and Benjamin Harrison in the White House, admission for such a politically reliable territory was assured. Yet other reasons account for the swiftness of the process. A homogeneous population prevented the rise of ethnic questions which delayed matters in Arizona and New Mexico; similarly, the absence of bitter sectional animosities precluded the difficulties experienced by Dakota. Most important of all, with the exception of Cleveland's land policy, the territorial experience had touched Wyoming very lightly. All the promotional techniques attempted by governors and delegates could be more effectively implemented by senators and representatives, and the problems of economic growth could be the subject of more direct action when Wyoming had its own spokesmen in Washington. Devoid of loyalties to their territorial past, the residents of Wyoming accepted statehood as a foregone conclusion, and this attitude helped to make it so.

Placed on the defensive by the statehood issue, Wyoming Democrats had also mishandled the last session of the territorial legislature. The Democrats had a majority in the upper house and did everything possible to humiliate Warren and the Republicans. The governor's nominees for auditor and treasurer were rejected, and the party sought to whittle down the contingency funds of Warren and the territorial secretary. Warren then asked Carey to secure legislation to allow him to unseat the holdover Democrats and appoint a Republican treasurer and auditor. "It is probably true that this action of the Council will secure us votes,

---

Congressional Record, 51st Cong., 1st sess. (Mar. 26, 1890), pp. 2710–12; Erwin, *Wyoming Historical Blue Book,* pp. 663–703.

but, having secured those, we could secure still more if I could have the axe in hand for keeps and to right ourselves. Voters always love the successful one and the successful party, hence they would follow the band wagon, if we were able to outwit and out do, this strongly partisan, foolish Council."[17]

Carey could not manage that feat, but the Democrats overplayed their hand on the contingency fund question, enabling Warren to defeat them. On the last day of the session, the Republican House adjourned before the Democratic Council could finish action on the general appropriation bill. Since the Democrats refused to alter their resolve to rebuke Warren by cutting down his contingent fund, the Republicans decided to leave their opponents with the onus for the failure of the appropriation measure to pass. The House "very properly determined," said Warren, "that the Governor and Secretary appointed by the present republican administration should not be insulted in the way contemplated by the democrats."[18] The success of this maneuver had the happy dividend, in Warren's eyes, of promoting unity among the Republicans: "I have never seen the time when there was a better prospect of a close adherence to party lines with a sharpened desire to work, than I have found yesterday and to-day. . . . If we measure our own comfort by the discomfort of our enemies, we certainly ought to feel good here now."[19]

Warren's skillful handling of the Republicans prevented any real opposition breakthrough in the legislature, but he

17. Warren to Carey, Feb. 14 and 26 and Mar. 11, 1890, Warren Papers.

18. Warren to Carey, Mar. 13, 1890, Warren Papers; *Leader,* Mar. 15 and 16, 1890.

19. Warren to Carey, Mar. 13, 1890, Warren Papers.

watched with more concern Democratic preparations for the first statewide campaign. "I am trying to get some action and some enthusiasm into representative republicans in the different counties as I can get hold of them, and quite a number of them are waking up to the fact that an early campaign is imminent, that the democrats are wary and working, that the republicans are careless and sleepy."[20]

To seize the initiative, the Republicans relied on an effective exploitation of Democratic opposition to the movement for Wyoming statehood. As Carey put it, "the Democratic party have gone crazy and I think are making fools of themselves to day. If they are not fools, the great mass of the people of Wyoming Territory are." After the House had passed the admission bill, Carey told Van Devanter that the time had come to "put the Democratic party on the defensive; our campaign is to be the offensive one."[21]

Republicans also had to consider how to distribute the spoils of office in the event of an electoral victory. After his labors in Congress, Carey would have no difficulty in securing election to the Senate if a Republican legislature was returned. To insure this result, Warren urged him to seek the cooperation of the railroads in the Republican campaign. He told Carey to go to Boston, see Charles Francis Adams, the president of the Union Pacific, ask his help, and "tell him the importance . . . of his instructing 'the powers that be' at Omaha the necessity of having republicans at the helm in Wyoming in the interests of the U.P., and what a lot of 'blatherskites' and anti-monopoly, workingman's

20. Warren to Carey, Feb. 26, 1890, Warren Papers. For Democratic preparations, see James B. Beck to George T. Beck, Feb. 17, 1890, C. H. Burritt to George T. Beck, July 3, 1890, George T. Beck Collection, Western History Research Center, University of Wyoming.

21. Carey to Van Devanter, Apr. 21, 1890, Van Devanter Papers.

friend, lot of pretenders the democrats are, who will assume to control the next election; and fix the thing up generally."[22]

Through Willis Van Devanter, Warren sought from Carey an expression of his desires about the Senate. The delegate offered Van Devanter only evasive assertions of his fidelity to the Republican party in answer to these inquiries.

> I have never wanted to consider myself a prospective candidate for the Senate or any other place that would be open by reason of Wyoming becoming a state. I have put this matter off as something to be decided by the circumstances that might hereafter arise. My great ambition for the last two years has been to see the territory admitted as a state. As soon as that is accomplished, my most earnest desire will be to have the state take its place in line with the party that shall have made its admission possible.[23]

A latent thread of hostility complicated the negotiations between Carey and Warren over the allocation of offices. Never close except in politics, the two men had begun to realize that the state of Wyoming was not large enough to accommodate their conflicting ambitions. As their differences emerged, tension grew. Because the Warren-Carey feud shaped and dominated Wyoming Republican politics for two and a half decades, it would be convenient if the historian could fix with precision the exact moment when Warren and his associate drew apart permanently. This is not possible, and the evidence indicates only a gradual drift from uneasy collaboration to open hostility.[24]

22. Warren to Carey, Apr. 8, 1890, Warren Papers.
23. Carey to Van Devanter, Apr. 8, 1890, Van Devanter Papers.
24. Warren's biographer, Mr. F. Duane Rose, who has interviewed

Whatever the real explanation for the break, by April 1890 Warren had lost much of his patience with Carey. In a letter in which he acknowledged that "perhaps [I] have written too frankly," adding however that "frankness is not the worst fault in the world," Warren listed his complaints against the delegate:

It has been and is my aim and desire to aid you in all possible ways in your political ambitions and success, and I don't propose to be turned aside until you are safely landed, or, with the rest of us, finally busted; but I am considerably handicapped. First, by not receiving as frank expressions and as much information from you as I am willing and anxious to give. Second, by feeling that some things I write may be in danger; and Third—and this is the most galling—by constant and numerous injuries and attacks, mainly underhanded, made upon me by over zealous relatives and friends of yours, who seem to have the peculiar idea that your greatest success must be secured by tearing me down. Doubtless they have the idea (which is totally untrue) that I am in some manner in your way. Now, Judge, I *am not* laying this up *against you,* nor am I entering a complaint upon which I wish you to act at present, but write because these matters are facts and bother me much, and will explain how I am handicapped.[25]

Unity between Carey and Warren, while strained, lasted through the first state election campaign. As expected, the

surviving members of Warren's firm, told me in the summer of 1964 that the Warren camp saw Mrs. Carey as one of the main disruptive forces between the two men.

25. Warren to Carey, Apr. 22, 1890, Warren Papers.

Senate passed the Wyoming bill 29–18 on June 27, 1890, and President Harrison signed the measure on July 10. The Republicans celebrated with the rest of Wyoming but wasted no time in preparing for the election. At the Republican convention in Cheyenne on August 11, the delegates nominated Warren to run for governor even though he had not pursued the office; when the convention met, he was seriously ill and only agreed to seek the governorship because "it seemed . . . a coward's part for me to decline it."[26]

Warren's opponent was the former territorial governor, George W. Baxter, and the focus of the whole campaign became the gubernatorial canvass. "The dirt of the entire campaign has all been aimed at me," Warren complained, "and from the Wyoming democratic newspapers one would be led to presume I was the only man running on the Republican ticket and Baxter the only one on the other side." Until Warren recovered Carey bore the brunt of the Republican effort, stumped the state, and engaged in a series of public debates with Baxter. The Democrats meanwhile asserted that Warren was using illness to his own advantage: "The Republicans figure, and we do not believe the governor himself overlooks the fact, that if it is given out that he is dangerously ill this fact grants him a certain degree of immunity from just criticism, while his own henchmen, newspaper and otherwise, may resort to any method however disreputable and scurrilous to further his candidacy."[27]

Republican newspapers countered by reviewing Baxter's record in Wyoming and warned voters to beware of the

26. Warren to Byron Weston, Aug. 25, 1890, Warren Papers; *Leader,* Aug. 16, 1890.
27. Warren to Thomas Sturgis, Sept. 1, 1890, Warren Papers; *Leader,* Aug. 16, 1890.

Democratic candidate, a Tennessee native, and other south-
erners who wanted to fasten their own kind of carpetbagger
rule on the state. "Vote the Republican ticket and loosen the
hold of the southern vampires who have long enough been
sucking the life-blood of Wyoming." Toward this end,
Warren arranged with the commanding officer at Fort
McKinney, near Buffalo, to have the soldiers vote at the
post, and when he learned that the Union Pacific planned
to bring Chinese workmen back to Rock Springs, scene of
the 1885 riot, he sought the cooperation of the railroad in
keeping the political effect to a minimum after the election.[28]

Their prestige as the party of statehood swept the Republicans to victory on September 11, 1890. Warren carried
every county and defeated Baxter by seventeen hundred
votes, 8,879 to 7,153. The leading Republican counties,
Uinta, Laramie, and Albany, were all along the route of
the Union Pacific; to the north, the Republican majorities
fell off to sixty-two votes in Sheridan, twenty-two in Natrona,
and seventy in Fremont. The legacy of the Rock Springs riot
kept Warren's majority in Sweetwater down to twenty-seven
ballots. Clarence D. Clark, an Evanston attorney and the
Republican congressional candidate, ran ahead of Warren
and trounced his opponent by more than twenty-five hundred votes; the G.O.P. controlled the legislature with thirty-
nine members in a forty-nine seat body. After a cursory
examination of the returns, the Republicans had good
reason to believe that they had established themselves as
the dominant party and would put the state in the Republican column in 1892. Nevertheless, their electoral coalition

28. *Wyoming Commonwealth,* Sept. 7, 1890; Warren to J. S. Tebbits,
general manager Union Pacific Coal Company, Sept. 11, 1890, Warren
Papers.

had numerous soft spots in northern and central Wyoming which would be tested in the event of a statewide crisis.[29]

Francis E. Warren's election to the Senate in 1890 placed the first strains on Republican dominance and proved to be one of his rare political setbacks. During the campaign Republican orators, especially Judge Carey, had assured audiences that Warren would serve a full term as governor and that he had no secret ambitions for higher office. Whether these platform promises reflected Warren's own feelings is doubtful; years later, he described Carey as "dishonorable" in making such declarations without asking Warren's permission. In any case, the electorate, especially the Republicans, believed that Warren would be governor, Carey the senator from Cheyenne, and some Republican from outside the capital the other senator.[30]

The legislature quickly named Carey and turned to picking the other Republican fortunate. On the seventh ballot Warren was chosen. Even now it is difficult to say whether he had sought the nomination directly in the legislature. In 1894, in the course of a spirited campaign for Carey's seat, he referred to events in 1890: "I was not a candidate until he [Carey] had been safely landed and then when a disagreement on an outside man arose, I became a candidate and was elected. I would not permit the use of my name to his detriment. I believed, then, that the state wanted J. M. Carey as their first choice for Senator, I acquiesced."[31]

29. Erwin, *Wyoming Historical Blue Book,* pp. 1176–77; O. H. Platt to Benjamin Harrison, Sept. 13, 1890, Harrison Papers.

30. Laramie *Weekly Sentinel,* Nov. 22, 1890; Fenimore Chatterton, *Yesterday's Wyoming* (Denver, 1957), p. 45; Warren to George E. Brimmer, Oct. 23, 1910, Warren Papers.

31. Warren to Merris C. Barrow, Dec. 12, 1894, Warren Papers; *Leader,* Nov. 15, 18, and 19, 1890.

Since Warren's historical perspective always took into account the demands of the moment, it is hardly surprising that his actions in 1890 belie his words in 1894. Before the legislature met, Warren had indicated to his friends his desire to avoid the chores of being governor in favor of the more hospitable duties of a senator:

People will fight about my leaving the Governor-ship, on the ground that I am elected for four years, that I am competent and experienced in executive business and also in politics. Of course they understand the office was crowded onto me, that I have a right to leave it, and they must understand, sooner or later, that I am liable to leave it any way by resignation, if I should not be Senator therever; because the way I am feeling now, I believe it will be necessary for me to spend some part of the time for the next one, two or more years at sea level in order to get rest from the effects on my nervous system of the high altitude.[32]

The defeated candidates, especially the president of the University of Wyoming and former governor John Wesley Hoyt, had no doubts that Warren had betrayed them for his own purposes. Yet as the Cheyenne newspapers pointed out, Warren's competition was lackluster, and he had great strength among the legislators from counties outside Cheyenne and Laramie. A figure of prominence throughout the state, Warren overshadowed his opponents who were, to put it charitably, second-rate.[33]

Warren's selection outraged large sections of his party.

32. Warren to W. C. Irvine, Oct. 18, 1890, Warren Papers.
33. Kepler Hoyt, *Life of John Wesley Hoyt,* typescript, Wyoming State Historical Society, pp. 365–66; *Leader,* Oct. 26 and Nov. 13, 1890.

The Republican Laramie *Weekly Sentinel* was "sorry because it justifies the charge that ring rule and political boss-
ism is so early and so thoroughly inaugurted [sic] in the
republican party in the very infancy of our statehood."
Among ambitious Republicans like Fenimore Chatterton
of Saratoga and DeForest Richards of Douglas, a movement
grew to oppose Warren's reelection. This resolve hardened
when Warren and Carey, in Washington for the opening of
Congress in December, drew lots, and Warren received the
two-year term, Carey the four-year term. If Warren sought
election in 1893, he would face determined opposition.
Meanwhile he was content: "Well, I guess two years will
be all I want of it and perhaps more than I can really afford
to take. Carey should have the long term as he is the senior
and I am not at all put out about it, but on the contrary
really glad."[34]

Warren's elevation to the Senate left the office of governor
vacant after his resignation on November 25, 1890. By the
provisions of the constitution, the secretary of state, Amos
W. Barber,[35] would succeed to the office as acting governor.
But after Warren's election, a movement began among the
members of the Albany County delegation to have the
legislature elect a successor to Warren, preferably Edward
Ivinson, a Laramie banker. Members of the Albany County
contingent visited Warren and "wanted to pin me down
(they asked the matter be *private*) to say that if bill for

34. Laramie *Weekly Sentinel,* Nov. 22, 1890; Warren to A. J.
Parshall, Dec. 3, 1890, Warren Papers.

35. Barber was a Pennsylvania doctor who came to Wyoming in
1885 as director of the military hospital at Fort Fetterman. While
practicing medicine at Douglas, he was nominated for secretary of
state. Harry B. Henderson, "Governors of the State of Wyoming,"
Annals of Wyoming, 12 (1940), 13–14.

legislature to elect Governor passed, I would help Albany County and support Ivinson."[36]

According to Willis Van Devanter in 1894,[37] the idea for legislative action originated with Carey, who managed to convince E. A. Slack, the editor of the Cheyenne *Sun,* to support it. Carey also promoted interest among Albany County Republicans on Ivinson's behalf. Warren believed that the plan was unconstitutional on its face, but he realized as well that the scheme would draw renewed attention to his resignation. The Albany County effort floundered because of the unfortunate constitutional precedent it would set. Van Devanter reported to Warren on December 11, 1890, that "the matter relating to the election of the Governor by the Legislature has all fallen through." Carey's covert sponsorship did help to persuade Warren that he must be careful of his colleague, and relations between the two Senators became still more distant.[38]

The possibility of tension between the two men disturbed some elements in the Wyoming Republican Party, but Warren vowed to them that he would not be the one to break the truce. "By the way, Billy," he told the prominent rancher W. C. Irvine, "you gave me some good advice about not having our knives out, must agree on every thing, not fight, etc. Now I can assure you that the matter shall be so handled at this end of the line that no disturbance or bad blood shall occur. There is too much at stake for Wyoming.

36. Warren to Van Devanter, Oct. 28, 1890, Van Devanter Papers. From internal evidence, I believe this letter should be dated Nov. 28, 1890.

37. Van Devanter to W. A. Richards, May 8, 1894, Van Devanter Papers.

38. Van Devanter to Warren, Dec. 11, 1890, Van Devanter Papers; *Leader,* Nov. 30, 1890.

On the other hand, if the friends of either and of both at that end of the line shall hold things there level on the same issue every thing will come out O.K., you may depend upon it."[39]

Among Warren's friends in Cheyenne, Willis Van Devanter now came to occupy a preeminent place. The son of an Indiana lawyer, Van Devanter had arrived in Wyoming in 1884 as a young attorney only three years out of the Cincinnati Law School. He had offered his services to Warren in 1885 and during the next four years had worked in a number of minor offices, until his appointment as territorial chief justice. This activity enabled him to win a greater and greater measure of Warren's confidence. Thirty-one years old in 1890, Van Devanter possessed limitless ambition, an immense capacity for hard work, and a never-failing commitment to Warren's cause. In him, Warren found the perfect lieutenant—discreet, loyal, and knowledgeable. Behind Van Devanter's thin face and neat moustache was an alert and perceptive mind, equally adroit at drafting bills, arguing election contests in court, supervising legislatures, or running political campaigns. From 1890 to 1897, the team of Warren and Van Devanter functioned with efficiency, and Warren owed much of his success to the contributions of his faithful aide.[40]

Reapportionment was the most pressing issue that Van Devanter faced in dealing with the first state legislature. The constitutional convention had allotted Laramie County only three senators and six representatives, while allowing the northern counties more members than they deserved. Since the next official redistricting of the state would not occur

39. Warren to W. C. Irvine, Jan. 11, 1891, Warren Papers.
40. Lewis L. Gould, "Willis Van Devanter in Wyoming Politics, 1884–1897," unpublished Ph.D. thesis, Yale University, 1966, pp.1–102.

until 1895, Warren would have to run for reelection in 1893 at a severe disadvantage. Consequently, he suggested to Governor Barber, "that if possible whole number [of legislators] should be kept about what it is cutting off from counties now having too many, rather than make big, unwieldy expensive legislature."[41]

The failure of Albany County to obtain a United States senator, coupled with the resentment of the northern counties at the arrogance of the Cheyenne delegation, combined to thwart Warren's plan. Van Devanter was kept busy fighting bills to give each county only one senator in the legislature, a scheme which had failed in the constitutional convention, while hammering out a bill to safeguard Cheyenne's interests. Unwisely, the Laramie County members allowed the apportionment bill to be deferred until the end of the session, when the accumulated resentments of the other legislators made passage impossible.[42]

On the last day of the session, the Laramie County forces tried to push the bill through. At that point, confusion over whether the clerk of the house had falsified the legislative record of the bill convinced opponents of the measure that Cheyenne and Warren had engaged in fraud to achieve their ends. Though the charge was false, the bill failed, to Warren's intense disappointment: "It seems a pity if the bill had a proper place of record that its friends could not have protected its honor, even if voted down; but, of course, I am incompetent to judge of matters and things at this distance."[43]

41. Warren to Van Devanter, Nov. 13, 1890, Van Devanter Papers.
42. Van Devanter to Warren, Dec. 24, 1890, Van Devanter Papers; S. B. Tuttle to Warren, Jan. 15, 1891, Warren Papers; *Leader,* Jan. 13, 1891.
43. *Leader,* Jan. 13, 1891; S. B. Tuttle to Warren, Jan. 15, 1891, Warren Papers; Warren to Van Devanter, Jan. 20, 1891, Van Devanter Papers.

In the meantime, Warren plunged into his work in Congress to establish his reputation as a spokesman for Wyoming. He asked Van Devanter to draft various bills for the construction of military roads to Yellowstone Park and for a federal court for Fremont County, adding, half-jocularly, "and in fact all such other matters as are desirable from your standpoint to get for the people of Wyoming or for me to receive glory from in introducing."[44]

The new state whose interests Warren wanted to serve had outgrown some of the economic handicaps it had possessed as a territory, but large problems remained to vex politicians and business leaders. Of Wyoming's sixty-two thousand residents in 1890, forty-four thousand lived in the five southern counties along the line of the railroad. Cheyenne, with eleven thousand inhabitants, and Laramie, with six thousand, were the largest towns, followed by Rock Springs, Rawlins, and Evanston; significantly, all five towns were seats of the Union Pacific counties. In the north, the seven smaller counties, Converse, Crook, Fremont, Johnson, Natrona, Sheridan, and Weston, tried to carry on efficient government under the twin burdens of a low population and a declining tax base. Their legislative representation gave them importance in senatorial elections, and the expectation that their inhabitants were the vanguard of large numbers of settlers caused southern politicians to pay attention to northern sensibilities.[45]

Predominantly native-born, Protestant, and rural, Wyo-

44. Warren to Van Devanter, Dec. 6, 1890, Warren Papers.

45. For evidence of a recognition of sectional concerns, see Warren to Carey, Dec. 12, 1889, Warren Papers; Van Devanter to Mortimer Jesurun, Aug. 11, 1894, Van Devanter Papers; "Report of the Governor of Wyoming," *Report of the Secretary of the Interior, 1889* (Washington, 1890), 5, 605–14.

ming's people earned their living in stock raising (13.5 percent), crop agriculture (12.4 percent), mining (10.4 percent), manufacturing (9.1 percent), and railroad work (7.2 percent). Consequently, the state's industrial structure looked more promising than it had in 1870. Agriculture no longer lagged behind the rest of the West, largely because of the cattle business; but the percentage of those engaged in crop agriculture still was the lowest of all the states and territories of the Rocky Mountain region. The number working in transportation, especially railroads, had drawn nearer the total of the other western states, but Wyoming's percentage continued to exceed its neighbors'. Finally, manufacturing and mining had shown small percentage increases over the two decades, but neither had attained a size commensurate with the hopes of Wyoming inhabitants.[46]

The role of the federal government as an alternative resource had receded. Statehood threw the expenses of governing back on the people, a drawback which seemed a small price to pay for an augmented voice in the legislative process in Washington. The military presence did not disappear from Wyoming without some laments from the natives. In the 1880s, as the focus of Indian conflict shifted to Arizona and New Mexico, Wyoming's number of soldiers fell off from thirteen hundred at the start of the decade to eight hundred and seventy-one in 1890. Despite Warren's efforts and the complaints of his constituents, the troop total persisted in its decline, reaching a low point of four hundred and fifty-six in 1900. The closing of forts and the withdrawal of soldiers in the 1890s was a trend which Warren labored ceaselessly to reverse.[47]

46. Arrington, *Changing Economic Structure,* pp. 32, 43.
47. Ibid.

In addition to the demand for increased military expenditures, the tariff started to loom as a factor in Wyoming politics. Sheep had become an important secondary product of the stock raising industry, especially in Carbon, Converse, and Sweetwater counties; as a result, the fortunes of the wool tariff received new attention in Wyoming. Protection for hides naturally claimed supporters among cattlemen, while railroad employees saw a virtue in duties on steel rails, iron, and coal. For many voters in Wyoming, Republican assertions of a connection between the tariff and their prosperity acquired much plausibility.[48]

Francis E. Warren recognized the importance of tariff bills and forts, but they did not provide a solution to Wyoming's major difficulty—an abundance of potential farmland which lay useless because of its aridity. In 1890, three-quarters of Wyoming's land was unimproved because so much of it lay in areas that received less than fifteen inches of rain per year. Looking at the waters which fell as snow on Wyoming's mountains and ran useless through the state as spring floods, Warren, under the guidance of Elwood Mead, became an ardent proponent of irrigation during his second term as territorial governor.[49]

His interest in reclamation led Warren into the front ranks of the western irrigation movement, but originally his involvement was a pragmatic answer to the needs of his constituents. At the same time, his struggle for an arid land cession bill represented a striking early example of Warren's legislative technique and his commitment to the use of the federal government as a promotional agent in the economic development of Wyoming. Most important, the wave of

48. Julian Ralph, *Our Great West* (New York, 1893), pp. 368–72.
49. "Report of the Governor of Wyoming," *Report of the Secretary of the Interior, 1889* (Washington, 1890), 5, 626–31.

criticism of his proposal within Wyoming brought home to Warren the necessity for solidifying his political base in his own state.

The idea of ceding the arid public lands to the states had gained popularity in the West after the failure of John Wesley Powell's irrigation survey to quicken the pace of reclamation. Warren believed that the states should use the proceeds from the sale of public lands to aid capitalists in construction of irrigation facilities. This would simultaneously stimulate private enterprise and prevent the federal government from exercising control over the development of irrigation. Working with Elwood Mead, Warren drafted a bill which he submitted on February 16, 1891. "The bill will receive little or no attention this session," Warren correctly predicted, "but I shall introduce something in its place upon the assembling of the next Congress."[50]

In the interval, Warren proceeded to marshal western support for cession. He spoke with railroad executives, government officials, and irrigation engineers on the bill's behalf. Through Elwood Mead and a Cheyenne colleague, Frank Bond, Warren persuaded the First National Irrigation Congress at Salt Lake City in September 1891 to endorse the arid land cession idea. Within Wyoming, Warren worked to swing public opinion behind his scheme. "In Cheyenne all of the State officers have signed the petition," Mead reported in January 1892, "all of the newspaper men except [E. S. N.] Morgan and [A. S.] Mercer of the Live Stock Record who were opposed. The Board of Trade has

50. Lewis L. Gould and William Lilley, III, "The Western Irrigation Movement, 1878–1902: A Reappraisal," *The American West: A Reorientation,* ed. Gene M. Gressley (Laramie, 1967), pp. 68–69; Warren to Joseph Nimmo, Feb. 25, 1891, copy of S. 5087, 51st Cong., 3d sess., Warren Papers.

endorsed it or will do so and I want to secure the individual signatures of all the members."[51]

Warren, meanwhile, labored over a new bill setting forth the cession principle, which he introduced on March 9, 1892. As submitted by Warren, the measure envisioned the total granting of the arid lands to the states, without restrictions. Once the state had received the portions of the public domain within its borders, it must set up irrigation districts, provide for the allocation of water to them, and supervise the actual work of reclamation. The state was also allowed to mortgage or use the land as collateral for bonds, a provision indispensable for the financing of future irrigation systems.[52]

Warren maintained that his bill was designed only to aid the people of Wyoming and that he had "no interest in this legislation whatever except the prosperity of the State and to provide for the new settlers the poor men and those of moderate means." Only by reclamation and irrigation, argued Warren, would Wyoming attain decent farmland to "put the arid region somewhere near on a par or basis with the eastern and more favored states whose settlers had farm land that was as good as ours will be after reclamation—perhaps even better."[53]

The Senator believed that his bill solved most of the difficult problems of irrigation. His optimism may have

51. Frank Bond to S. W. Irish, Sept. 29, 1891, to A. C. Botkin, Dec. 4, 1891, Frank Bond Letterbook, Wyoming State Historical Society; Elwood Mead to Warren, Jan. 22, 1892 (the quotation is from this letter), to John R. Arnold, Jan. 22, 1892, to Charles H. Burritt, Jan. 29, 1892, Wyoming State Engineer's Records, Wyoming State Archives.

52. Copy of S. 2529, 52d Cong., 1st sess., Warren Papers.

53. Warren to E. A. Slack, Feb. 3, 1892, to E. E. Lonabaugh, Feb. 19, 1892, Warren Papers.

been excessive,[54] but his sincerity was genuine. Warren's position as a leading landowner and stock raiser in Wyoming, however, allowed his political opponents to charge that the arid land bill was simply a device to enable him to monopolize more land. Once the state owned the land, they asserted, Warren would manipulate the administrative machinery to increase his own holdings. The small farmer and rancher who should obtain the benefits of irrigation would in reality achieve nothing. Some of this opposition Warren saw as politically motivated, some as simply misguided, but all of it frustrated him. "The more I have worked on this problem of getting out a bill covering the necessary points and also assurances of protection and restriction to the weak minded and 'shakey kneed' the harder I find it [to] make a garment that in one piece will fit all shapes, sizes and colors of people and their prejudices and beliefs, to say nothing of the political capital that the ungodly are always sure to undertake to make."[55]

Warren's bill died in committee, but he was undaunted by this temporary reverse. He felt certain that legislative success grew from persistence, and he planned to keep up his campaign to educate his constituents and Senate colleagues to the value of cession. His ability to do this hinged on his reelection in 1893, and in the spring of 1892 he had to face the problems attendant on running again. Aware of the opposition to his elevation in 1890, he urged his supporters to avoid premature discussion of his chances. "Knowing the joggle that the senatorship may create in politics, it is probably better for me to neither declare myself entirely out nor to assume that I will be a 'hot on the

54. Gould and Lilley, "Western Irrigation Movement," p. 69.
55. Warren to Slack, Mar. 3, 1892, Warren Papers.

trail' candidate. If it is considered that I am liable to be a candidate to succeed myself, it will probably hold things together for the present in better shape until the time arrives for definite avowals."[56]

At the same time, Warren's experience in Washington had not brought all the anticipated rewards. The abuse of his enemies, particularly over the irrigation question, as well as the incessant demands of his friends, wearied him. "These and other matters are heaped high enough upon me to render it no self-denial for me to say that they can take their Senatorship and stick it in their—pocket or into the hat of some ambitious man who will come down here and draw his salary and let the public in his locality be damned, etc."[57]

In this restless mood, Warren wrote Van Devanter in search of sound advice:

> I therefore, ask you confidentially, to sum the matter up and express to me your judgment without regard to personal feelings, which you think would strengthen the party most in Wyoming in the coming struggle—for me to have it understood that I am a candidate, to have no expression at all but let matters drift along, or for me at some time soon to have it unmistakably understood that I am entirely out of the race, say that it should be advertised in the coming convention about the 1st of May."[58]

Adding that "I am frank and desire your best judgment," Warren sketched for Van Devanter the rewards that might come from an extension of his public career but balanced them against the drawbacks and frustrations of political

56. Warren to A. J. Parshall, Feb. 23, 1892, Warren Papers.
57. Warren to S. B. Tuttle, Feb. 26, 1892, Warren Papers.
58. Warren to Van Devanter, Mar. 19, 1892, Van Devanter Papers.

life. Describing politics as "a dog's life," Warren noted, "there is perhaps much that might come to me and through me to Wyo. and my friends, should I succeed myself, but there is also much that I could shake off, much that I could retain, which now flows on down stream past me, and a great deal of personal comfort which I could enjoy if entirely out of politics and political offices."[59]

Van Devanter's reply chided Warren for his tendency to decline offices prematurely, thus placing his position in jeopardy unnecessarily. "It seems to me much better for you to say nothing respecting any desire for re-election. Do not announce yourself as a candidate, and by all means do not decline the position in advance. It will be advantageous to the party in the coming campaign for it to be generally accepted (as it is) that you desire re-election. At the same time it leaves the field open."[60]

Van Devanter's detachment may have been shaped by Warren's evident concern with the gubernatorial race and its effect on his senatorial chances. Following his effort in the legislature of 1890, Edward Ivinson had retained his support in Laramie and Albany counties, while picking up adherents elsewhere. Warren had no particular objection to Ivinson, but he urged the banker's supporters to improve his popularity throughout the state. In the meantime, Warren indicated that he would be available for financial help if needed.[61]

Warren's associates did not see Ivinson as a strong choice. "In my judgment," wrote Van Devanter, "the mention of his name is not well received and the great majority of those

59. Ibid.
60. Van Devanter to Warren, Apr. 9, 1892. Van Devanter Papers.
61. Warren to E. P. Camplin, Mar. 30, 1892, to Otto Gramm, Mar. 7, 1892, Warren Papers.

135

with whom I have talked concerning the matter have predicted certain defeat if he were nominated." Disregarding the claims of Ivinson's adherents that he would acquire big majorities in Cheyenne and Laramie, Van Devanter advised Warren "that the sooner we look in another direction the better." But Ivinson's support remained too powerful for Warren to risk a party split, and Van Devanter's counsel was overruled.[62]

By the end of March 1892, Warren had decided to continue his strategy of watchful waiting on his reelection, while making the best of the Ivinson candidacy. The arid land bill had not gone as he hoped, but a victory in the autumn would allow him to resume his irrigation agitation with renewed strength. On the basis of his own soundings and those of his aides, Warren could anticipate a Republican victory in the state, Wyoming securely behind the Republican national ticket, and his own return to the Senate. Two years after statehood, Warren seemed to be on the verge of a political dominance which would permit him to carry out his design for the economic development of Wyoming. By the second week of April 1892, however, Warren's plans were in disarray. The Republicans were split, the Democrats were on the offensive, and Warren's candidacy was in trouble. Into the calm political scene of Wyoming, a band of cattlemen had thrown a bomb—the Johnson County War.

62. Van Devanter to Warren, Mar. 3 and Apr. 9, 1892, Van Devanter Papers.

CHAPTER SIX: THE JOHNSON COUNTY WAR

HE Johnson County War began on April 5, 1892, when a band of Wyoming cattlemen and Texas mercenaries left Cheyenne for northern Wyoming with the avowed purpose of exterminating the rustlers in Johnson County. At Casper the invaders left the train, stopping at the ranch of state Senator John N. Tisdale to rest. On April 9, acting on news brought by an agent, they rode to the KC ranch where they trapped and killed two suspected thieves, Nathan Champion and Nick Ray.

The day long fight at the KC roused the countryside, and by April 10 the cattlemen were forced to seek refuge at the TA ranch on Crazy Woman Creek. A two-day siege ensued, in which the vigilantes were badly outnumbered by the angered citizenry of Johnson County. On Tuesday, April 12, the Johnson County forces made plans for the final attack on the beleaguered stockmen. Using a portable breastwork loaded with dynamite, the attackers hoped to explode the ranch house in which the invaders had taken cover.

The next day, just as the climactic assault was being readied, a troop of cavalry dispatched by President Harrison arrived at the scene. They dispersed the Johnson County forces, took the stockmen into custody, and averted wholesale bloodshed. The invaders, much the worse for their ordeal, were held at Fort McKinney near Buffalo for a week, then transported to Fort Fetterman, and finally to Fort D. A. Russell outside Cheyenne to await their trial.

As the last epic range war, the Johnson County conflict has received much attention from historians of the West. Unhappily, their accounts are more distinguished for partisanship, incomplete research, and inaccurate presentation than for scholarly analysis and thoroughness. Relying on inadequate reminiscences, biased newspapers, and occasionally their own imaginations, historians have focused on the colorful events of the war itself, missing the significance of an event which changed the shape of Wyoming politics in the 1890s.[1]

The cattlemen's raid was a last desperate measure in a struggle between large rancher and settler-rustler which had flared up occasionally from 1887 to 1891. After the hard winter of 1886–87, the ranchers in Wyoming, forced to pay more attention to their herds to gain a profit, began to complain of rustling, while the influx of settlers and small ranchers brought competition to the members of the WSGA. "If it was difficult for the associations to distinguish the small cattleman from the cattle thief, it was becoming equally difficult for newcomers to escape the conclusion that an association like that in Wyoming, which represented the whole range-cattle business in that section, might easily use its power to dominate the cattle range and to exclude all but a few wealthy companies."[2]

To combat rustling, the WSGA sought legislative approval for its policing measures of range detectives and

1. Lewis L. Gould, "A. S. Mercer and the Johnson County War: A Reappraisal," *Arizona and the West*, 7 (1965), 9; Smith, *War on Powder River*, is the best single history of the episode, while George T. Watkins, "Johnson County War," *The Pacific Northwesterner*, 5 (1961), 17–28, is a thoughtful discussion of the literature on the conflict.

2. Osgood, *The Day of the Cattleman*, p. 238.

railroad inspectors who would work to check the shipment of stolen cattle. The legislation of 1888 neglected to supply funds to support the system, and the Association tried in 1890 and 1891 to persuade the legislature to give governmental status to their organization. The first state legislature set up a board of live-stock commissioners which possessed large powers to regulate the cattle business. Packed with members of the WSGA, the board acted in the interest of its patron.[3]

The WSGA's efforts were frustrated, however, by the refusal of local juries to convict rustlers, even on the strongest evidence. For the big cattlemen, convinced that all nesters were rustlers, this failure to obtain what in their view was simple justice demonstrated that legal means would hardly suffice to meet a threat to their property and profit.[4]

The situation deteriorated further in 1891. In October the board of live-stock commissioners declared all cattle with brands not on the commission's list subject to confiscation and sale by commission inspectors. This move outraged settlers in northern Wyoming, who in the winter of 1891–92 laid plans for their own roundups in May 1892, disregarding edicts of the board. To the cattlemen, this apparently illegal roundup appeared as a scheme to rustle their cattle.[5]

Members of the WSGA believed that they were confronted with an organized band of cattle thieves, supported

3. Ibid., pp. 239–40; Jackson, "The Wyoming Stock Growers Association: Its Years of Temporary Decline," pp. 260–70.

4. F. G. S. Hesse to Horace Plunkett, July 10, 1889, to Frank Wolcott, Jan. 25, 1893, F. G. S. Hesse Papers, Western Range Cattle Industry Study, Colorado State Historical Society; Smith, *War on Powder River*, pp. 114–20.

5. Osgood, *The Day of the Cattleman*, pp. 246–47.

by the bulk of the populace in the north. Since legal means were of no avail, they turned to selective elimination of the rustlers. Several killings in the fall of 1891 poisoned the atmosphere and drove the two sides farther apart. In this welter of acrimony and bad faith, it is impossible to decide who was right. Some settlers engaged in rustling, but not on the vast scale which the cattlemen claimed. Northern juries would not convict rustlers, but whether this was from coercion by the thieves or solidarity against the stockmen is unclear.[6]

Even piecemeal killings did not accomplish the cattlemen's object, and the more violent members of the WSGA decided to organize a punitive expedition to go north and eliminate the leaders of the rustlers. On the theory that fifty or sixty deaths would clean up the mess, the stockmen made their plans. After the failure of the expedition, the conspirators destroyed much of the incriminating evidence, and the erosion of time has aided the process. Documentary proof of the planning of the raid has not turned up, but the far-flung recruiting and procurement of equipment by the plotters indicates the dimensions of the effort. For present purposes, however, it is only important to define the extent of the conspiracy among the politicians.[7]

6. A. S. Mercer, *The Banditti of the Plains* (Norman, Oklahoma, 1954), pp. 21–27. The Johnson County War is so clouded with controversy that even the judgment that the cattlemen believed there was an organized group of rustlers would be questioned by partisans of the settlers. Still, this conception helped guide the stockmen's plot. C. H. Burritt to Hesse, May 29, 1892, Hesse Papers.

7. The files of the WSGA are bare for 1892–93, but the letters displayed in Helena Huntington Smith, "Mystery Man of the Johnson County War," *Montana, 13* (1963), 40–49, indicate the involvement of the members of the organization; Clay, *My Life on the Range,* pp. 268–69; Lois Van Valkenburgh, "The Johnson County War, The

Senator Carey was intimately involved with the expedition from its inception. As the invaders complained after their capture, Carey "encouraged them to go into this thing & when they got into trouble deserted them." Since Carey was not up for reelection in 1893, he did not suffer politically to the same degree as Warren, but the stockmen had long memories and turned their backs on Carey's campaign in 1894. Carey reaped temporary political benefits from Warren's embarrassment in 1892, but his vacillating course at the height of the crisis eventually cost him dearly.[8]

Warren knew nothing of the expedition before it left Cheyenne. His personal letters are full of vehement denials of any part in the plot, and there is no evidence that these assertions were untrue. Warren's papers are so complete, frank, and indiscreet as to make it improbable that he destroyed any relevant materials. Indeed, he made a deliberate effort to preserve his correspondence concerning the Johnson County War, much of which was less than flattering to him personally. For Warren to have sponsored an expedition that unified his opponents, split his own party, and cost him his Senate seat would be a striking departure from the consistent cleverness of Warren's career.[9]

Attempts to link Warren with the planning of the invasion have proceeded on the assumption that he shared the confidence of Senator Carey and the other plotters. This was not the case. The invaders kept the details of the raid from

---

Papers of Charles Bingham Penrose in the Library of the University of Wyoming with Introduction and Notes," unpublished M.A. thesis, University of Wyoming, 1939.

8. Henry G. Hay to Warren, Apr. 15, and July 25, 1892, Warren Papers (the quotation is from the second letter).

9. James Marsh to Warren, Apr. 8, 1892, Warren to S. B. Tuttle, July 27, 1892, to O. H. (Jack) Flagg, Jan. 28, 1895, Warren Papers.

even their most intimate associates. Henry G. Hay, the Cheyenne banker who was close to Carey, told Warren on April 15, 1892, that "those of us who were consulted at all were only consulted as to general results, and knew nothing whatever of the plan or purposes in detail." In the absence of firm evidence of Warren's involvement, statements to the effect that the Senator must have known about the invasion are little more than unsupported guesses.[10]

When the news of the raid trickled into Cheyenne, the dimensions of the fiasco became apparent. On April 12, 1892, Governor Amos W. Barber learned of the cattlemen's plight at the TA ranch. Wiring President Harrison that evening, Barber claimed that "an insurrection exists in Johnson County, in the state of Wyoming, in the immediate vicinity of Fort McKinney, against the government of said state." Barber called upon the President to send the troops at McKinney to the rescue.[11]

When Warren and Carey in Washington received word of the events, they roused President Harrison, who was soon "up and dressed and using every minute upon receipt of Governor's request."[12] The troops were sent, the cattlemen saved, and the besiegers dispersed. This federal intervention has been interpreted by numerous historians as evidence of the dimensions of the stockmen's influence. President Harrison, so goes the story, "sent troops to bail them out" when the invaders got into trouble. According to Warren, however, Harrison acted on the basis of Governor Barber's telegram which made no reference to the character of the invading party beyond the statement that the "lives of a

10. Hay to Warren, Apr. 15, 1892, Warren Papers.
11. Amos Barber to Benjamin Harrison, Apr. 12, 1892, Mercer, *Banditti,* pp. 74–75.
12. Warren to Hay, Apr. 20, 1892, Warren Papers.

large number of persons are in imminent danger." After asking Warren if Barber was the legal governor, the President concluded, "my duty is plain. The Governor has made a requisition on me for troops according to the statutes made and provided for such cases and I will order them placed at his disposal for the purpose of preserving life and property only."[13]

Because Barber's telegram was less than candid about the situation in Wyoming, legal and political complications began to trouble Warren and Carey within hours after the invaders were rescued. On April 13, Warren's private secretary summarized the problem for the Senator:

> Stockmen surrendered to Colonel Van Horn this morning. They are at Fort McKinney and will be given protection there. Many friends and good citizens are involved. Civil authorities want them for serious offences and may be entitled to detain them for trial. May not be admitted to bail. Much excitement in Johnson county. Violence may occur to captives if protection of troops is not continued. It is suggested by friends that troops be requested by Governor to escort captives to railroad at once. Decisive measures necessary if serious prosecutions are to be avoided. What do you and your colleague suggest and what action do you advise executive to take?[14]

These questions by Warren's secretary suggest the dilemma in which Republican politicians found themselves in

13. Smith, *War on Powder River*, p. xii; Barber to Harrison, Apr. 12, 1892, Mercer, *Banditti*, pp. 74–75; Warren to W. F. Williams, May 4, 1892, Warren Papers.
14. S. B. Tuttle to Warren, Apr. 13, 1892, Warren Papers.

the spring and summer of 1892. Johnson County, through its duly elected officials, would surely make a request for the custody of the cattlemen. Since the crime had been committed in their county, the case was theirs. Yet every Republican state officer believed that abandoning the invaders to the mercies of Johnson County would mean a lynching, either informally or with legal sanction.[15]

The day after the cattlemen were captured, the Johnson County sheriff, W. G. (Red) Angus,[16] asked Governor Barber to "Make a request on General [John R.] Brooke to have the commanding officer at Fort McKinney to surrender the 44 men, now held by him as prisoners, to the civil authorities for trial under the charge of murder." Barber rejected this demand because, as he told the commander at McKinney, Colonel J. J. Van Horn, "there seems to be too much danger of the civil authorities not being able to give the men adequate protection against violence."[17]

Willis Van Devanter, sensitive to the political implications of the raid, knew that the prosecution of the invaders must go forward, but he shared the governor's reluctance to allow Johnson County custody of the men. "The members of this expedition," he wrote Warren, "are charged with murder and other serious offences, and the State can do nothing less than vigorously prosecute them. They should, however, be removed to a place of entire safety and there kept in custody until the time of trial." This process began

15. Amos Barber to Warren, Apr. 29, 1892, Warren Papers.

16. For biographical details on Angus, see W. G. Angus to Richard Olney, May 18, 1893, Wyoming Appointment Papers, Justice Department, NA, RG60.

17. W. G. Angus to Amos Barber, Apr. 14, 1892, Barber to Colonel J. J. Van Horn, Apr. 15, 1892, *Leader,* Apr. 16, 1892.

on April 17, 1892, when the army sent the prisoners south to Cheyenne on a special train.[18]

The arrival of the prisoners in Cheyenne under army guard provided the cattlemen's attorneys, led by Van Devanter, with a delicate problem in legal strategy. Given the probable fate of the prisoners in Johnson County, they could not be released to the civil authorities; but the Harrison administration, anxious to end its interference in Wyoming affairs, might decide at any time to insist that the state take charge of the stockmen. If forced to do this, Governor Barber would have to hand the prisoners over to the sheriffs of Johnson County, the only officials legally able to take custody of them.[19]

The histories of the war give the impression that the attorneys for the stockmen did not desire a speedy initiation of criminal proceedings against their clients. This was not their view. As soon as Johnson County filed criminal informations against the prisoners, Van Devanter could seek a change of venue to a southern county, but if Johnson County proved dilatory, the army might be forced to abandon its protective guarding of the prisoners.[20]

18. Van Devanter to Warren, Apr. 20, 1892, Van Devanter Papers; *Leader,* Apr. 20, 1892; Robert A. Murray, "The United States Army in the Aftermath of the Johnson County Invasion," *Annals of Wyoming, 38* (1966), 67.

19. Van Devanter to Warren, Apr. 20 and May 9, 1892, Van Devanter Papers; Warren to Van Devanter, June 24, 1892, Warren Papers; Benjamin Harrison to C. J. Hogerson et al., Apr. 22, 1892, Benjamin Harrison Papers.

20. Wayne Gard, *Frontier Justice* (Norman, Oklahoma, 1949), pp. 143–44; Smith, *War on Powder River,* p. 260; Mercer, *Banditti,* pp. 91–93, 123–24; Van Devanter to Warren, Apr. 20, 1892, Van Devanter Papers.

Johnson County's officials also confronted difficult problems. The expense of trying the cattlemen was their responsibility, but the county was in no position to assume the financial burden. If proceedings began, the costs would mount; but while the army held the prisoners, Johnson County could seek funds around the state. Johnson County made periodic requests to the governor for the custody of the stockmen, but this tactic was meant more for home consumption than as a serious alternative. It also had the happy effect of embarrassing Governor Barber.[21]

These demands began in late April as soon as the cattlemen had reached Cheyenne. Armed with warrants for the arrest of the prisoners, the prosecuting attorney asked Barber to turn the stockmen over to Johnson County deputies. If the request had been granted, the invaders would have been taken to Buffalo for a preliminary hearing, but no opportunity would have been offered to file a motion for a change of venue.[22]

Coached by Van Devanter, Barber told the prosecutor on April 25 that the prisoners would be held "until you shall have had a reasonable and sufficient time within which to prepare and commence in the district court of your county any criminal proceedings against any of them which, upon consideration, you shall deem justified and warranted by the evidence which investigation may disclose to you." Stressing the alleged unrest in Johnson County, Barber added that "the prisoners at Fort Russell will be delivered to the civil authorities whenever the status of the prosecutions, in the judgment of the court requires it, and order is

21. On the financial problems of Johnson County, see C. H. Burritt to F. G. S. Hesse, July 18, 1892, Hesse Papers; C. H. Burritt to Henry G. Hay, July 2, 1892, *Buffalo Bulletin,* June 8, 1961; *Sun,* May 18, 1892.
22. *Leader,* Apr. 26, 1892.

restored and excitement so abated as to render it safe to do so."[23]

Further attempts were made to secure custody in May, but Barber stood by his decision. With the assurance that they could seek a change of venue immediately after the filing of charges, the attorneys for the stockmen were anxious to begin proceedings. While Johnson County procrastinated, Governor Barber and the invaders' lawyers attempted to ensure that the army would not give up the prisoners before the trial could open. On May 9 the governor wrote General Brooke and Warren to obtain their aid in having the army maintain custody for at least thirty days. "If you concur in my views and can assist in securing the retention of the prisoners by the military authorities at Fort D. A. Russell until the change of venue, a considerable service will be rendered to the state." Warren's intercession and the efforts of the large cattlemen brought army agreement within nine days; Van Devanter reported on May 18 that "Gen. Brooke has written to Governor Barber that the prisoners will be maintained in their present position according to present arrangements, for a period of time, but does not state how long."[24]

The months of May and June passed without change in the prisoners' status. National political conventions occupied the attention of state officials, while Johnson County's

23. Amos Barber to Alvin Bennett, Apr. 25, 1892, *Leader,* Apr. 26, 1892; Barber to Warren, Apr. 29, 1892, Warren Papers.

24. Barber to Warren, May 9, 1892, John W. Lacey and Willis Van Devanter to Warren, May 18, 1892, Warren Papers; Lacey and Van Devanter to Warren, May 9, 1892, Van Devanter Papers; Barber to General J. R. Brooke, May 9, 1892, quoted in Murray, "Aftermath of the Johnson County Invasion," p. 68; *Sun,* May 11, 12, 15, 17, and 18, 1892.

representatives fanned out over the state seeking money for their prosecution without success. At the end of June, the stockmen's attorneys tried, to no avail, to arrange an "amicable change of venue." While it was evident that the prosecution was stalling in a vain effort to raise funds, the prisoners themselves broke the logjam over their fate. After a squabble between the Wyoming cattlemen and the Texas gunmen at the fort, Governor Barber learned of possible escape attempts by the prisoners, who despite their captivity were armed. To forestall the break, "Governor Barber telegraphed to Johnson County requesting the immediate presence of an officer prepared to serve warrants upon the men and to take them into custody."[25]

Barber's wire to Johnson County sparked negotiations between prosecution and defense which produced an agreement to have the prisoners transferred to Laramie City, where a motion for a change of venue would be argued before the trial itself began. After setting forth the defense plans, Henry Hay informed Warren, "we have reason to hope that it will proceed without very much more delay," unless the question of expense came up, and in that case Johnson County might have to "put up the entire amount of the expenses of the trial in cash in advance."[26]

On July 5, 1892, the stockmen appeared in the district court at Laramie before Judge J. W. Blake, and arguments for a change of venue commenced immediately. A mass of testimony taken proved little except that opinion was

25. Lacey and Van Devanter to Warren, May 18, 1892, Warren Papers; Van Devanter to Warren, June 23, 1892, to Carey, June 27, 1892, Van Devanter Papers; Carey to Louis Kirk, June 3, 1892, M. A. Chapman Collection, Western History Research Center, University of Wyoming; *Sun,* June 25 and 26, 1892.

26. Hay to Warren, July 2, 1892, Warren Papers; Van Devanter to Carey, June 27, 1892, Van Devanter Papers.

divided over whether the prisoners could obtain a fair trial at Laramie, Cheyenne, or anywhere else in the state. Finally on July 19 Judge Blake granted a change of venue to Cheyenne because there was a better chance of finding an unbiased jury in the most populous county. Judge Blake's decision had a sound practical basis, since the defense had twelve peremptory challenges for each defendant.[27]

While the arrangements to protect the captured stockmen were in progress, Warren had engaged in a scheme to accomplish the extermination of the rustlers with the help of the federal government. The campaign, begun as soon as the invaders were taken, reached its peak in June and July, when Warren induced President Harrison to support the cause of the WSGA. For different reasons, the politicians and the cattlemen forged an alliance to achieve their separate, if equally unsavory, objectives.

All parties concerned wanted to eliminate the lawless elements in Johnson County. The stockmen, anxious about their herds, believed that the entire county was dominated by rustlers who must be driven from the state, dead or alive. Politicians like Warren wanted to stamp the leaders of Johnson County as criminals to offset the political damage done to the Republican cause by the raid itself. Despite the nonpartisan nature of the invading band, the Republicans had been identified as the sponsors of the expedition, and this posed a threat to Warren's campaign for reelection to the Senate.[28]

Several possibilities were suggested, but the most attractive initial proposal was a declaration of martial law. After some discussion, it was agreed that a proclamation by

27. For the discussion of the trial, see *Leader, Sun,* and Laramie *Daily Boomerang,* July 6–20, 1892.

28. Warren to A. J. Parshall, May 7, 1892, Warren Papers.

Governor Barber would not suffice. The governor, linked in the popular mind with the cause of the cattlemen, could not be sure that the militia would respond to his commands; and effective implementation of martial law required the intervention and assistance of the United States Army. Early in June, Warren and Carey investigated the possibility of a declaration by President Harrison. On June 1 the stockmen and their attorneys wired Carey to have troops moved to Fort McKinney "preliminary to declaration of martial law." Warren added that letters he received from northern Wyoming "implore martial law." The first part of this campaign succeeded when twelve troops of cavalry were ordered into summer encampment in Johnson and Converse counties. President Harrison, however, was aware of the precedents against a declaration of martial law by the federal government and showed no desire to usurp the functions of a state government until it demonstrated itself incapable of handling its own affairs. By June 10 it was clear that some other tack would have to be taken, but the situation remained at an impasse until the Republican National Convention ended.[29]

With Harrison's renomination, Warren initiated a further attempt to obtain federal aid by "trying to get military support U.S. Marshal instead of marshal law."[30] Through

29. Hay, Van Devanter, George W. Baxter et al. to Carey, June 1, 1892, Warren to Carey, June 1, 1892, quoted in Murray, "Aftermath of the Johnson County Invasion," pp. 70–71; Warren to A. T. Butler, July 8, 1892, to Hay, July 31, 1892, Warren Papers; Mercer, *Banditti*, p. 115. On the reluctance of presidents to declare a formal state of martial law, see Bennett M. Rich, *The Presidents and Civil Disorder* (Washington, 1941), pp. 209–11.

30. Warren to Hay, July 31, 1892, to General J. R. Brooke, June 10, 1892, G. W. Holdrege to Warren, June 23, 1892, Warren to Holdrege, July 3, 1892, Warren Papers.

the compliant federal courts, the cattlemen procured an injunction against unauthorized roundups in Johnson County, but attempts to serve the writ were frustrated. Then an effort was made to burn a barracks at Fort McKinney where the prisoners had been housed.[31] Finally, various men were charged as parties to a conspiracy to murder George Wellman, a Johnson County foreman and deputy U.S. marshal who had been killed on May 9, 1892. Wellman, a popular young cowboy, had been traveling to Buffalo when he was shot down from ambush by a group of thieves. His death convinced the cattlemen that extreme actions would still be necessary. "For myself," remarked Frank A. Kemp, "I don't see how the hell we can do anything as long as the opinion is so strong against violent measures. I don't see the slightest use in declaring marshall law, or calling out the troops, without they are willing to do what the late expedition failed in doing, namely exterminate the rustlers."[32]

Warren's plan was to have Marshal Joseph P. Rankin[33] attempt to serve warrants on these charges and meet with resistance of some kind to provide an excuse for federal intervention. Whether Warren expected Rankin to be harmed is not clear; certainly the large cattlemen looked for such a result.[34] As W. C. Irvine told a Justice Depart-

31. *Sun,* May 3 and 19, 1892; *Leader,* May 4, 1892; Hay to Warren, July 25, 1892, Warren Papers.

32. *Sun,* May 11, 1892; C. H. Burritt to F. G. S. Hesse, May 29, 1892, Frank A. Kemp to Hesse, May 29, 1892, Hesse Papers; J. Elmer Brock, "Who Dry-Gulched the Hoe Ranch Foreman?" *The Denver Westerners' Brand Book,* ed. Maurice Frink, *9* (Denver, 1954), 19–30.

33. Rankin had first gained fame in 1879 with his ride for help in the Meeker massacre. He had been appointed marshal over Warren's misgivings in 1890. Warren to Carey, Mar. 11 and 30, 1890, Warren Papers.

34. Joseph P. Rankin to W. H. H. Miller, June 21, 1892, Papers

ment official, "he [Irvine] '*hoped* and *expected*' that, when Marshal Rankin attempted to serve the warrants for the arrest of the Rustlers in Johnson County, he would meet with the resistance threatened, namely that they would die in their tracks before they would allow service to be made, thereby placing the Marshal, if he lived, in a position to call for the assistance of the U.S. troops."[35]

Presented with the warrants in June 1892, Rankin declined to serve them without the help of federal troops. Happy to settle for this, Warren and Carey met with Harrison on June 21, 1892, to seek his backing for their cause. When the President repeated his reluctance to declare martial law, they reminded him that they sought only aid for the federal marshal. The President replied: "I can scarcely see my way clear to do that and I advise you strongly to have civil process instead; Let the marshall take a sufficient number of deputies to make necessary arrests." Warren and Carey underlined their predicament, but the President remained adamant. At the conclusion of the interview, Warren asked Harrison to direct Attorney General Miller to "send such instructions to our United States Marshall as would compel him to immediately act or give way to another who will, and that all necessary expense in the way of paying deputies, etc. be authorized."[36]

Harrison's reluctance to endorse Warren's original scheme

---

on the "Johnson County War," Justice Department, NA, RG60 (hereafter cited as Johnson County Papers).

35. F. B. Crosthwaite to W. H. H. Miller, Dec. 22, 1892, Johnson County Papers.

36. Warren to Van Devanter, June 21, 1892, Warren Papers. For the President's authority to use troops to aid in the enforcement of federal law, see Rich, *The Presidents and Civil Disorder*, pp. 195–98.

did not stem from political considerations. Later in the summer the use of federal troops at Coeur d'Alene, Idaho, and the intervention of state militia in the Homestead Strike would damage Republican chances in the campaign. Once these incidents erupted, Harrison's innate caution about martial interference would be strengthened by an appreciation for the political consequences, especially in the South, of federal soldiers intruding on the sovereignty of a state. On June 21 both these crises were several weeks in the future, and Harrison rejected the Wyoming plea on the basis of his general conviction that the "civil authorities must gather sufficient help from the body of the people to maintain order and execute the law."[37]

In Cheyenne Marshal Rankin began to feel pressure to take a posse north. The attorney general wired on June 21, asking him to describe the character of the warrants. Rankin appreciated his predicament and had to be cajoled into signing a letter written by Willis Van Devanter outlining the charges against the Johnson County men and requesting federal support in serving the warrants. Further persuasion by Van Devanter induced Rankin, after some hesitation, to send the letter to the Attorney General; but Van Devanter wrote Warren of Rankin's fear of trying to serve the warrants in Johnson County.[38]

While Rankin's letter made its way to Washington, Warren repeated his doubts of Rankin to Van Devanter but added, "I do believe he would take sufficient deputies to

---

37. Warren to Van Devanter, June 21, 1892, Warren Papers; Benjamin Harrison to Norman B. Willey, July 4, 1892, Harrison Papers.

38. W. H. H. Miller to Joseph P. Rankin, June 21, 1892, Rankin to Miller, June 21, 1892, Johnson County Papers; Van Devanter to Warren, June 23, 1892, Van Devanter Papers.

defend himself; would risk the capture or a fight, that, upon resistance an urgent demand from the spot for troops, they would be furnished instanter from the commands nearest the seat of troubles." Warren had scant patience with the bureaucratic delays involved in obtaining troops, but as he told Henry Hay, "custom and law has made it necessary that everything should be of record, where political enemies constantly have access to record and everything is done openly and with public knowledge so that it is pretty hard to cut across corners and get any benefit whatever from administration or troops except in the prescribed way."[39]

On July 1, 1892, the Attorney General answered Rankin's ghost-written letter and directed him to proceed with serving the warrants. The letter was unsatisfactory for Warren's purpose because it did not make clear that the demand for action was a command. Rankin continued to waver, and on July 14 Miller, under Warren's prodding, telegraphed the marshal, "What have you done about execution warrant referred to in my letter of July 1st? It was expected you would organize posse and proceed to make arrests at once." In a subsequent wire Miller told Rankin, "to act or to give way to someone who will act."[40]

Rankin replied to these attacks that there seemed to be some "radical misrepresentations" regarding the manner in which he was executing the duties of his office. He added that he had tried to assemble a force of deputies, but a lack of funds had hampered his recruiting. This continued procrastination annoyed Warren, who was under considerable pressure from cattlemen like W. C. Irvine and John Clay to

39. Warren to Van Devanter, June 24, 1892, to Hay, July 31, 1892, Warren Papers.

40. Miller to Rankin, July 1, 14, and 15, 1892, Johnson County Papers; Warren to Hay, July 15, 1892, Warren Papers.

have the army complete the extermination of the thieves.[41]

The Harrison administration was not satisfied with Rankin's stalling, either, and proved more receptive to Warren's pleas. On July 30, 1892, President Harrison, pointing to the alleged obstructions put in the way of federal officers, commanded all persons engaged in resisting the laws and process of the United States courts, "to cease such opposition and resistance and to disperse and retire peaceably to their respective abodes on or before Wednesday, the 3rd day of August next."[42] Warren was pleased and wrote to Hay:

> It is coming our way now. Possibly there will be still the one little string on it that Marshall must wire Washington for troops when arrived on ground and resistance offered but shall have this arranged if possible so can have troops glued to officers back & no further request necessary but if any common sense exercised troops can be 'hanging around' post [Fort McKinney] where wanted & *do* before hand just what they know they will be *ordered to do* later i.e. act first and get authority afterward—They will all know what President will do & be keen for action.[43]

This elaborate preparation proved unnecessary, for when Rankin finally rode north with a posse, the President's message had preceded him. "In obedience to the President's proclamation the sympathizers of these parties charged with murder, went to their homes or dispersed, and the defendants themselves left the Country in various directions." In

41. Rankin to Miller, July 19, 1892, Johnson County Papers; Warren to John Clay, July 15, 1892, to G. W. Holdrege, July 3, 1892, to W. C. Irvine, July 23, 1892, Warren Papers.

42. Mercer, *Banditti,* pp. 117–18.

43. Warren to Hay, July 30, 1892, Warren Papers.

September Rankin informed the Attorney General, "the securing the posse which I sent there and the President's proclamation have together brought about general good order in the community, and with very few exceptions the people have turned to their original avocations, and I do not look for any reorganized defiance of the United States authority."[44]

The rustlers' departure eased the pressure on Rankin, though Warren would soon seek fitting retribution for the marshal's seeming cowardice. In the meantime Willis Van Devanter resumed his defense of the cattlemen, whose trial began in Cheyenne on August 6. The process of selecting a jury had commenced when, on August 9, Sheriff A. D. Kelley of Laramie County asked the court to guarantee his payment of the expenses of housing the prisoners in Cheyenne. Since the cost was $100 a day, he had sought money from Johnson County, but no funds were available. After deliberation, Judge Richard Scott, of the First Judicial District, announced that if Johnson County would not provide for the prisoners, he had no choice but to admit them to bail.[45]

The prisoners signed their bail bonds, and the case was bound over until the next term of court. On August 10 the stockmen were released, and the Texas gunmen immediately left for home, never to return. The rest of the cattlemen resumed their business activities while the politicians occupied themselves with the fall election. After the campaign, on January 3, 1893, the invaders' trial began again in Cheyenne as the legislature prepared to elect a senator.

---

44. Rankin to Miller, Sept. 4, 1892, Johnson County Papers.
45. *Leader*, Aug. 7 and 11, 1892; Mercer, *Banditti*, pp. 127–30; Clay, *My Life on the Range*, pp. 272–74.

Selecting a jury became the first problem because, with twenty-three defendants, the defense had nearly three hundred peremptory challenges. Since the controversy had influenced the minds of some men and awakened the fears of others, the chances of finding twelve men to sit in the jury box were very slight. The prosecution, with two thousand eligible voters to pick from, insisted on making the effort, however, and the selection process began.[46]

Their hopes proved illusory. By January 21, 1893, over nine hundred men had been examined and eleven impaneled. This has led some historians to assume that only one more man was needed, but the defense had yet to use one of its peremptory challenges. Before the trial could start, the defense would empty the jury box and the laborious task would begin again. By that time all jurors from Cheyenne had been questioned, and the sheriff was ready to go out into the outlying districts to seek more men.[47]

Johnson County gave up. Faced with mounting expenses which they could not pay, the prosecution decided to seek a dismissal of the charges. Van Devanter, ever alert, saw that this would not protect his clients completely. Arranging a deal with the Johnson County attorneys, Van Devanter allowed a jury to be seated, but when the prosecutor moved to have the cases against the cattlemen dismissed, Van Devanter objected. The judge overruled the objection, but the record of Van Devanter's action protected the stockmen from any further prosecution on the same charges in the future.[48]

46. Van Devanter to Warren, Dec. 28, 1892, to Isaac Van Devanter, Jan. 4, 1893, Van Devanter Papers; *Sun,* Jan. 4, 1893.

47. *Sun,* Jan. 22, 1893.

48. Ibid.; Mercer, *Banditti,* p. 133; Clay, *My Life on the Range,* pp. 275–76.

Historians now agree that the Johnson County War, like a summer thunderstorm, cleared the air and allowed the cattle business in northern Wyoming to take a more tranquil course. On the political side, there were more immediate repercussions in the campaign of 1892: the ensuing effect on the fortunes of Warren and the Republicans enabled the Democrats to win a temporary ascendancy in state politics. Though innocent of direct participation in the preparation for the invasion, Warren ended the summer of 1892 firmly fixed in the popular mind as the champion of the cattlemen. As his campaign against Marshal Rankin makes clear, this was a fair evaluation, but at the same time it posed serious obstacles to the achievement of Warren's economic and personal goals. Under the pressure of this crisis, Warren began to move toward the creation of a more durable form of political organization which could withstand such unexpected shocks as the Johnson County War.

CHAPTER SEVEN. DEMOCRATIC REVIVAL: THE ELECTION OF 1892

HE Democrats' success in the Wyoming election of 1892 depended on their ability to saddle the Republicans with the blame for the Johnson County War. Though the invaders were largely Democrats, the participation of Senators Warren and Carey, Governor Barber, and President Harrison in saving the cattlemen gave the Democrats an opportunity on which they quickly capitalized. Warren, at first hopeful of assigning a portion of the blame to the Democrats, reluctantly concluded that "we cannot afford to raise that issue, because pot cannot call kettle black I suppose when it comes to the cattle troubles as it applies to the two parties."[1]

Sensing victory, Democratic leaders for once proved more adept than their rivals. They seized on the invasion issue at the outset and kept it before the public. Since the legal process of trying the cattlemen consumed several months, opposition newspapers could point to every action of Governor Barber's as evidence of his connection with the stockmen. The Republicans also suffered from the gross stupidity of the invaders and their sympathizers, who showed themselves to be without the slightest understanding of the depth of popular feelings against them.

To support their imprisoned comrades, the cattlemen tried to repress any dissent in Wyoming. When the *Cheyenne Daily Leader* attacked the invasion, George W. Baxter

1. Warren to N. J. O'Brien, Apr. 20, 1892, Warren Papers.

and Frank A. Kemp, as stockholders, sued the management on the pretext that their interests were being violated. The suit was correctly interpreted as an attempt to silence effective opposition.[2] Still more damaging was the case of A. S. Mercer, editor of the *Northwestern Live Stock Journal.* Mercer, a wandering journalist with a low price tag, had been a paid agent of the WSGA until the invasion, but financial reverses made him an easy prey for Democratic cash. After Mercer revealed his defection, the stockmen, in a fit of pique, withdrew their ads from the *Stock Journal,*[3] and transformed Mercer from a discredited editor into a martyr in the battle for free speech. As one of Mercer's particular targets, Warren sensed the political overtones and remained reluctant to take out the Warren Live Stock Company advertisement. "I had sometime since decided to discontinue there when I could do it in a way not to turn the heads of some honest but misguided people who are sensitive about boycotting, free speech, etc."[4]

With the assets of the invasion, the Warren arid land bill, and the mistakes of the WSGA, the Democrats had only to maintain unity to have a good chance of victory. Like the Republicans, however, the Democratic Party had elements which supported the purposes of the stockmen. George W. Baxter, representing this group, urged his friends in the party to "steer clear of the cheap demagogues, who desiring to get in front by every breeze that blows, are at present loudly championing the cause of theft and dishonesty."[5]

2. *Leader,* June 19, 1892; Frank Kemp to F. G. S. Hesse, May 11 and 29, 1892, Hesse Papers.

3. Gould, "A. S. Mercer and the Johnson County War," pp. 9–13.

4. Henry Hay to Warren, July 25, 1892, Warren to Hay, July 30, 1892, to S. B. Tuttle, July 27 and August 2, 1892, Warren Papers.

5. George W. Baxter to William Daley, June 11, 1892, William

By July, when their state convention met, anti-invasion Democrats had marshaled enough strength to oust the pro-stock elements and nominate a ticket opposed to the invasion. After a stormy conclave in the "handsomely decorated" opera house in Rock Springs, the seventy-five delegates picked John E. Osborne, a Rawlins druggist and sheepraiser, to run for governor, nominated the Sheridan journalist Henry A. Coffeen as the congressional candidate, and made a concession to the conservative stockmen by naming Gibson Clark, a Cheyenne lawyer, to run for the Supreme Court.[6]

In their platform the Democrats held the Republicans "largely responsible for the fact that a considerable body of armed men were collected without the state and permitted to march into Johnson county in open and armed defiance of the constitution and laws and in resistance to the local civil authorities." They also condemned "the Warren arid land bill . . . as an infamous measure covertly designed to aid land sharks in obtaining control of large areas of land and thus defraud the people of their rightful heritage."[7]

The party launched their campaign in August and dispatched speakers across the state. The poverty of former years was forgotten as all the senatorial aspirants tried their best to insure a Democratic legislature properly sympathetic to their cause. For a brief time, the presence of strong individual ambitions within the Democratic ranks worked to the advantage of the party. "I believe the chance is good," remarked Henry A. Coffeen in September, "to elect our

---

Daley Collection, Western History Research Center, University of Wyoming.

6. *Leader,* July 28, 1892.

7. *Leader,* July 30, 1892.

entire state ticket and redeem Wyoming to democracy where she properly belongs."[8]

The Wyoming Populist Party, given new life by the invasion issue, proved another liability to the Republicans.[9] Until 1892 the Populists had tried vainly to adapt their national program to the inhospitable Wyoming environment; solutions well-suited to Kansas or Nebraska had little relevance in a state where, in 1889, farm products had a value of two million dollars as compared with the thirty-three millions in livestock. Populism in Wyoming was confined to the northeastern counties of Crook and Weston, adjacent to South Dakota, until the Johnson County War made Populism in Laramie, Albany, and Johnson counties an avenue for protest which drew off normally Republican voters.[10]

Warren estimated that the total number of Populist voters could not exceed two thousand, but for the state Democratic leadership and the managers of the national party, this bloc might supply the margin which would throw Wyoming to the Democrats on the state level and keep its three electoral votes from Benjamin Harrison's column. Acting on the instructions of the Democratic national committee, the party's state chairman, A. L. New, proposed fusion to the People's Party convention at Douglas in late September. A rancorous debate ended in a vote of twenty-seven to nineteen for fusion. James B. Weaver and James G. Field replaced Grover Cleveland and Adlai E. Stevenson on the

8. Henry A. Coffeen to George T. Beck, Sept. 21, 1892, George T. Beck Collection.

9. Thomas Kreuger, "Populism in Wyoming," unpublished M.A. thesis, University of Wyoming, 1960.

10. Warren to W. F. Sanders, Oct. 6, 1892, Warren Papers; *Sun*, Sept. 22, 1892; Kreuger, "Populism in Wyoming," pp. 13–14.

Democratic ballot, while the Populists began to campaign for Osborne and Coffeen. This arrangement did not please all the loyal Democrats, but it did offer the possibility of funneling the bulk of the Johnson County protest vote to their ticket.[11]

Republicans, thrown off stride by the invasion, never regained their balance. Senator Carey was hardly heartbroken by Warren's identification with the raid, and he contented himself with offering foolish suggestions to buy juries and occasional attempts to influence the choice of candidates. Outside Cheyenne anti-Warren sentiment persisted, especially in Converse County where DeForest Richards nursed a grudge and political ambitions of his own. In the north, normally Republican counties like Johnson could not be relied upon for their usual majorities.[12]

Edward Ivinson's candidacy for governor, so powerful before the Johnson County War erupted, continued to gather strength, but he began to encounter some competition. State Senator Frank W. Mondell of Newcastle, ambitious and handsome, joined Surveyor-General William A. Richards and DeForest Richards, the leader in Converse, in

11. *Leader,* Sept. 22, 1892; George L. Miller to William C. Whitney, additional note by A. L. New, Oct. 7, 1892, The Papers of William Collins Whitney, Manuscripts Division, Library of Congress; John Hunton to Phillip Zehner, Oct. 27, 1892, Hunton to John Taylor, Nov. 17, 1892, John Hunton Papers, Western History Research Center, University of Wyoming; J. S. Clarkson to Grenville M. Dodge, Oct. 7, 1892, Box 23, Dodge Papers.

12. Warren to Helen Warren, May 19, 1892, to J. D. Woodruff, Nov. 16, 1892, Warren Papers; Van Devanter to Carey, June 27, 1892, to W. A. Richards, May 8, 1894, Van Devanter Papers; *Sun,* Sept. 3, 1892; Denver *Rocky Mountain News,* Aug. 15, Sept. 27, and Oct. 10, 1892.

the gubernatorial field; but Ivinson's cause had several strong points which enabled him to surpass his rivals. As a banker of some substance, Ivinson could finance the campaign in a year when there would be no aid from the Republican national committee. Ivinson, a political novice, was "anxious [to] run but fearful of expense" and asked Warren "confidentially how much it would cost him to make the campaign for Governor." Ivinson hazarded the guess that "five [thousand] ought to cover," but Warren told him it "would be nearer ten; and he still seeks place."[13]

Ivinson's backers also argued that Albany County would roll up such large majorities for the Republican ticket as to outweigh possible losses in the northern part of the state. It became evident to Warren and Van Devanter that Albany County "was so earnest in its advocacy of Ivinson that it would be likely to be quite injurious to Senator Warren for him or his friends to oppose the nomination of Ivinson."[14]

The Republican convention, held at Laramie on September 14, announced its opposition to "all class legislation" and pronounced itself "in favor of the equal and exact enforcement of all the laws of the state, the equal and full protection of life and property and the equal fostering and encouragement of every industry."[15] Ivinson won the nomination on the tenth ballot over DeForest Richards, after Mondell dropped out of the race. Clarence D. Clark was renominated for Congress, while Carroll H. Parmelee, a Johnson County land office incumbent, sought the vacancy on the Supreme Court. Several days later the state committee

13. Warren to J. S. Taylor, June 21, 1892, to Van Devanter, Aug. 27, 1892 (letter and telegram of the same date), Warren Papers.
14. Van Devanter to W. A. Richards, May 8, 1894, Van Devanter Papers.
15. Laramie *Weekly Sentinel,* Sept. 24, 1892.

met and chose Willis Van Devanter as chairman of the Republican campaign.[16]

Van Devanter brought his usual thoroughness and flair for organization to his work as chairman, but his management of the campaign faced several difficult obstacles. The Republican national committee had allotted no funds for the Wyoming campaign on the theory that Harrison had little chance in the West, and this decision threw Van Devanter back on the resources of the state politicians, whose contributions were necessarily limited. By mid-October, Van Devanter had to solicit $1,000 from Carey and tell Warren that the committee needed fifteen thousand more, ten from Ivinson and five from Warren.[17]

Aware that his campaign was not going well, Ivinson became reluctant to contribute to the Republican coffers. His failure to send his pledged share irritated Van Devanter, who had contracted numerous debts on behalf of the committee. To meet these obligations, Van Devanter reminded Ivinson of his responsibilities; when Ivinson persisted in an unwillingness to aid the committee, Van Devanter threatened more drastic action. "Unless you send me a favorable telegram at once," he told Ivinson, "I shall be compelled to take such action as will be necessary to protect me against financial embarrassment." Under this pressure, Ivinson contributed $2,500 to the Republican war chest, but his penny-pinching tactics imposed serious limits on the state committee's ability to match the Democratic canvass.[18]

16. *Sun,* Sept. 17 and 24, 1892.

17. Van Devanter to W. C. Anderson, assistant secretary of the Republican National Committee, Oct. 6, 1892, to Carey, Oct. 18, 1892, to Warren, Oct. 19, 1892, Van Devanter Papers; statement by Van Devanter, Feb. 11, 1893, Warren Papers.

18. Van Devanter to Edward Ivinson, Nov. 1 and 2, 1892, Van Devanter Papers.

WYOMING: A POLITICAL HISTORY

With the money that he did receive, Van Devanter directed a multitude of activities. Acting through a loose network
of county chairmen, newspaper editors, and faithful Republicans, as well as the members of the state committee, Van
Devanter dictated letters of solicitation, exhortation, and
encouragement to such party stalwarts as Merris C. Barrow,
Converse County editor of *Bill Barlow's Budget,* and Otto
Gramm, a Laramie druggist and political hopeful. In Cheyenne, Van Devanter could rely on the help of Warren's
secretary, S. B. Tuttle, and such local minions as N. J.
"Nick" O'Brien, A. J. Parshall, and the erratic but useful
editor of the Cheyenne *Sun,* E. A. Slack. They arranged the
rallies and entertainment which enabled the voters to see
and hear the candidates, distributed party literature, and
sent Van Devanter daily reports on changing sentiment
among the electorate. These men had not yet become the
smoothly functioning team of 1894–97, but they managed
to execute campaign plans with some degree of efficiency.

Even under Van Devanter's direction, the Republican
effort went from bad to worse as soon as it was launched.
Their late start put them at a disadvantage, and Warren's
conviction, expressed to correspondents, that the Republicans would gain strength proved ill-founded. The state ticket
was colorless. Ivinson, the Laramie banker, or "Old Gilded
Guts" as his unkind opponents labeled him, had a speaking
style which bored audiences instead of inspiring them; and
on October 6, Warren concluded, "if an election was to
occur to day, I fear the result would be disasterous to 'me
and mine.' "[19]

19. For the Ivinson nickname, see W. H. Root to John E. Osborne,
Dec. 1, 1892, John E. Osborne Papers, Carbon County Historical
Society, Rawlins; Warren to W. F. Sanders, Oct. 6, 1892, Warren
Papers; *Bill Barlow's Budget* (Douglas, Wyo.), Oct. 15, 1892.

Republican hopes for victory demanded that the issue of the Johnson County War be neutralized. Instead, the invasion rose up at every turn to plague them. In September the Justice Department, acting under Warren's pressure, finally asked for Marshal Rankin's resignation. Warren's zeal for revenge could not have been more poorly timed. Rankin's complaints about the bad treatment he received supplied the Democratic press with ample material for further denunciations of Republican connection with the infamous cattle barons.[20]

To repair this damage to their cause, Warren and Van Devanter adopted a pose of detachment. Warren pretended that the Justice Department had acted on its own, while Van Devanter assured restless Republicans of his earnest solicitude for Rankin's fate. "I am very sorry to see Joe burn the bridges behind by threatening people who have been his constant friends, but probably this is only a temporary madness, which his own good judgment will cause him to regreat later on." This strategy did not deceive Rankin, who told the attorney general,

> The sentiment in this state is such today that the men, whom it would seem had represented to you that I have not performed my duty, and who, no doubt, are secretly asking for my removal, are afraid to come out openly and advocate it; but are themselves anxious and willing to have the matter held in abeyance until after the election. They do not dare go before the people of the state and accuse me of failure to perform my official

20. Warren to John Clay, Aug. 30, 1892, Warren Papers; Clarence D. Clark to W. H. H. Miller, Sept. 26, 1892, Wyoming Appointment Papers, Justice Department, NA, RG60; Carey and Warren to Benjamin Harrison, Sept. 3, 1892, Benjamin Harrison Papers.

duties, or to advocate my removal. In fact, they refuse to put in writing any statement of charges against me.[21]

Despite their pious assertions, Warren and Van Devanter continued to seek Rankin's ruin. When the marshal managed to obtain an investigation by a Justice Department inspector, Warren used every means to secure a verdict unfavorable to Rankin; but the lawman proved equal to the challenge, convincing the inspector that he had done his best. The attorney general had no alternative, in the face of the inspector's report, but to retain Rankin. Yet only with Warren's departure from the Senate in 1893 did the campaign against Rankin come to an end.[22]

The Democrats capitalized briefly on the Rankin issue, but they were saving their bombshell for a more propitious time. On October 14, 1892, the *Northwestern Live Stock Journal*, A. S. Mercer's paper, printed the text of a confession by George Dunning, an invader who had escaped from the TA ranch battle and had been captured by the Johnson County authorities. In early October Dunning affixed his signature to a statement which set forth his part in the raid and accused every prominent Republican of complicity in the conspiracy. Subsidized by the Democratic state committee, Mercer printed numerous copies for distribution across the state.[23]

21. Van Devanter to Homer Merrell, Sept. 17, 1892, Van Devanter Papers; Warren to A. T. Corlett, Sept. 26, 1892, Warren Papers; Rankin to W. H. H. Miller, Oct. 31, 1892, Johnson County Papers.

22. Warren to Van Devanter, Dec. 20, 22, and 25, 1892, to Carey, Dec. 22, 1892, Warren Papers; F. B. Crosthwaite to W. H. H. Miller, Nov. 2 and Dec. 22, 1892, Johnson County Papers.

23. Mercer, *Banditti,* pp. 152–95; Smith, "Mystery Man of the Johnson County War," pp. 40–49.

Van Devanter was alone in Cheyenne when the *Stock Journal* appeared. Taking over the Cheyenne *Sun* in the absence of editor Slack, Van Devanter secured statements of denial from Governor Barber, Judge Blake, and Attorney General Charles N. Potter. He also composed an editorial which attempted to refute the "Stock Journal's slanders." After a lengthy examination of Dunning's charges, Van Devanter concluded "were these men capable of this thing, they could not, while yet in possession of their faculties, engage in an undertaking which could have as it [sic] only outcome ruin and lasting disgrace for themselves and their friends."[24]

Reasoned editorials were not the only Republican response to Mercer. They resurrected a damage suit against the editor and closed his printing office. With this action Mercer, who had left for Chicago to attend the opening of the World's Fair, became identified as an object of Republican repression. The cattlemen added to this impression when John Clay sued Mercer for libel in Chicago. Though he was quickly freed, Mercer and his plight gave the Democrats fresh evidence of the extent of the Republican conspiracy.[25]

Warren's sponsorship of the bill to cede arid lands to the states became another tempting target for the opposition.

24. *Sun,* Oct. 18, 1892; *Leader,* Oct. 18, 1892; Denver *Rocky Mountain News,* Oct. 22, 1892; Van Devanter to Warren, Oct. 16 and 19, 1892, to Carey, Oct. 18, 1892, Van Devanter Papers.

25. *Leader,* Oct. 18 and 27, 1892; *Wyoming State Tribune,* Oct. 21, 1892; *Chicago Tribune,* Oct. 26 and 27, 1892; A. S. Mercer v. St. Louis Type Foundry Company, Civil Appearance Docket, 5–130, and Annie Mercer v. St. Louis Type Foundry Company, Civil Appearance Docket, 5–329, Laramie County District Court Records; Gould, "A.S. Mercer and the Johnson County War," pp. 14–16.

Easily linking "land-grabbers" with "cattle barons," the Democrats harped on Warren's huge holdings, and heated editorials denounced his attempt to drive out the small farmers and ranchers. In an October issue the *Leader* printed a report on the Warren Live Stock Company which purported to show Warren's plans to accumulate more land. Once again Van Devanter tried to rally Republican newspapers to the defense of the Senator. "The article has been going the rounds of the democratic press, and it was positively known by the one who started it that it was a bare faced lie. As soon as this is published please send a marked copy to every republican paper in Wyoming."[26]

Van Devanter also had to contend with the spirited young chairman of the Democratic campaign, A. L. New, a former Evanston land office appointee and scion of a prominent Indiana political family. New challenged Van Devanter to allow public debates between the two congressional candidates, Coffeen and Clark. Pleading the exigencies of Clark's schedule, Van Devanter refused the request, but Democratic editors noted that his reply "reminded people of the letters signed by Governor Barber at the time when the state invaders were being shielded from the civil processes of Johnson County, and which it is understood that Van Devanter wrote for the governor."[27]

In the closing days of the campaign, both state chairmen exhorted their lieutenants to a final effort on behalf of the state and national tickets. Van Devanter assured eastern newspapers that Wyoming would be safely in the Harrison

26. *Leader,* Oct. 9, 11, and 20, 1892; Van Devanter to Merris C. Barrow, Oct. 23, 1892, Van Devanter Papers.

27. Laramie *Daily Boomerang,* Oct. 15, 1892; *Sun,* Oct. 13 and 14, 1892; Van Devanter to A. L. New, Oct. 11, 1892, Van Devanter Papers.

column with a sufficient majority in the legislature to elect a Republican senator. The Democrats exuded similar confidence as what one observer described as "the *dirtiest* and *meanest* campaign the country ever saw" drew to a close.[28]

For all their exertions, the Republicans suffered defeat on November 8, 1892. As the returns trickled in, it became evident that though the state had voted for Harrison electors by a narrow majority, the Democrats had elected Osborne, Coffeen, and Gibson Clark and stood a good chance of controlling enough votes in the legislature to name a senator. Among Democrats, starved for victory, the sweetness of the unexpected fact of success provoked jubilation. "The gang is dead with no political mesiah to save or resurect them," wrote an ecstatic party worker, "I feel that life is safer and property more valuable in Wyo. than it was up to the 8th inst." According to the *Leader,* victory meant that "Wyoming has not only been redeemed but rejuvenated, and it is a proclamation to the world that this free, sovereign state, handicapped though it is and has been, cannot descend to the level of a political pocket borough for any man or clique of men."[29]

The Republicans, unaccustomed to postmortems, could only ask with Warren, "where are we at?" Their joy at carrying the state for Harrison was tempered by Cleveland's national victory, which would deny them federal patronage for four years. The causes of defeat on the state level were all too clear. As Ivinson himself admitted, "The Cheyenne

28. John Hunton to Blanche Hunton, Oct. 26, 1892, Hunton Papers; Van Devanter to A. A. Fowle, *Boston Globe,* Nov. 2, 1892, to Frank Hadsell, Nov. 5, 1892, to Frank M. Foote, Nov. 5, 1892, Van Devanter Papers.

29. *Leader,* Nov. 11, 1892; A. W. Jones to John E. Osborne, Nov. 11, 1892, Osborne Papers.

Ring[30]—the Invasion & the great Land Steal [Warren's arid land bill] has been so crammed with those people it was impossible (in the short time) to counteract the mischief."[31]

Naturally enough, Ivinson overlooked his own sorry performance. In Albany County, where his backers had promised a large majority, his vote trailed Warren's 1890 total by 179 ballots, and his "majority" turned out to be a 166 vote deficit. In ten of the twelve counties, Ivinson ran behind Warren's showing in 1890; he carried only Laramie County and acted as a drag on the rest of the Republican candidates. Clarence D. Clark ran better than Ivinson, but even his popularity could not pull him through. After 1892, Warren did not pay much attention to the squeals of Albany County politicians; their candidate had proven a loser—on the stump, with the cash, and most disastrously, at the polls.[32]

The electoral evidence suggests that a weak gubernatorial candidate and the Johnson County War combined to defeat the Republicans. These factors permitted the Democrats to improve their showing over 1890 all across Wyoming. John E. Osborne increased his party's vote in every county and did especially well in Carbon (his home county), Johnson, and Sheridan. The presence of Henry A. Coffeen, a Sheri-

30. Democratic newspapers throughout the late 1880s and early 1890s referred to the Republican organization in Laramie county as the Cheyenne Ring. In view of the strained relations between Warren and Carey, the term has little relevance. There is no evidence, more-over, that any of the cattlemen enjoyed the political influence which such a name suggests.

31. Warren to Ivinson, Nov. 10, 1892, Warren Papers; Ivinson to E. A. Slack, Nov. 12, 1892, E. A. Slack Scrapbook, Wyoming State Historical Society.

32. Erwin, *Wyoming Historical Blue Book,* pp. 1180–83

dan resident, gave a boost to the Democrats in that area. Since the Harrison electors won narrow victories, it seems probable that the protest vote against the invasion by unhappy Republicans was registered for the Democratic state candidates and then returned to its normal allegiance in the national contest. Of course, some conservative Democrats, as well, may have voted for their state ticket and then declined to cast a ballot for the Weaver and Field electors. In either case, the Democrats had gained control of the Wyoming state government after a decade of defeat; their resurgence, part of a national pattern, placed Wyoming in the category of a doubtful state and presented the Democratic Party with a splendid opportunity to establish itself as a genuine rival to the Republicans in 1894.[33]

The tragedy of the demise of the Republican state ticket, as Warren saw it, was the blow it dealt to his chances of winning reelection to the Senate. In order to reach his goal, Warren had to win twenty-five votes from the forty-nine-member Wyoming legislature meeting in joint session. If the Republicans had a clear majority, Warren would seek to win a vote in the party caucus binding the whole Republican delegation to vote for him. On the other hand, if the Democrats and Populists had a majority, Warren would try to unite the Republicans into a solid bloc behind him and then add the necessary votes from the opposition by persuasion, force, or bribery.[34] In the days after the election, while results accumulated in Cheyenne, Warren kept a count on the legislative situation; but on November 10 he wrote Clarence D. Clark that "it looks pretty gloomy, though we may yet get a scrimping majority."[35]

33. Ibid., pp. 1176–77, 1180–81.
34. Warren to J. D. Woodruff, Nov. 16, 1892, Warren Papers.
35. Warren to Clarence D. Clark, Nov. 10, 1892, Warren Papers.

Even with a Republican majority, Warren would have difficulty in collecting all the party's votes. Outside Laramie County, Republicans like Fenimore Chatterton, Bryant B. Brooks, and John Ludvigsen had pledged to their constituents that they would never vote for Warren's candidacy. DeForest Richards of Converse County had senatorial designs, while Clarence D. Clark sought to compensate for his defeat in the general election by becoming a member of the Senate. All these considerations, however, had to wait on the final composition of the legislature.[36]

As the situation developed in November, Warren could count on twenty-three Republican votes, while the Democrats had seventeen and the Populists five. In dispute were four votes, two from Carbon and Natrona, one from Fremont, and one from Converse. All these contested seats were in the House of Representatives, the control of which would, in all probability, determine the election. If the Democrats could organize the House, they could decide election contests, seat the desired members from their party, and with an increased delegation, unseat enough Republicans to free themselves from the necessity of relying on the Populists. With the four seats at stake, the House stood twelve Republicans, twelve Democrats, and the five Populists.[37]

Willis Van Devanter managed all the election cases for the Republicans in November and December as chairman of the state committee and as the custodian of Warren's

36. Warren to Mondell, Nov. 24, 1892, Warren Papers; Fenimore Chatterton, *Yesterday's Wyoming* (Denver, 1957), p. 47.

37. On the contested seats, see, for Carbon and Natrona, *Sun,* Nov. 29, 1892; for Converse, *Sun,* Nov. 22, 1892; for Fremont, Warren to Mondell, Nov. 24, 1892, Warren Papers. The Republican candidate from Fremont, J. B. Okie, was declared elected by his county canvassing board in November, over the protests of the Democrats.

fortunes. The first problem was the disputed seat in Converse County, where the Republican nominee, John Scott, had apparently run behind the Democratic candidate, Nat Baker, a rancher and advocate of fusion, by a scant seven votes. In the course of compiling the returns, the county canvassing board had reduced Scott's total by ten votes because of an obvious clerical error. Van Devanter procured a writ of mandamus from the district judge which compelled the board to count the returns as originally given on the grounds that the board could not go behind the certified returns. By this process, Scott finished with 450 votes while Baker received 447. The county board had no alternative but to declare Scott elected.[38]

Democratic newspapers greeted Van Devanter's strategy as further proof of Warren's willingness to stop at nothing. The *Leader* charged that Van Devanter had tried to count Baker out "by misquoting the law and legal decisions, but his devious trail has been unearthed and the scores of telegrams which he and Warren flashed forth will be of little avail." The sole consolation of the defeated Democrats was that they believed themselves assured of two representatives from Carbon County, sufficient to control the house in January 1893. "Baker is not yet counted out, as will be discovered at the proper time."[39]

But Van Devanter and Warren understood the decisive nature of the Carbon County delegation, and Van Devanter hurried to Rawlins to be present at the deliberations of the county canvassing board. The Democrats, alert by this time, had a full team of their own present, including Chairman

38. Van Devanter to DeForest Richards, Nov. 17 and 18, 1892, to Charles Maurer, Nov. 18, 1892, Van Devanter Papers; Warren to Van Devanter, Nov. 23, 1892, Warren Papers; *Leader,* Nov. 19, 1892.

39. *Leader,* Nov. 19 and 25, 1892.

New and Thomas M. Patterson, publisher of the *Rocky Mountain News* and a Colorado Democrat. The decision of the county board might resolve the fate of all the Senate candidates, and the *Leader* pleaded, "No matter what the cost the people of Carbon county should not permit a steal of the legislative and county ticket which they have elected."[40]

The issue was simple. The returns from Hanna, as the board received them, lacked indications of the precinct, district, or county in which the election had been held; in addition, the poll list had not been signed. If the votes of the precinct of Hanna were counted, the two Democratic candidates for the house, S. B. Bennett, a Snake River rancher and resident of Rawlins, and Harry A. Chapman, a cowboy and "a rather fine looking gentleman," would receive enough votes to triumph over their Republican opponents. If the Hanna returns were thrown out, the two Republicans would be elected. By law, the canvassing board consisted of the county clerk, S. B. Ross (Republican), whose own reelection depended on excluding Hanna, together with the two justices of the peace, W. E. Tilton (Republican) and C. P. Hill (Democrat).[41]

For Van Devanter, the omissions, however technical, provided sufficient evidence that the returns from Hanna were invalid. At his urging, Ross decided not to accept the Hanna returns. Once Ross had been won over, the other Republican, Tilton, became the focus of attention; but according to Van Devanter, "the opposition threatened to boycott his meat markets at Carbon and Hanna, and to otherwise injure him in his business, and the pressure was too much for him to withstand." By a vote of two to one, the board accepted

40. *Leader,* Nov. 25 and 27, 1892.
41. *Sun,* Nov. 26 and 29, 1892; *Leader,* Jan. 10, 1893.

the Hanna returns and declared Bennett and Chapman elected. Democratic dominance in the House was, for the time being, assured.[42]

Republican tactics at Rawlins, however, left the Democrats concerned and anxious. The results of Carbon County were still subject to review by the state canvassing board, composed of the state auditor, the state treasurer, and Governor Barber, acting as secretary of state. Two characteristics of the state board disturbed the Democrats. The members were all Republicans, and none was noted for his independence of Francis E. Warren.

Since County Clerk Ross, under the prodding of Van Devanter, had obligingly supplied a set of returns which did not include Hanna, the Democrats foresaw a situation where the state board would accept Ross's returns and unseat the Democrats. The election laws which discussed the state canvassing board had been taken from the territorial laws and consequently made no reference to the office of governor. If the Republicans seized on this technicality, it was conceivable, argued the Democrats, that no certificate of election would be issued to John E. Osborne until after the legislative question had been settled to Warren's entire satisfaction.[43]

The only solution, as the Democrats saw it, was for Osborne to anticipate the Republican strategy, take office, and then "as it is made the duty of the governor to give certificates to the persons having the highest number of votes, you can issue certificates to the persons (especially members of the lower house) who are actually elected. This

42. Van Devanter to DeForest Richards, Nov. 28, 1892, Van Devanter Papers; *Leader,* Nov. 29, 1892.
43. *Leader,* Nov. 30 and Dec. 1, 1892; Warren to Van Devanter, Nov. 26 and 30, 1892, Warren Papers.

will give the democrats and populists a majority in the lower house and control of the situation."[44]

After satisfying themselves that the Republicans intended to delay matters as long as possible, the Democrats resolved to act, and in the early morning hours of December 2, 1892, Osborne appeared at the capitol and attempted to gain access to the governor's office. Acting under Republican orders, the janitor refused. As Warren reported, "Later Osborne broke in & is now sitting in Gov's office & reported to [J. W.] Meldrum or [R. H.] Repath, [Van Devanter's secretary], who went through door unlocked by themselves that he had taken possession as Gov. & demanded they receive for filing his oath of office."[45]

Democrats applauded Osborne's bold move, calling him "Brave Governor Osborne," and urging him to "Hold the fort. Be Governor of Wyoming is the wish of the people at Casper." Warren, on the other hand, complained of Republican confusion, adding, "we are sucking our thumbs in Cheyenne like a lot of old women." From his new office, Osborne issued proclamations, pardons, and a decree summoning the state canvassing board to meet with him at the capitol.[46]

The board was required by law to meet in the presence of the governor, if possible, and issue certificates to those

44. Samuel T. Corn to John E. Osborne, Nov. 25, 1892, J. C. Hamm to Osborne, Nov. 26, 1892, Osborne Papers; Osborne to Grover Cleveland, Nov. 14, 1893, Cleveland Papers.

45. Warren to Van Devanter, Dec. 2, 1892, Warren Papers; *Sun,* Dec. 3, 4, and 5, 1892; *Leader,* Dec. 3, 4, and 5, 1892. The Wyoming legend that Osborne made his entry by forcing a window open is probably accurate.

46. Denver *Rocky Mountain News,* Dec. 3, 1892; J. J. Hurt to Osborne, Dec. 4, 1892, Osborne Papers; Warren to Van Devanter, Dec. 3, 1892, Warren Papers.

elected. The Republicans contended that Osborne's term of service would not commence until January 1893, when he formally took the oath of office. Osborne replied that the oath he took in December was binding, that he was now the governor, and the canvassing board must conduct its proceedings at his pleasure.[47]

In order to forestall Osborne's strategy, Warren urged Van Devanter to convince the members of the board to issue certificates to Osborne which specified clearly the date on which he would become governor. Warren hoped this would eliminate the possibility of a question being raised about the legislature's authority to elect a senator, in the event a Republican was named. "It seems to me that if the Governor's certificate is not to designate the time his service commences and if such certificate is issued before or at the same time with the legislative ticket there will be very serious trouble and in the contest on the Senate floor or Committee room if made there the matter might turn against us upon this one point."[48]

The board proceeded as Warren directed, ignored Osborne's claims, and began a canvass of the crucial returns, the county legislative results. When the board reached Carbon County, Van Devanter advanced the argument that the election law specified only the county clerk as the official agent to tabulate the results. The members of the board, said Van Devanter, did not have equal authority. The justices could only assist the county clerk; they could not overrule him.[49]

47. A. L. New to Amos Barber, *Leader,* Dec. 3, 1892.
48. Warren to Van Devanter, Dec. 7, 1892, Warren Papers.
49. The language of the statute said that the clerk should certify the returns, "taking to his assistance two justices of the peace of his county." *Session Laws of Wyoming Territory passed by the Eleventh*

Democratic lawyers disputed Van Devanter's interpretation and claimed that all three men were equal members of the county board and that a majority of the panel should determine the result. After some discussion, devoted largely to getting Warren's instructions clear, the state board concluded,

A return has been made by the county clerk of Carbon county which complies with the statute. We cannot go beyond that to anything either within or without his returns to contradict his certified abstract. We therefore conclude that it is our duty to act upon the abstract from the county which is certified to have been made by the county clerk at the time and in the manner provided by our laws.[50]

The board's acceptance of County Clerk Ross's returns gave Carbon County and the House to the Republicans, but the Democrats had one avenue of appeal left. On December 9, 1892, the Democratic attorneys asked Chief Justice H. V. S. Groesbeck "for a writ of alternative mandamus to compel the board to canvass the return of the majority of the county board." Groesbeck issued the writ, whereupon Van Devanter requested the full Wyoming Supreme Court to quash the writ on the grounds that a single judge of the court could not issue such an order while the court was recessed.[51]

Legislative Assembly (Cheyenne, 1890 [?]), p. 177, Sec. 137; *Leader,* Dec. 9, 1892; S. B. Tuttle to Warren, Dec. 9, 1892, Warren Papers.

50. *Leader,* Dec. 9, 1892. One is dependent on newspapers for the official acts of the Wyoming state government in 1892. The papers of Governor Barber and other state officials are no longer in the Wyoming archives.

51. *Leader,* Dec. 10, 1892; Van Devanter to Warren, Dec. 15, 1892, Van Devanter Papers.

The ultimate issue to be decided by the court, composed of three Republicans, was whether the county clerk or the justices of the peace constituted the county canvassing board; but Van Devanter did not intend to let the question be argued until all legal methods of delay had been exploited. "We will make the opposition decidedly weary before they get any consolation or relief from the litigation." Van Devanter hoped that the legal proceedings might drag on through December and into January. This would prevent the Democrats from organizing the House and give the Republicans a chance.[52]

After two days of argument, the supreme court overruled Van Devanter's motion to quash the writ. Next Van Devanter moved to have "certain allegations in the petitions" of the Democrats struck out and also endeavored "to throw Governor's controversy into the fight." He asked the court to make the Democrats specify in their petitions that the state canvassing board had acted in the presence of the governor as required by law. If the Democrats conceded this, they would admit that Amos W. Barber, and not Osborne, was the legal governor of Wyoming.[53]

The court granted some portions of Van Devanter's motion but turned aside his attempt to ensnare the Demo-

52. Van Devanter to Warren, Dec. 18, 1892, Van Devanter Papers.
53. For the court's decision, see "On Motion to Quash the Alternative Writs of Mandamus," *State Ex Rel. Bennett v. Barber Et Al., State Ex Rel Chapman v. Same,* 4 *Wyoming Reports,* pp. 59–67, and for Van Devanter's next step, "On Motion to Strike Out Certain Allegations in the Petitions and to make the petitions more definite and certain," *Bennett v. Barber,* 4 *Wyoming Reports,* pp. 67–68; Van Devanter to Warren, Dec. 18, 1892, Van Devanter Papers. The Wyoming Supreme Court decided against the legality of Osborne's actions in *In Re Moore,* 4 *Wyoming Reports,* pp. 98–115.

crats. Warren was disappointed at this result. "Sorry court didn't rule upon presence of Governor consider it very important court in some way pass upon that question especially in view two sets certificates by two Governors." Warren had gone to Washington for the lame duck session of Congress, where he was attempting to gather senatorial support in the event of a contest over the choice of a Wyoming senator.[54]

With the Republican obstructions removed by the court, the argument became focused on the real issue. Van Devanter repeated his contention that the language of the statute made the county clerk the sole judge of the validity of the returns, while the Democrats renewed their assertion that the two justices of the peace also belonged on the board. On December 27, 1892, the supreme court upheld the Democratic claim. Justice A. B. Conaway outlined the precedents and concluded, "The rights of the people in choosing their officers are certainly safer in the hands of a canvassing board of three persons, of different political parties when practicable, than in the hands of one man."[55]

Van Devanter informed Warren of the defeat, characterizing the decision as producing "real cause for complaint,"

54. *Bennett v. Barber, 4 Wyoming Reports*, p. 68; Warren to Van Devanter, Dec. 21, 1892, Warren Papers. Both the Republican and Democratic national committees showed a great deal of interest in the Wyoming Senate race in December and January 1892–93. It was not clear until the end of December which party would control the Senate. *Chicago Tribune*, Dec. 12, 1892; John P. Irish to George F. Parker, Dec. 17, 1892, "Letters Written by John P. Irish to George F. Parker," *The Iowa Journal of History and Politics, 31* (1933), 421–512.

55. "On Demurrer to Petitions and Alternative Writs of Mandamus," *Bennett v. Barber, 4 Wyoming Reports*, p. 78.

but he conceded that "the question was in truth a very close one, with the usual prejudice against 'one man power' ever present against us in the arguments and in the consideration of the question." Even with the granting of the writs by the court, Van Devanter had one more line of attack against the Democrats, and the same day he filed a motion to have the election of Bennett and Chapman set aside because lawful certificates of nomination had not been submitted. He also alleged that Chapman was not a citizen.[56]

After several days of deliberation, as well as an examination of the nominating certificates, the court decided that while the certificates were not in the precise form required by law, "There is no such defect in this instrument as could possibly affect the result of that election. There is no provision of the statute indicating an intent on the part of the legislature that the statute prescribing what the certificate should contain and how it should be verified is so mandatory that a mere formal defect, incapable of affecting the regular and orderly conducting of the election or its result, should invalidate an election."[57]

With this decision the Republicans abandoned the legal fight, and the two Democratic representatives were seated in the House, giving the Democrats fourteen seats to the Republicans' twelve and the Populists' five. Two seats were still in dispute, but now the House itself would decide.[58] The second session of the Wyoming state legislature in January 1893 was bitter, faction-ridden, and indecisive.

56. Van Devanter to Fenimore Chatterton, Nov. 18, 1892, to Warren, Dec. 28, 1892, Van Devanter Papers.
57. "On Demurrer to Reply," *Bennett v. Barber,* 4 *Wyoming Reports,* p. 92.
58. Van Devanter to J. B. Okie, Jan. 2, 1893, Van Devanter Papers.

Thirty-one ballots failed to produce a senator to succeed Warren, and few laws of any consequence were passed. The reasons for this stalemate are still not entirely clear because of the dearth of Democratic manuscripts, and even on the Republican side, Warren's papers give only hints of all the forces at work.

When the session began, the Democrats organized the House, wooed the Populists by electing their leader, L. C. Tidball, a rancher, onetime Greenbacker, and later a Socialist editor, as speaker, and commenced the serious business of unseating Republicans. In the two weeks before the balloting opened, the Scott-Baker contest was decided in favor of the Democrat, and J. B. Okie of Fremont was removed in favor of L. D. Pickett. Later in January State Senator J. N. Tisdale, a Johnson County Republican, a supporter of the invasion, and a resident of Salt Lake City, "was made to walk the plank by enough republican votes, added to the Democrats, to make a majority." With the membership of the legislature reduced to forty-eight, the Republicans had twenty-two votes, the Populists five, and the Democrats twenty-one.[59]

Success for both major parties depended on uniting behind a candidate from their ranks who would be acceptable to the Populist bloc that held the balance of power. On the Republican side, Warren faced the resolute opposition of two groups. DeForest Richards led a loose coalition of five or six members who had pledged not to vote for Warren, but who felt less reluctance about furthering Richards' ambitions. Another half dozen preferred Clarence D. Clark to Warren. After exerting all his influence, Warren could only

59. Warren to Isaac Trumbo, Jan. 8, 1893, to M. M. Estee, Jan. 21, 1893, to Carey, Jan. 31, 1893, Warren Papers; *Chicago Tribune,* Jan. 22 and 23, 1893; *Sun,* Jan. 22, 1893.

count on the eight-man Laramie county contingent and a few votes from Albany County.[60]

The Democrats were, if possible, more divided than the Republicans. The state chairman, A. L. New, sought to parlay his effective leadership in the campaign into six years in Washington and commanded solid support from Uinta, Carbon, and Natrona counties, with a scattering elsewhere. His candidacy conflicted with the desires of old-line Democrats like George W. Baxter, W. H. Holliday, and George T. Beck. Baxter, a conspirator in the Johnson County invasion, could never obtain a vote from the Populists. Holliday and Beck were hacks. Since New's ability and ruthlessness might become a threat to Republican dominance, Warren's forces were not above giving enough support to Baxter and others to thwart New without breaking the stalemate.[61]

60. The journals of the first two state legislatures were not printed, but the *Sun* and *Leader* gave a full account of how each legislator voted in the senatorial contest. In the usual tradition of Wyoming journalism, the reports of the maneuvering of each candidate reflect more of the political outlook of the management than the realities of the situation. The above outline of the Republican lineup is based on the reports of ballots 1–10 in the *Sun* and *Leader,* Jan. 24–31, 1893; Warren to Van Devanter, Dec. 17, 1892, to Kilpatrick Bro. & Collins, Jan. 17, 1893, to Carey, Jan. 30 and Feb. 3, 1893, to L. C. Baker, Jan. 25 and Feb. 4, 1893, Warren Papers.

61. Baxter, the candidate for governor in 1890, had the quiet backing of the *Leader,* Holliday was a perennial candidate for any office from Laramie, and Beck, son of a late Kentucky senator, hoped to translate his economic interest in Wyoming into political power. Material on the Democratic side of the conflict can be found in the Cleveland Papers, which reflect the continuing scars left by the struggle. The appointment papers of the Interior, Justice, and Treasury Departments for Wyoming in the National Archives all contain some useful letters that shed much retrospective light. See, for instance, M. C. Barkowell to A. L. New, Oct. 18, 1893, J. D. Hurd to New, Oct. 22, 1893, Cleveland Papers.

For the Populists the situation looked promising as the session began. Without their five votes, no candidate could be elected on a party vote, and they were well aware, perhaps too aware, of their position. "The populists are inflated with their importance," wrote Warren, "until they are as big and round and full as a bladder of wind, totally unable to handle themselves, and seemingly without the slightest idea of what they finally expect to do." As Warren saw, the Populist delegation, small as it was, had internal divisions; the Johnson County members were Populists only because of the invasion and did not share the reforming outlook of their colleagues.[62]

The first ten ballots were indecisive in choosing a senator, but they demonstrated to Warren that he could not be elected. Instead of standing united in the caucus, Republican hopefuls pursued their own ends and made separate overtures to the Populists. "De Forrest [sic] Richards is sleeping with from one to four of the populists," reported Warren, "beseeching them on bended knees to accept him that he will be a populist and S.O.B. generally if they will do so. Others from our side are pressing them to their bosoms, and the democrats are, a part of them praying with them, some more sleeping with them, and still more clubbing them." Blaming the "personal ambition" of Richards and others for his failure, Warren complained bitterly about the

62. Warren to L. C. Baker, Jan. 30, 1893, Warren Papers. The Populists from Johnson County, D. A. Kingsbury and E. U. Snider, were former Republicans whom Warren considered certain to return to the fold. Warren's feeling that the Populists might defect may also have been based on his lifelong precept that most people had their price. The Populists held a similar balance of power in Montana and North Dakota. They failed to elect a senator in Montana but combined with the Democrats successfully in North Dakota.

unwillingness of Republicans to support him in the caucus. "Had all of the republican members accepted the will of a majority of the caucus in the first place I should have been nominated, and if so supported by all the republicans, should have undoubtedly been elected last week." Frustrated and angry, Warren resolved to repay the political slights he had suffered in the canvass.[63]

In future years Richards, Brooks, and Chatterton all experienced the perils of offending Warren, but Warren ascribed some of the blame for his defeat to Carey. Warren's secretary in Washington, L. C. Baker, described Carey's lukewarm attitude, pointing out that Carey was ready to swing to Clarence D. Clark and adding "if a man has no first and only choice, I do not think he is much of a man. To be looking for a second choice when the prize should go to another is anything but fair." Warren referred to Carey's alleged indifference in a letter to a California friend: "I note carefully what you say about C., and while I do not wish to make any accusation, I am carefully noting events, and I know I am not receiving the same co-operation from colleagues etc. that I would extend to them under similar circumstances."[64]

Warren's bland assertions that he would gladly throw his support to any Republican with a chance of being elected were in part hypocritical; but his conviction that the Republicans could achieve victory only through unified action was well-founded. Characteristically, all the Republican candidates placed their own personal goals ahead of the gains that the party would obtain from the election of a senator. Judging from their letters and actions, the senatorial hope-

63. Warren to Carey, Jan. 31 and Feb. 3, 1893, Warren Papers.
64. L. C. Baker to Warren, Jan. 22, 1893, Warren to M. M. Estee, Jan. 29, 1893, Warren Papers.

fuls had little sense of party loyalty, especially when that ephemeral emotion came up against even the remotest possibility of being senator. In the jungle of Republican intrigues, any contender foolish enough to step aside would have found his enemies publicly grateful but privately amazed at his stupidity. The inevitable result was a standoff.

With Warren's concession at the end of January that "there is scarcely a ghost of a show for any republican now,"[65] the initiative swung to the Democrats. Presented with a superb opportunity to win the greatest prize in Wyoming politics, the Democratic leadership also degenerated into small disorganized groups, whose excesses discredited the party as a whole.

In early February, A. L. New attempted to win by stealth what he could not gain honestly. Obtaining the promise of eighteen Democrats to vote for him on February 4, 1893, New would have twenty-three supporters if the Populists could be persuaded to back him. With forty-eight members of the legislature, New would still be two short of a majority, but he devised a plan to reduce the number of lawmakers to forty-six. Once he was within one vote of victory, New believed he would be able to procure the needed assistance from the remaining Democrats. On the morning of February 4, a Republican state senator, John L. Russell of Uinta County, left for Denver, ostensibly on business but with strong indications that his trip had been subsidized. Then another state senator, James Kime, was escorted on a drinking spree by a New henchman, and when properly inebriated, was given a drugged "cocktail" to prevent his attendance at the joint session.[66]

65. Warren to Carey, Jan. 31, 1893, Warren Papers.

66. *Leader,* Feb. 5, 21, 22, 23, and 24, 1893; *Sun,* Feb. 5, 21, 22, 23, and 24, 1893. Warren believed, until convinced otherwise, that the

Kime recovered, perhaps with Republican help, but New's scheme collapsed anyway when the Populists balked at voting for him. A few days later New withdrew, and the Democrats united around a Cheyenne lawyer, John Charles Thompson, who won the support of twenty of the twenty-one Democrats on the twenty-fourth ballot on February 15, 1893. Thompson's candidacy also gained the backing of four Populists, bringing him within one vote of success, but the fifth Populist and one Democrat, Nat Baker, refused to cast their ballots for Thompson. Since Baker had earlier voted for a bill appropriating money for the hated livestock commission, the Democrats suspected Republican money as the cause of Baker's treachery. In any case, the failure to elect Thompson made the stalemate permanent, and subsequent ballots closed out the session with no result except Democratic frustration. Believing that Governor Osborne could now appoint a senator, the *Leader* asked that Thompson be designated since he would represent the choice of the majority of Democrats in Wyoming.[67]

Union Pacific had helped New. Though his connection with the railroad is not clear, New was probably associated with the UP's coal department in some capacity. The railroad did not aid him on this occasion, however. Warren to L. C. Baker, Feb. 4, 1893 (two letters), to Ed Dickinson, Feb. 4, 8 and 11, 1893, to G.W. Megeath, Feb. 6, 1893, Warren Papers.

67. *Chicago Tribune,* Feb. 12 and 13, 1893; *Leader,* Feb. 16, 1893; *Sun,* Feb. 16, 1893. "John Charles Thompson came within one vote of getting in to-day, but I guess we have got his eye knocked out now," Warren to Carey, Feb. 15, 1893, Warren Papers. Chatterton, *Yesterday's Wyoming,* p. 49, claims credit for defeating Thompson, but his account is inaccurate as to date and details. For Democratic reaction to Nat Baker's action, see A. C. Beckwith to Richard Olney, Mar. 16, 1893, Wyoming Appointment Papers, Justice Department, NA, RG60.

Warren's hopes were dashed by the failure of the Republicans, and he returned to Washington to wind up his affairs. When Governor Osborne announced that he would go to Washington for Cleveland's inauguration in March, Willis Van Devanter saw another opportunity to achieve Warren's desire. If Osborne left the state, Barber would again become acting governor and could then appoint Warren. Unfortunately, Osborne's lawyers were as vigilant as Van Devanter and canceled the trip. On that inauspicious note, Republican dominance in Wyoming politics came to a temporary end.[68]

The spectacle of the ineffectual legislature had, however, made the Democrats the butt of political criticism and popular ridicule. Their brave campaign promises of renewed integrity in government had become tarnished by the sordid infighting of the senatorial squabble. Reviewing the session, the Lander *Clipper* begged, "May the good Lord deliver us from another reign of such base deceivers as they have proven themselves to be." To Wyoming voters, disposed to regard the Democrats as proponents of economy, free trade, and land reform anyway, the patent inability of the minority party to organize its forces gave the apparent order and regularity of Republican methods, as exemplified by Warren, new appeal. The Johnson County War for a moment averted the Democratic collapse which Grover Cleveland had started in the 1880s, but the Wyoming Democrats, with their propensity for disaster, managed to turn victory into defeat by the spring of 1893.[69]

68. Van Devanter to Warren, Feb. 27, 1893, Van Devanter Papers; S. B. Tuttle to Warren, Feb. 25 and 28 and Mar. 3, 1893, Warren Papers.

69. Quoted in the *Sun,* Mar. 2, 1893.

A month after Cleveland took office, Warren sang his familiar refrain to a correspondent: "Glad to say of myself that I am again 'a white man' a United States citizen partly well of body, entirely easy of mind & red-hot in business interests."[70] This interlude of calm would not last. Warren knew that Carey would be up for reelection in 1895, and if the Senate did not seat Osborne's appointee, two senators would be elected when the next legislature met. At the most, Cheyenne would have a claim to only one of the places, and Warren was determined that he would be the man. For all his protestations of disinterest, Warren's campaign for reelection never ended, a fact which only Joseph M. Carey failed to grasp.

In planning for the next campaign, Warren could pick out the errors of 1892 with ease. He must find some way to overcome the lack of cohesion within Republican ranks which had plagued him in 1893. As long as political success depended solely on the twin factors of personality and money, Warren's ambitions might be blocked by other men with similar assets. To counter this possibility, he must find a way to make party loyalty the dominant political emotion. In short, from 1893 to 1895 Warren had to move from the classic pattern of frontier politics to the more regular and orderly techniques of the older states. Until he did, his career would be at the mercy of such unforeseen events as the Johnson County War and such unreliable associates as DeForest Richards and Carey.

In 1892 the Warren organization was not able to offset the liabilities of Johnson County and Warren's ill-advised elevation to the Senate in 1890. In the next campaign, how-

70. Warren to W. A. Taylor, Apr. 1, 1893, Warren Papers.

ever, Warren's enemies would possess the weaknesses, and he would be in command. To some extent, this would be a result of Warren's popularity and Willis Van Devanter's skill, but success in 1894 would owe much to two strange bedfellows: Joseph M. Carey and Grover Cleveland, whose collective mistakes returned Warren to his senatorial place.

CHAPTER EIGHT. WARREN TRIUMPHANT: THE ELECTION OF 1894

HE adjournment of the 1893 legislature was the low point of Warren's political career in the 1890s. Deprived of his Senate seat, cut off from federal patronage, and repudiated at the polls, he turned to private affairs after a year of defeat and disappointment. Yet the inauguration of Grover Cleveland did not, as Wyoming Democrats hoped, mark the beginning of their era of dominance within the state, but only the high point of their abortive resurgence. In the spring of 1893, fortune and circumstance, Warren's enemies in 1892, repaid with indecent haste their debt to the Republican Party. In the process, the Democrats suffered a series of setbacks which foreshadowed their long decline as a party in Wyoming.

The fundamental cause of the Democratic enfeeblement was the Panic of 1893, from which all their subsequent ills stemmed. The failure of banks[1] and the continued lassitude of the cattle industry[2] made assurances of the prosperity that Cleveland would bring sound very hollow in Wyoming. When the Union Pacific went into receivership, the trustees instituted wage-cutting and retrenchment policies which produced more hardship among the normally Democratic railroad workers.

By the spring of 1894, the *Cheyenne Leader* urged its

1. *Leader,* July 26, 1893, recounts the dramatic collapse of T. A. Kent's bank in Cheyenne.

2. Frink, *Cow Country Cavalcade,* pp. 62–63.

readers to look on the bright side of things: "When complaining of hard times don't overlook the fact that Cheyenne is really better off than any other town in the west. There is no big army of unemployed and there are no hungry and desperate men such as abound elsewhere."[3] Warren painted a darker picture:

> Here in Cheyenne, stores are empty, rooms in blocks empty and the business streets look as quiet and uninteresting through the busiest part of the day as they used to look at daylight on a Sunday morning.—While poverty shows in some quarters in unpainted houses, broken fences, dead trees and burnt up grass, yet the greater percentage of the yards, gardens, flowerbeds, trees, etc, look perhaps better than usual because their owners have less to do in a business way and more time for "chores."[4]

Hard times alone did not, however, wound the Democrats beyond repair. It was the determination of Grover Cleveland to repeal the Sherman Silver Purchase Act of 1890 which ruined Democratic dreams of glory, for Cleveland's use of the patronage so divided and discredited the Wyoming party as to make it easy prey for the Republicans in 1894.

This disintegration began shortly after the adjournment of the legislature, when Governor Osborne appointed A. C. Beckwith, an Evanston businessman associated with the Union Pacific, to fill the Senate vacancy. This nomination, supposedly an attempt to mediate between A. L. New and John Charles Thompson, outraged the Thompson forces,

3. *Leader,* May 4, 1894; E. P. Oberholzer, *A History of the United States Since the Civil War* (New York, 1939), 5, 256.
4. Warren to T. A. Kent, June 16, 1894, Warren Papers.

who claimed that their candidate had the support of the bulk of Wyoming Democrats. Beckwith, they charged, had only his free silver beliefs to recommend him; his anti-labor attitudes, particularly his use of Chinese workers and his reluctance to pay decent wages, made him "a tyrant whose merciless lash has often brought the blood from the bared back of drudgery."[5]

For Beckwith, his designation was the prelude to further difficulties. The Senate questioned the power of a governor to fill a vacancy left by the failure of the legislature to act, and Beckwith's case, like that of several other senators appointed from western states, was referred to a committee for investigation. The prospects for favorable action were small, since the appointed senators were free silver men, a circumstance which offered little incentive to the Cleveland Democrats and Republicans in the Senate to overturn the clear precedents against seating Beckwith and the others. The issue was not decided against the western appointees until after the special session of Congress opened in August 1893, but it became clear in the spring that Beckwith had little hope.[6]

Even as an interim senator, Beckwith tried to exercise a determining voice in the distribution of the spoils of office; but in this effort he ran afoul of the designs of A. L. New, who intended to keep control of the patronage in his own hands. In July Beckwith resigned in disgust. New had never abandoned his ambitions for higher office, even in the face of

5. *Leader*, Feb. 24, 1893; Erwin, *Wyoming Historical Blue Book*, pp. 1305–06; A. L. New to John E. Osborne, Feb. 22, 1893, Governor's Incoming Correspondence, Wyoming State Archives.

6. *Compilation of Senate Election Cases from 1789–1913*, 62d Cong., 3d sess., Senate Document 1036 (Washington, 1913), pp. 52–84; Warren to J. B. Okie, Mar. 6, 1893, Warren Papers.

Beckwith's appointment, and he convinced Governor Osborne to appoint him in Beckwith's place. The Senate's unfavorable action thwarted New, and the deterioration of the Democratic position in Wyoming made a special session of the legislature to elect a senator a dangerous tactic. By general agreement, the Democrats decided to let the election of 1894 settle the senatorial problem.[7]

If New's scheme for the Senate did not prosper, it had no effect on his campaign to make himself the master of the Wyoming Democratic Party. After Cleveland took office, the crafty chairman embarked on an incredibly devious course which found him in pretended alliance with Beckwith, Osborne, and Congressman Coffeen, while actually he was reminding the President at every opportunity that all three men were tainted with extreme free silver sentiments. Using the influence thus gained with Washington, New sought to establish his supremacy in patronage matters.[8]

In so doing, New had to steer a course between the overwhelming resolve for free coinage of silver among the Wyoming Democrats and the even more resolute determination of Cleveland to deny patronage to all who were not unequivocally for repeal of the Sherman Act. To some degree, New's task was impossible. By 1893 the craze for free silver in Wyo-

7. *Leader,* July 30 and Aug. 3, 1893; John G. Carlisle to Grover Cleveland, Aug. 7, 1893, A. L. New to Grover Cleveland, Aug. 11 and 19, 1893, Grover Cleveland Papers.

8. A. L. New and Henry A. Coffeen to Hoke Smith, Aug. 7, 1893, Appointment Papers, Cheyenne Land Office, Interior Department, NA, RG48; New to W. F. Harrity, Oct. 5, 1893, Appointment Papers, Wyoming Surveyor-General, Interior Department, NA, RG48; New to Grover Cleveland, Oct. 31, 1893, Wyoming Appointment Papers, Justice Department, NA, RG60; New and Coffeen to Hoke Smith, Dec. 14, 1893, Appointment Papers, Douglas Land Office, Interior Department, NA, RG48.

ming had taken hold. Surrounded by states which were strong for the white metal, Wyoming residents received a shower of pamphlets, editorials, and letters singing the praises of bimetallism. The Panic of 1893, with its privations, gave the silver arguments force in both the agricultural and urban centers of Wyoming, although the electorate seems to have had an equally fervent faith in the tariff as a panacea. While the state had no silver mines to provide a direct connection with the attack on gold, the optimistic residents of the state shared the conviction of one observer that Wyoming "has hundreds of square miles that contain rich silver . . . bearing ores, and all that is necessary to develop them is capital." These factors were of a passing nature, and the free silver movement never gained the frenzied allegiance in Wyoming which characterized politics in Nevada and Colorado; but in the 1890s a politician in Wyoming could disavow silver only at the risk of his electoral fortunes.[9]

For a time it seemed that New would succeed. In his favor were the simple factors of greed and necessity; Democrats in Wyoming lusted after the spoils voraciously. New's position gained more strength when Cleveland decided to name him collector of internal revenue for Colorado and Wyoming in June 1893. This office, ordinarily a prize for Colorado, went to Wyoming because of the deep split among the Democrats in Denver; and the unexpected acquisition gave New more jobs to dispense among the faithful.[10]

9. Laramie *Weekly Boomerang*, Nov. 24, 1892, quoted in Kreuger, "Populism in Wyoming," p. 52.

10. C. S. Thomas to Grover Cleveland, Apr. 13, 1893, Grover Cleveland Papers; A. L. New to John G. Carlisle, June 1, 1893, Appointment Papers, Colorado Collector of Internal Revenue, Trea-

The patronage whip was New's most potent weapon, but forces beyond his control lessened its value and enabled his enemies to expose his duplicity. To establish his power, New needed to make some of his appointments before his anti-silver beliefs, so necessary to remain in Cleveland's good graces, became known. Unfortunately, the President would not distribute the spoils until he was assured of favorable action on the Sherman Act repeal, and he laid down a series of rules on appointments, including an order that Republican officeholders should be allowed to finish their terms before being dismissed.[11]

Such regulations seemed like unforgivable pettiness to Wyoming Democrats, and complaints soon appeared in the press. New pleaded with Washington to "relieve us of some of the offensively Republican Partisans, which are being kept alive by holding on to the 'Government teat.' " Part of New's urgency stemmed from the pressure placed on him in the summer of 1893 to call a state-wide silver convention. In a public letter a committee of Wyoming Democrats asked him to summon the conclave "to take such action and pass such resolutions as they may deem proper and wise to strengthen our delegation in congress in their defense of silver and to reflect the sentiments of the democrats of Wyoming upon the proposed action in congress upon this vital and important question."[12]

---

sury Department, NA, RG56; New to Daniel S. Lamont, June 20, 1893, Daniel S. Lamont Papers, Manuscripts Division, Library of Congress.

11. Nevins, *Grover Cleveland,* pp. 515–16.

12. A. L. New to S. W. Lamoreaux, Sept. 15, 1893, Appointment Papers, Sundance Land Office, Interior Department, NA, RG48; *Leader,* May 19, July 15 and 18 and Sept. 27, 1893.

After a month's hedging, New refused to act,[13] and his curt dismissal of Democratic efforts for silver caused the "silver fanatics" to claim "that I am too much in sympathy with the Administration," and helped widen the Democratic split. In return for his loyalty, Cleveland appointed New's candidates to the Cheyenne Land Office in the late autumn, provoking the *Leader* to complain that the men were not truly representative of the Wyoming Democratic Party. Since the *Leader's* editor, John F. Carroll, had been an unsuccessful applicant for the post of receiver of public monies in the office, one of New's kept papers complimented the chairman for blocking the ambitions of "a set of vultures, hypocritical in their lofty professions of love for the grand principles of democracy as handed down from the days of Jefferson and Jackson." This feuding led one Democrat to conclude in January 1894 that "this state has gone to hell entirely as far as democratic politics are concerned."[14]

With the liabilities attendant on the split over the silver issue, patronage allocation, and the policies of New, the Democrats badly needed a strong champion in Washington. Instead they had Congressman Henry Asa "Grandma" Coffeen, who possessed a short, unkempt beard, a taste for overblown rhetoric, and no political sense whatever. As a first term member of free silver persuasion, he was banished to an obscure committee where he had no power. In the face of financial reverses, Wyoming residents looked to the government for aid; but Coffeen, a discredited member of an economy-minded Congress, could not garner the subsidies,

13. *Leader,* Aug. 8, 1893.
14. John Hunton to Charly [?], Jan. 15, 1894, Hunton Papers; New to Cleveland, Aug. 11 and Sept. 30, 1893, Cleveland Papers; *Carbon County Journal,* Oct. 28, 1893; *Leader,* Sept. 27 and 30 and Oct. 13, 1893.

contracts and projects to which his constituents had become accustomed during Warren's tenure. Still more damaging, Coffeen weakened his standing in northern Wyoming by wavering on the question of a tariff on wool and by raising the possibility of a shift or removal of Fort McKinney at Buffalo.[15]

By the end of 1893 the Democratic Party in Wyoming was a group of blundering factions without any directing force or sound leadership. In January 1894 Governor Osborne pleaded with the President to make more appointments, for "Unless we receive merited recognitions at an early date, I fear that it will be too late, since our party leaders are at present almost completely discouraged, and are only buoyed up by the hope, that those to whom they must look for relief will be brought to a realizing sense of our deplorable condition before it is too late."[16]

Democratic reverses enabled the Republicans to bear with equanimity the second Cleveland administration, but Warren was especially cheered by the way the free silver issue had eroded Carey's popularity. As public opinion in Wyoming and in the Republican party rallied behind silver as the answer to the depression, Carey remained a consistent opponent of free coinage. He voted for repeal of the Sherman Act in 1893 and in 1894 was recorded against the Bland seigniorage bill. This stance, a matter of principle with the Senator, won Carey admiration in the East, but all conceded that it would cost him dearly with his constituents. "I know I did what I believed to be right in the matter of the repeal

15. *Rawlins Republican,* Sept. 13, 1894; S. B. Tuttle to Warren, Feb. 27, 1894, Warren Papers; Henry A. Coffeen to Grover Cleveland, Sept. 14, 1893, Grover Cleveland Papers.

16. John E. Osborne to Grover Cleveland, Jan. 12, 1894, Cleveland Papers.

of the Silver purchase bill," Carey wrote in November 1893, "I am being pounded hard in this western world, but I think I can stand it." At the end of the year, Carey's chances of returning as the one senator from Cheyenne looked remote.[17]

Warren, less principled, or perhaps more sensitive to the change in the political climate, had not taken such an adamant stand against silver in 1893. Indeed, he had demonstrated an eager willingness to abandon his earlier opposition to the white metal and speak out strongly for bimetallism. In September Willis Van Devanter, as state chairman, summoned leading Republicans to a convention in Cheyenne for a discussion of the silver question. Warren asserted that the Republicans had always been friendly to silver and that it was through the G.O.P. that relief "must come . . . if any is to come." Democratic newspapers were not impressed. Warren "has paraded too long as a grasping monopolist to suddenly become an enemy to that class of human sharks, and although he now has on a sackcloth if he should be elected to the senate he would immediately resume his broadcloth and gold collar."[18]

What effect Warren's about-face would have was uncertain. A Democratic analyst believed that "the recent flop of ex-senator Warren as a free silver champion when he has been so long known as an earnest advocate of the gold standard disgusts hundreds who readily discern his object. His race is run." But a Democratic editor assessed the situa-

17. Joseph M. Carey to Robert Underwood Johnson, Nov. 21, 1893, Robert Underwood Johnson Papers, Bancroft Library, University of California; George W. Paulson, "The Congressional Career of Joseph Maull Carey," *Annals of Wyoming*, 35 (1963), 53–63.

18. *Leader*, Sept. 3, 1893; *Sun*, Sept. 3, 1893, *People's Voice*, Sept. 2, 1893, clippings in Warren Scrapbooks, Warren Papers.

tion more perceptively: "While Carey is floundering laboriously in a hopeless slough of public condemnation, Warren prances to the front, and with the attributes of Ananias and the audacity of the devil, claims to be the leader of the free silver cause and the moulder of public sentiment in this matter."[19]

In later years Carey attributed his defeat in 1895 solely to his gold sentiments, a point of view which enabled Carey to assert that it was his fidelity to principle which brought him down. This is true to some extent, but Carey and his apologists overlook the Senator's other weaknesses. There is much circumstantial evidence that he did not keep his fences mended and even more substantial indications that many Republicans believed Carey had received enough rewards at the hands of his party. "I am opposed to Senator Carey's re-election," a Republican editor told the *Leader* in the spring of 1894, "not on the ground of his silver views but because he has been amply honored for his services by his party."[20]

Senator Carey did record one legislative achievement in the summer of 1894, but ironically it had little effect on his political hopes. An amendment to the Sundry Civil Appropriations bill, later known as the Carey Act, bestowed one million acres on each state of the arid region with the proviso that the land be irrigated within ten years. Once again the absence of Senator Carey's personal papers prevents a conclusive judgment on the act's relationship, if any, to the Warren arid land bill or on the Senator's motives in introducing his amendment. As an answer to the problems of

19. J. D. Hurd to A. L. New, Oct. 22, 1893, Grover Cleveland Papers; *Wyoming Derrick,* Sept. 22, 1893, clipping in Warren Scrapbooks, Warren Papers.

20. *Leader,* May 8, 1894.

irrigation, the Carey Act was far from a success. Amended many times, it was finally superseded by the Newlands Act in 1902. As a political tactic in Carey's race for reelection, it passed generally unnoticed in the Wyoming press.[21]

With his major antagonists in difficulty, Warren remained ostensibly uninterested in the Senate race. He would not make a formal announcement, or an active canvass, "but like many men have been before 'I am in the hands of my friends.'" Meanwhile he gave Van Devanter the duty of putting together a strong state ticket which would insure a Republican victory. In so doing, Van Devanter drew liberally on the lessons of 1892 and sought to correct the oversights which had hampered the campaign and hurt Warren's chances. He advocated a longer period for electioneering, a change which the state committee approved when it scheduled the nominating convention early in August. The delicate problem of Cheyenne domination, so crucial a factor in Warren's senatorial hopes, was sidestepped by making Casper the site of the gathering.[22]

Warren's quest for the Senate seat required two ingredients for success: a unified Republican organization and an unqualified endorsement of free silver. His timely shift in 1893 had done much to counteract his earlier "goldbug" activities, but the campaign would demand that the Republican platform spell out a desire for silver on the part of the party. As Warren foresaw, this would have the happy effect of placing Carey in a most difficult position. If Carey con-

21. Gould and Lilley, "The Western Irrigation Movement," pp. 69–70.
22. S. B. Tuttle to Warren, Feb. 27, 1894, Warren to Charles Kingston, July 17, 1894, Warren Papers; Van Devanter to J. C. Davis, Mar. 13, 1895, to J. M. Carey, June 12, 1894, to W. A. Richards, May 8, 1894, Van Devanter Papers.

tinued to oppose silver, Warren had only to retreat to the high ground of party principle and ask why his rival refused to abide by the express will of Wyoming Republicans.

The means which Warren and Van Devanter used to promote this end were the Republican League Clubs which had been formed throughout the country in 1887 to work for party enthusiasm. Van Devanter encouraged the founding of league clubs in Wyoming as a device to rally support and to recruit workers in advance of the campaign. He organized the Laramie County Republican League Club himself and called a state convention in June 1894, which met shortly before the opening of the League's national convention in Denver. After electing delegates to Denver, the convention declared that "the republican state league of Wyoming favor the free and unlimited coinage of both gold and silver at the ratio of 16 to 1, with full legal tender functions accorded to each, in payment of all public and private debts."[23]

The national convention at Denver evaded the question of silver, but Warren had achieved his object of establishing a party-wide consensus on the issue which would appeal to the voters and isolate Carey. While strengthening the organizational framework of the Republicans, Warren also sought to arrange a potent state ticket which would help elect legislative candidates favorable to his cause. Ignoring the weak claims of Edward Ivinson, Warren decided that Frank W. Mondell and William Richards would be ideal selections for the two top places, congressman and governor. The problem was that both men wanted to be governor.[24]

23. *Sun,* June 25, 1894; *Leader,* June 26, 1894; Van Devanter to C. C. Hamlin, May 8 and 11, 1894, to Clarence D. Clark, May 31, 1894, to Frank Mondell, June 11, 1894, Van Devanter Papers.

24. *Leader,* June 27 and 28, 1894; Warren to W. A. Richards, May 22, 1894, Warren Papers.

From the first, Warren and Van Devanter considered Richards the stronger choice for governor, since Mondell, as a former employee of the manufacturing firm of Kilpatrick Brothers which had Burlington Railroad connections, appealed less to the workers in southern Wyoming. Moreover, if Richards had to take the congressional nomination and won, his residence in Laramie County might impair Warren's Senate chances by raising the question of whether Cheyenne had valid claims to more than one federal office. Richards, however, felt that he could not make an active campaign for the gubernatorial nomination but would rather be chosen by acclamation. Van Devanter warned him in April 1894 that the "tide is turning perceptibly in favor of Mondell," and asked Richards to "confide in me enough (confidentially) to give me your personal position with reference to the coming campaign."[25]

After an equivocal response from Richards, Van Devanter, on May 8, 1894, set forth the situation in detail and indicated that Richards had many friends and much strength throughout the state, especially in Carbon and Converse counties; but while the outlook was favorable, Richards would have to act. Mondell continued to solicit support, making it clear that he and Richards could only wound the party by their separate campaigns because Warren had concluded that "the general feeling was that yourself and Mondell should receive the nominations for Governor and Congressman if the two nominations could be agreed upon between you." As Warren explained to Mondell, "with yourself and Richards on the same ticket, all elements would be reached."[26]

25. Van Devanter to Richards, Apr. 18 and May 8, 1894, Van Devanter Papers.
26. Van Devanter to Richards, May 8 and June 11, 1894, Van Devanter Papers; Warren to Mondell, July 4, 1894, Warren Papers.

The matter fluctuated during June and July 1894, but it was evident that a deal between Mondell and Richards was the logical solution to the impasse. Few records of the negotiations have survived, and these indicate that at one point Warren swung behind Mondell when Richards, whom Warren regarded as badly advised, pulled out of the race. Van Devanter stepped in at once and attempted to restore the balance. By the end of July the situation was static, with the answer obvious, but the issue in doubt. Meanwhile a serious split in Laramie County threatened to destroy the smooth organization in the most important Republican stronghold.[27]

Dissension had arisen in Cheyenne over the activities of the American Protective Association (APA) and its attempts to use the Republican party to promote its anti-Catholic goals. The organization had begun to take hold in the West after 1890, and a branch was established in Cheyenne in 1891. By 1892 the question of membership had become a factor in local elections. Because of its secrecy, few traces of APA activity emerge until January 1893, when its influence helped elect a Republican mayor.[28]

The Association's historian, Donald Kinzer, attributes its success in the West to "its ability to capitalize on local incidents and to pursue rather limited objectives." In Cheyenne and later in Laramie, the order grew in response to the presence of nearly four thousand Catholics whose foreign backgrounds aroused nativist feelings. The economic depression after 1893 may have fed resentment against

27. Warren to Richards, May 22, 1894, to Mondell, June 11–12 [?], and July 4 and 8, 1894, Warren Papers.
28. Warren to G. R. Palmer, Mar. 14, 1892, S. B. Tuttle to Warren, May 3, 1892, Warren Papers; *Sun,* Sept. 27 and Oct. 11, 1892; *Leader,* Jan. 4, 1893.

Catholic workers holding jobs with the railroad, but the secret nature of the APA makes firm conclusions impossible. From all accounts, the APA in Wyoming shared the aims of the national body: oust Catholics from public office, maintain the nonsectarian public school, and end the use of public funds to support religious education.[29]

As in other states in the West, the Republican Party furnished the bulk of the APA membership, but the order in Laramie County seems to have been a vehicle for Republicans seeking to express their dissatisfaction with the dominant faction in Cheyenne. Many of the movement's adherents resented the "aristocratic" tendencies of the group led by Frank and Fred Bond, A. J. Parshall, and C. W. Riner, which had controlled city politics for several years. The greatest strength of the APA was centered in Cheyenne's first ward, a less well-to-do area than the second ward where the Republican leaders lived, so that economic jealousy and class antagonism probably played as great roles in the actions of the APA as religious conviction.

During the early part of 1894, feuding on the city council drove the APA contingent and their foes farther and farther apart. Encouraged by their local success, the nativist organization prepared to strive for larger goals. Using their power in Laramie County, they hoped to advance the cause of one of their leaders, a lawyer named Ralph Emerson Esteb, to acquire one of the Senate seats or the chairmanship of the state committee.[30]

29. Donald Kinzer, *An Episode in Anti-Catholicism: The American Protective Association* (Seattle, 1964), p. 111; U.S. Bureau of Census, *Census Bulletin: Statistics of Churches, 101* (Washington, 1891), 23.

30. *Leader*, Feb. 7 and 21, March 6, April 1, and May 8, 11, and 13, 1894; S. B. Tuttle to Warren, Feb. 19, 1894, Warren Papers. Van Devanter had written a letter of recommendation for Esteb in 1893,

Willis Van Devanter's response to the APA's threat to his position combined caution and compromise. The movement had little following outside Laramie and Albany counties, so that Van Devanter did not want it to have too large a voice on the state level. Attacking the APA might be the most effective technique the Democrats could use among Catholic railroad workers, a group which Grover Cleveland's anti-labor policies had alienated. At the same time, Van Devanter could not afford to support a full-scale battle to wipe out the APA in Cheyenne because too many loyal Republicans backed the order and might resist a purge. In May 1894, Van Devanter told Richards that there might be trouble, and "If there is to be a conflict then I am with the Bonds; but I am very much opposed to such a conflict, and I believe that if a less threatening attitude were taken by the anti-A.P.A.'s some kind of a truce could be declared and a satisfactory division of county nominations made."[31]

Conciliation suffered several reverses in the spring of 1894. The anti-APA faction started a rival organization in Cheyenne, the Lincoln Club, with a ten dollar admission fee. Since the bulk of the APA membership was drawn from the lower strata of the Republicans, this move was seen as an attempt by the "creased-pants," or aristocratic faction to shut out the less well-to-do element. Warren regarded the club as an overzealous device which could only add to the existing problem, but since it had been set up without his knowledge, Warren's disavowals had little pacifying effect.[32]

---

calling him a "stalwart Republican," Van Devanter to J. M. Thurston, July 15, 1893, Van Devanter Papers.

31. Van Devanter to Richards, May 8, 1894, Van Devanter Papers.

32. *Leader,* Apr. 21, July 22, 1894; Warren to W. E. Chaplin, May 2, 1894, Warren Papers.

Bad feeling increased when the Cheyenne *Sun* started an editorial offensive against Esteb in June, calling him a "phototype" of A. L. New and inquiring whether "the Republican party will tamely submit, like oxen, to be yoked and driven as the Democratic party is now being goaded on to destruction by the unscrupulous trickster at its head." Slack attacked Esteb's habit of putting up prearranged slates of county and city nominations and urged all decent Republicans to reclaim their independence. As might have been expected, the result of Slack's onslaught was renewed hostility.[33]

In early June, Esteb abandoned his hopes to become a senator and decided to be content with the state chairmanship. With the solid backing of the APA members in Laramie and Albany counties, he sought support outside Cheyenne for his accession to the post. Warren could not throw his weight behind either wing without risking an irreparable break, and the situation festered. As conditions deteriorated, Warren moaned that "To fool away the present almost heaven born opportunities by internal dissention [sic] would be very unusual and mournful 'asinity' [sic] for the republicans."[34]

The moment of crisis would come in the primaries to elect delegates to the Laramie County convention which would, in turn, make county nominations and pick a slate of delegates for the meeting at Casper. Esteb wanted to secure a delegation pledged to vote for his choices for county offices, as well as bound to support him for state chairman, and he intended to use the APA method of packing the elections with his adherents to drive through the desired

33. *Sun,* July 1, 6, and 20, 1894; Warren to Mondell, July 8, 1894, Warren Papers.
34. Warren to Mondell, July 8, 1894, Warren Papers.

candidates. Van Devanter's first mission was to defeat this plan and obtain a county convention in which the APA would not have control. To accomplish this, he urged the voters to select men unpledged to any particular candidates in the primary to be held on July 23, 1894.[35]

Van Devanter's strategy required that all Republican voters in each of Cheyenne's three wards turn out for the balloting; the only way to counteract the APA's docile majorities was with larger numbers. On the day of the primary, Van Devanter, along with other prominent Laramie County Republicans, issued an address to party members which urged them to "attend the primaries of the party in their respective precincts and in the interest of the community and the Republican party and demand and participate in the selection of UNPLEDGED DELEGATES CHOSEN FROM REPRESENTATIVE CITIZENS, who shall go to the county convention not for the purpose of furthering the personal ambitions or selfish aspirations of any individual candidate, but who, FREE FROM ALL ENTANGLEMENTS, shall stand for the best interests of Laramie county and the Republican party and for those interests alone."[36]

Primary night saw a great outpouring of voters who turned back the Esteb candidates in two out of the three wards, giving the unpledged faction twenty-three of thirty-six places. The power of the APA to pick and choose local officers had been broken. Van Devanter realized, however, that crushing the APA would destroy all chance of unity, and he intended to see that the county convention did not

35. *Leader,* July 22, 1894; Warren to D. G. Thomas, July 13, 1894, Warren Papers.
36. *Sun,* July 23, 1894.

become a bloodletting. If this meant the sacrifice of the anti-APA wing, then Van Devanter was prepared to make this offering to the Esteb camp.[37]

The county convention went off smoothly with one exception. Van Devanter persuaded the delegates to hold a secret caucus at which, in exchange for a delegation to Casper of sufficient pliability and a legislative ticket agreeable to Warren, the APA was given its share of county nominations. When the caucus adjourned, the delegates set about acting out the script. Van Devanter's intrigues were exposed when the balloting for county attorney began. The anti-APA faction insisted that the caucus nominee, Esteb's law partner, be discarded and another man named in his place. The complaints of the APA prevented any further changes in the caucus agreement, and the rest of the convention proceeded as scheduled.[38]

The outcome of this convention met with general accord among Republicans, who were disposed to accept the *Sun's* judgment that "it is best not to be too curious about such transactions." With Laramie County at rest, if not at peace, Van Devanter could deal with the lingering problem of the state ticket. On the eve of the Casper convention, Warren telegraphed Van Devanter to convey his finding of a "Unanimous and enthusiastic desire, amounting to almost a command" among Republicans "that Mondell go Congress." Acting on Warren's warning that "Convention should make no mistake," a division of offices and unity were achieved. After Richards received the gubernatorial nomination, Mondell would be selected to run for Con-

---

37. *Leader,* July 26, 1894; Van Devanter to Warren, Apr. 17, 1896, Van Devanter Papers, discusses the events of the 1894 primary.

38. *Leader,* July 27 and 28, 1894.

gress. The rest of the offices were similarly allocated until the final ticket was arranged.[39]

As a result, the Casper convention was tranquil. Richards and Mondell triumphed over token opposition, and the rest of the ticket was ratified with only one change. The delegates declared for free coinage of silver at 16 to 1, using the exact words of the Republican league's resolution, and received a telegram of congratulations from Warren for their work.[40] With a strong ticket, as even the Democrats acknowledged, Warren could look forward to the campaign in an optimistic mood. The certainty of success was strengthened when Van Devanter was reelected chairman, "without a dissenting vote," insuring that the direction of the state canvass would be in capable hands.[41]

For Carey, on the other hand, the outcome of the state convention boded ill. Out of step with his party, repudiated by the platform, and removed from the centers of power, he was faced with a situation where Republican victory would work to his disadvantage. Aware of the strong cards which they held, Warren and Van Devanter moved to complete the ruin of their rival.

Republican anxiety about the campaign was considerably eased by the continued troubles of the Democrats. During the spring and summer of 1894, the discontent stemming from the Panic of 1893 briefly touched Wyoming. Following the example of Coxey's Army of the unemployed, which had moved east from Ohio to Washington in April 1894, bands of out-of-work men began capturing trains in the Far

39. *Sun,* July 28, 1894; *Leader,* Aug. 3 and 4, 1894; Warren to Van Devanter, Aug. 1, 1894, Warren Papers.

40. *Leader,* Aug. 5, 1894; Warren to Chairman, Casper Convention, Aug. 3, 1894, Warren Papers.

41. *Sun,* Aug. 4, 1894; *Leader,* Aug. 5, 1894.

West in the vague hope that they might travel to Washington, present their grievances, and receive governmental aid. Their tactic of train-grabbing aroused fears of social upheaval throughout the West; and the Union Pacific, in line with its general policy, directed its legal representatives in Wyoming, Van Devanter's law firm, to recover the stolen trains and see that the thieves were arrested. When the trains crossed into Wyoming, Van Devanter secured a writ barring damage to railroad property in the state, had the United States marshal seize one group of men, and turned the rest back into Idaho with the aid of the army.[42]

Later in the summer, the Pullman strike spread to Wyoming. Token compliance with the walkout lasted only a short time, and the power of the American Railway Union collapsed quickly. For all the rapidity of the victory over the railroad workers, Warren was not disposed to mercy toward the discontented. When a movement began to have the strikers rehired by the Union Pacific, Warren wrote the general manager of the railroad that "at this juncture when you have such an elegant opportunity to clean out these cranks with wheels in their heads etc., I think it would be better to let them go notwithstanding they may be old employees or that they have families and homes here."[43]

As the party in power, however, the Democrats received the onus for these manifestations of unrest; on the local level, the summer of 1894 was marked by even more crippling events. In July anti-New Democrats disclosed a nasty scandal involving the surveyor-general, Perry Bickford. A family man in his sixties, Bickford used his position

42. *Leader,* May 13, 15, and 16, 1894; *Sun,* May 23, 1894; Herman C. Voeltz, "Coxey's Army in Oregon," *Oregon Historical Quarterly,* 65 (1964), 291–92.
43. Warren to Ed Dickinson, Aug. 22, 1894, Warren Papers.

to support a prostitute in Cheyenne, an arrangement which came to light when the girl committed suicide. Since Bickford's nomination had been one of New's most praised appointments, the collector's enemies did not hesitate to seize their opportunity.[44]

President Cleveland placed public rectitude ahead of party regularity, and John Charles Thompson replaced Bickford. The Republicans, anxious to exploit their windfall, induced Bickford to defend himself; his refusal to step aside kept the issue alive during the campaign.[45] Meanwhile New's connection with the Bickford scandal had convinced the Justice Department to reject New's choices for the crucial posts of United States attorney and marshal and to appoint other men. When these nominations were made in September 1894, they marked the end of New's hegemony in Wyoming.[46]

44. Perry Bickford to Grover Cleveland, Aug. 9 and 13, 1894, Henry A. Coffeen to Hoke Smith, Aug. 10, 1894, A. L. New to Cleveland, Aug. 16, 1894, Appointment Papers, Wyoming Surveyor-General, Interior Department, NA, RG48; Coffeen to Cleveland, July 27, 1894, New to Cleveland, Aug. 14, 1894, Luke Voorhees to Henry T. Thurber, Aug. 22, 1894, Cleveland Papers.

45. George T. Beck et al. to Grover Cleveland, Aug. 11, 1894, J. D. Hurd to Henry A. Coffeen, Aug. 20, 1894, Coffeen to Hoke Smith, Aug. 20, 1894, to Cleveland, Aug. 27, 1894, Perry Bickford to Hoke Smith, Sept. 19, 1894, to Cleveland, Sept. 19, 1894, John E. Osborne to Hoke Smith, Jan. 2, 1895, to Cleveland, Jan. 2, 1895, Appointment Papers, Wyoming Surveyor-General, Interior Department, NA, RG48; J. S. Harper to Cleveland, Jan. 1, 1895, Bickford to Cleveland, Jan. 5, 1895, Cleveland Papers.

46. R. W. Allen to Richard Olney, Dec. 29, 1893 and July 18, 1894, John A. Riner to George W. Baxter, May 14, 1894, Henry G. Hay to Henry F. Sears, July 16, 1894, Andrew McMicken to A. L. New, July 17, 1894, New to Grover Cleveland, July 23, 1894, Wyoming Appointment Papers, Justice Department, NA, RG60.

Before his political eclipse, however, New bestowed a final gift of disunity on the party he had served so badly. At the Democratic state convention in August, New blocked a resolution condemning the Cleveland administration. This move, made in the interest of preserving the collector's influence with the President, further sharpened party differences at an already faction-ridden gathering. Several days of bargaining produced a lackluster ticket, an evasive platform, and a demoralized Democratic Party. Governor Osborne, seeking a senate seat, did not stand for reelection, and the perennial candidate, W. H. Holliday, won the dubious privilege of running at the top of the ticket. Congressman Coffeen, nobody's choice for a second term, was allowed to run again when the other candidates shunned the nomination.[47]

The refusal of the Populists to repeat the fusion of 1892 delivered another blow to Democratic hopes. After their exertions in behalf of the Democrats, the Populists had received scant rewards at the hands of Cleveland and New. The President's anti-labor, anti-Populist, and anti-silver policies had made him a hated figure among western Populists, and they saw little point in aiding his party. The Republicans also used financial influence to subsidize Populist newspapers and speakers on the condition that fusion be prevented. For these reasons, the Populists preferred to wage a separate campaign in the mistaken conviction that they could win on their own.[48]

47. New to Cleveland, Aug. 15, 1894, Cleveland Papers; *Leader,* Aug. 9 and 10, 1894; Denver *Rocky Mountain News,* Aug. 10, 1894.

48. *Leader,* Aug. 10, 1894; *Sun,* Aug. 24 and 25, 1894; Van Devanter to C. C. Hamlin, Sept. 14, 1894, Van Devanter Papers; Warren to Mrs. M. S. Burke, Sept. 7, 1894, Warren to J. S. Clarkson, Oct. 13, 1894, Warren Papers.

In September the Republicans were given another ready-made campaign issue when the army closed Fort McKinney at Buffalo. Congressman Coffeen had initiated a drive with the Secretary of War to have the fort moved to Sheridan, his home town. This, as Warren noted, was a serious mistake. "It has long been known by men of sense that to intimate to the War Department a desire to change the location of a post, or to cut down a reservation, is to invite its destruction." Already handicapped by his vote for free wool on the Wilson-Gorman tariff, Coffeen had endangered his waning popularity in the areas in which he needed every vote.[49]

The plight of the Democrats did not mean that the Republicans lacked problems. While the Republican state ticket was strong, the real prize remained the two Senate seats, and the Democrats were quite content to let their state candidates lose if they could salvage a legislative majority. Republican counterattacks would require large expenditures in each county, but the normal sources in Wyoming had gone dry. Repudiation by the convention, as well as his own Senate hopes, made Carey reluctant to contribute, while Warren had been stricken with business reverses which made his usual full participation doubtful. In July the Warren Livestock Company went into receivership, and "The Democratic tariff bill and Democratic administration have cost me several hundred thousand dollars, and leaves me much involved. However, I will expect to furnish a few dollars for the campaign, [but] nothing like what I have formerly done."[50]

49. Warren to Fred Bond, Sept. 22, 1894, to C. H. Parmelee, Sept. 22, 1894, to E. H. Smock, Aug. 25 and Sept. 22, 1894, Warren Papers; Burton S. Hill, "Buffalo-Ancient Cow Town, A Wyoming Saga," *Annals of Wyoming, 35* (1963), 151.

50. Warren to Mrs. M. S. Burke, Sept. 7, 1894, Warren Papers.

Faced with empty coffers, Warren and Van Devanter looked for outside assistance from the East. Van Devanter traveled to Washington and New York in August on a "business trip," soliciting help from prominent Republicans and the national committee. For the moment his requests for ten thousand dollars were turned aside, though the American Protective Tariff League did supply some literature for distribution. Because of this stringency, Van Devanter reminded his workers that "the most rigid economy must be practiced," and in rejecting a plea for a newspaper subsidy stressed "that the campaign will have to be conducted upon a basis in keeping with the times."[51]

Financial shortages nearly frustrated several of Warren's key campaign maneuvers, and they were finally made possible only by the united effort of the Republican leadership in the state. The most dramatic was the *Cheyenne Daily Leader's* defection from the Democratic camp. The paper's editor, John F. Carroll, had been badly treated by New and Coffeen after being the journalistic champion of Wyoming Democrats since the late 1880s. Because Carroll made no secret of his discontent, the Republicans approached him in early September concerning the price of his shift in allegiance.[52] To forsake the Democrats would cost Carroll the state and national printing which they had hitherto allotted him. The Republicans, on the other hand, could not bestow their patronage on the *Leader* without

51. Warren to O. H. Platt, Aug. 13, 1894, to Van Devanter, Aug. 20 and 22, 1894, Warren Papers; Van Devanter to C. H. Parmelee, Sept. 2, 1894, Van Devanter Papers; *Sun,* Aug. 30, 1894.

52. New and Coffeen to Hoke Smith, Dec. 14, 1893, Appointment Papers, Douglas Land Office, Interior Department, NA, RG48; New to Cleveland, Oct. 20, 1893, Cleveland Papers; W. E. Chaplin, "Some of the Early Newspapers in Wyoming," *Wyoming Historical Society, Miscellanies, 1919* (Laramie, 1919), p. 18.

hurting E. A. Slack and the *Sun*. Van Devanter indicated to eastern Republicans that with the allegiance of the *Leader* party success would be "absolutely insured," but "on account of our financial condition," they had to reject Carroll's terms.[53]

The prospect of picking up the *Leader* proved too tempting to ignore, however, and negotiations resumed within a few days. Drawing on the resources of Henry G. Hay, the candidate for treasurer, and of Clarence D. Clark, Carroll's price was met, and the *Leader* came out as an "independent" daily in late September. The exact nature of the agreement is not known, but Carroll sold out to Slack in 1895 and moved to Denver and later to Oregon. For the rest of the campaign, the *Leader* left the Republican partisanship to the *Sun* and concentrated its fire on Coffeen and his alleged disservices to Wyoming.[54]

By the end of September, Republican hopes in Wyoming were bright. The Democrats had not found an issue on which to focus, their campaign treasury was exhausted, and their candidates had become the butt of ridicule. In desperation the party attempted to revive the Johnson County War issue by subsidizing A. S. Mercer's history of the incident, *The Banditti of the Plains*. Despite an extensive selling tour of the state by Mercer and his family, the book

53. Van Devanter to J. W. Babcock, Sept. 20, 1894, Van Devanter Papers.
54. Van Devanter to W. F. Wakeman, Sept. 25, 1894, to Jay L. Torrey, Sept. 26, 1894, Warren to Van Devanter, Apr. 29, 1896, William A. Richards to Van Devanter, Sept. 20, 1903, Van Devanter Papers; John Hunton to John F. Carroll, Sept. 27, 1894, Hunton Papers; New to Cleveland, Sept. 27, 1894, Cleveland Papers; Warren to Mrs. H. E. Stanton, Jan. 21, 1895, Warren Papers; *Leader,* Sept. 26, 1894; Denver *Rocky Mountain News,* Sept. 28, 1894.

aroused little interest. Apologists for Mercer have claimed that the book's poor reception was the result of a concerted effort by the cattlemen to suppress it, but Democratic weaknesses and the voters' boredom with the rustler question account for the failure of Mercer's attempt to rake over old animosities.[55]

Improvement in Republican prospects made eastern political circles more receptive to Wyoming's needs, and money began to reach the state committee. Cornelius N. Bliss sent five hundred dollars to Warren in October, with a promise of five hundred more. With some money from Carey,[56] the party was able to look with confidence toward election day. "As to our state ticket," Warren said, "we are 'out of the woods.' As to our Member of Congress, think we have a little the best of it but we ought to make it more certain." But for Warren the crucial question was the legislative ticket, and he begged for more assistance. "We must keep speakers and workers, and lots of them, constantly in the field to patch up differences; to hold our own steadfast; to proselyte from the dems, turning those who wont come to us to the pops; to keep the pops in the field and prevent their fusing with the dems."[57]

In October, Warren and Van Devanter realized that only a major miracle could thwart Republican success. With this in mind, they opened Warren's senatorial campaign and looked for ways in which to sabotage Carey. As luck would have it, Carey picked that moment to write Van Devanter that if the state committee wanted him to participate in the

---

55. Denver *Rocky Mountain News,* Aug. 26 and 29, 1894; Gould, "A. S. Mercer and the Johnson County War," pp. 18–20.
56. Warren to J. S. Clarkson, Oct. 13, 1894, Warren Papers.
57. Ibid.

campaign, it should designate the times and places immediately:

> I very much regret that it is not the wish of the Committee that I should go to each of the counties in the State, which has at all times been so loyal and true to me and which I have served to the best of my ability. I feel that the Democratic speakers and the press are giving me more attention than I really deserve and it is my right, as a Republican, to reply. I presume I can find a way to successfully do it. I personally have no doubt whatever that I would be received, in each county of the State, and treated as I have always heretofore been which, without exception, has been of that character to which I could not take any exception.[58]

Van Devanter understood that Carey had played into Warren's hands, but he adopted a pose of neutrality and solicited advice from other members of his committee. "It places us in a very embarrassing position, because several of the counties, while indicating no hostility whatever toward Senator Carey, either personally or politically, have said that a sufficient number of their voters were opposed to his silver views and political course to endanger the legislative and other tickets if he actively participated in the campaign in their county."[59]

Warren, too, was told that he would not be welcome in some areas, and he quickly agreed to avoid speaking in those counties. "Senator Carey feels that he should speak in every county, and is inclined to feel hurt because the State Con-

58. Carey to Van Devanter, Oct. 6, 1894, copy in author's possession courtesy of Justice Van Devanter's son, Mr. Winslow B. Van Devanter.

59. Van Devanter to Jay L. Torrey, Oct. 8, 1894, to Cyrus Beard, Oct. 10, 1894, Van Devanter Papers.

vention adopted a silver platform, and does not believe that he would do any possible harm by actively participating in the campaign in every county." Van Devanter laid the matter before the Executive Committee of the Republican State Committee, who approved a letter which Van Devanter had drafted, and which outlined Carey's differences with the party.[60] In it Van Devanter told Carey that the committee had received complaints from various counties "that it would not assist the party for you to speak in their campaign." After expressing his regrets at this rebuff, Van Devanter offered to send a copy of Carey's letter requesting a speaking tour to each county committee who would then "inform us whether Republican success will be promoted in their respective counties by your participating in this campaign." When the answers were received, Van Devanter would "be glad to confer with you as to what is to be done."[61]

With the political amenities disposed of, Van Devanter reminded Carey of the action of the state convention in endorsing silver, a decision which was "carefully considered and honestly taken. We should do nothing which will erroneously cast upon the party any suspicion of insincerity in this matter." While some Republicans might not support every plank in the platform, "the campaign should not be so conducted by the committee as to in any sense justify the charge that we are doing otherwise than standing squarely and fairly upon our state platform."[62] Carey's isolation was completed by Van Devanter's pointed request that "in determining whether it will be advantageous to the party for you to speak in the several counties, it will assist the county

60. Van Devanter to T. D. Woodruff, ...

61. Van Devanter to Carey, Oct. 9, 1894, Van Devanter Papers.
62. Ibid.

committees if they know whether you endorse the declaration of principles adopted at our recent State convention, and for this purpose we ask that you state your position in this matter. If there be any portion of the platform which you do not endorse, we would then like your judgment as to whether your speaking throughout the State, under the auspices of this committee, would create a belief that the Republican party is not sincerely standing by its platform."[63]

Carey's response to this delicately phrased attack has not survived, but the evidence suggests that his speaking tours were sanctioned with the greatest reluctance by the state committee. In any case, Van Devanter believed that Carey's gold sympathies had sufficiently alienated the electorate to insure that the legislature would not "elect any Senator who is not a free silver man." With Warren's chief rival in Cheyenne crippled, Van Devanter resumed his supervision of the last-minute details of the campaign.[64]

As state chairman, Van Devanter affected a mood of cautious optimism, but the scent of victory stimulated Republican rallies in the days before election. Warren told a large cheering crowd in Cheyenne to "be assured from my own lips that I stand as firmly upon the silver plank of our platform as does the building which now shelters us stand upon its foundation—sixteen to one, or better yet, fifteen and one-half to one; with the cooperation of other first class countries if possible, but the United States alone if necessary, say I. And in either event at once and with vigor,

63. Ibid.
64. Van Devanter to M. M. Pettigrew, Oct. 12, 1894, to Mortimer Jesurun, Oct. 19, 1894, to Lewis D. Apsley, New York, Oct. 25, 1894, to J. W. Meldrum, Oct. 26, 1894, Van Devanter Papers.

press it to an issue, press hard and continually, until achieved. (applause)."[65]

Election results bore out Republican hopes. Their state candidates overwhelmed their opponents, Mondell swamped Coffeen, and forty-eight Republican legislative aspirants were returned to the fifty-five-man legislature. Among the successful lawmakers were some men who had triumphed by narrow margins, and Warren thanked eastern Republicans for their "liberality," which had enabled the candidates to squeak through. "In several localities," Warren wrote, "(enough to turn 3 whole counties) there are large number of foreign voters in the coal mines where you may rest assured, it was necessary to 'oil the wheels of progress' in order to carry their vote."[66] Vote buying, bribery, and coercion helped to swell the victory margins, but Republican triumph in 1894 owed as much to Democratic mistakes and ineptness. After two years of Grover Cleveland and his party, Wyoming voters returned to their Republican allegiance in the hope that Warren, Mondell, and Clarence D. Clark might restore the prosperity which New and Coffeen had seemingly destroyed.

The Republican resurgence in 1894 was part of a general political upheaval in the nation which signaled the opening of an era of supremacy for the G.O.P. While hardly a new center of Republican strength, like the cities, Wyoming responded to the same concerns which turned other states away from the Democrats. In the West Grover Cleveland completed in his second term the emasculation of his party that he had begun from 1885 to 1889. Wyoming voters believed that rigid economy, pro-gold policies, and the Wilson-

65. *Sun,* Nov. 4, 1894.
66. Warren to Cornelius N. Bliss, Nov. 13, 1894, to J. W. Babcock, Nov. 10, 1894; Erwin, *Wyoming Historical Blue Book,* pp. 1184–85.

Gorman tariff had led to their economic troubles, and they swung, as Carl Degler has argued, to the "party of progress, prosperity, and national authority" for relief.[67] Bryan's campaign in 1896 made a temporary dent in the Republican facade, but with that exception, the election of 1894 established a pattern of Republican dominance that persisted until 1912 in presidential elections and until 1932 on the state level.

Warren, his spirits buoyed by the election, announced his candidacy for the Senate several days after the final results were compiled. He told Mondell, "I propose to join you in Washington business," and began soliciting votes from Republicans around the state. Newspaper editors who were favorably disposed to Warren's cause obtained his assurance that "it takes money to run a newspaper and if you will give me your friendship, I ought to pay you for such space as you may feel is necessary to use."[68]

Warren's candidacy frightened some Republicans; they feared that an unseemly fight would ensue, to the detriment of the party. Warren recognized the genuine concern behind these apprehensions, but he found little merit in suggestions that he should step aside to avoid a quarrel. "I see no reason," he asserted, "why I should stand out of the way because Judge Carey desires me to." To one editor, Warren sketched ten reasons in support of his right to seek a Senate seat, citing his many services to the party and concluding, "I know of no reason on 'God's footstool' why I should always play second fiddle in the Carey-Warren or Warren-Carey com-

67. Carl N. Degler, "American Political Parties and the Rise of the City: An Interpretation," *The Journal of American History, 51* (1964), 41–59.

68. Warren to Mondell, Nov. 10, 1894, to J. F. Crawford, Nov. 25, 1894, Warren Papers.

bination. Now I am not *against Carey,* but I am *for Warren.*"[69]

The Senate struggle in 1894–95 was governed by two legacies of the 1893 fiasco, neither of which worked to Carey's advantage. Republicans felt that the party must avoid a long battle and that only one senator should be chosen from Cheyenne. Warren's generosity during the campaign, his silver views, and his effective organization made him the overwhelming choice of the legislators outside Laramie County for the senator from Cheyenne. Thanks to Willis Van Devanter's manipulation of the APA, Warren had the Laramie county delegation in his pocket.[70]

For the second senator from Wyoming, there were three men in the field, but only one had a real chance. Clarence D. Clark far outdistanced two rivals, J. C. Davis and Jay L. Torrey. According to Warren's analysis, Clark would collect the great majority of votes from outside Cheyenne, and any attempt to impose the election of two senators from the capital would meet with determined opposition. There was, in short, no chance whatever that Carey would be elected.[71]

Warren's strategy was to win a firm backing for his candidacy from the Republican legislative caucus, and in the balloting for the second senator, throw his weight behind the strongest candidate from outside Cheyenne. This would force Carey to go against the sentiment for limiting Laramie County to one senator, and if Carey was not careful, elim-

69. Warren to Merris C. Barrow, Dec. 12, 1894, Warren Papers.

70. Warren to L. R. Davis, Nov. 12, 1894, Warren Papers; *Sun,* Nov. 13, 1894, contains a planted interview with Van Devanter in which he dismissed reports that Cheyenne sought both senators; *Carbon County Journal,* Nov. 17, 1894.

71. Warren to J. D. Woodruff, Dec. 13, 1894, Warren Papers; *Natrona Tribune,* Dec. 13, 1894.

inate him from all consideration. In November and December 1894, Warren combined an extensive correspondence with Republican county leaders and a newspaper campaign in behalf of his candidacy on the basis that he should be the one senator from Cheyenne.[72]

The *Sun* led the drive for Warren, and its editorials gradually shifted from a desire to see Warren as the Cheyenne senator to an all-out attack on Carey. Slack complained of Carey's reluctance to share offices with other Republicans and charged that "What we need is men fresh from the people, who are not under the control of those who have no appreciation nor sympathy with the struggles of the pioneer." Carey could only suffer in contrast to Warren, "a man among men; a man of unbounded resources; a man of original ideas, who has never worn borrowed plumes; a man who is not afraid to tell where he stands on important questions; a man who will not arrogate to himself the right to antogonize [sic] the wishes of his constituents; nor will he seek to appropriate to himself all the power, all the glory and all the credit that belong to the Republican party of Wyoming."[73]

Slack's fulsome regard for Warren stemmed in part from Carey's attempt to set up a rival newspaper in Cheyenne. After insisting that the Republican *Cheyenne Tribune* be discontinued in October, Carey contributed ten thousand dollars to revive the journal in his own interest in November. The *Tribune* immediately initiated a series of

72. Warren to J. F. Crawford, Nov. 25, 1894, to D. H. Craig, Nov. 25, 1894, to Van Devanter, Nov. 25, 1894, to J. B. Schoenfelt, Nov. 25, 1894, to Mondell, Nov. 29, 1894, to J. H. Hayford, Dec. 1, 1894, Warren Papers.

73. *Sun,* Dec. 11 and 14, 1894.

attacks on the *Sun*, Warren, and Van Devanter. The chairman brushed off Carey's insults, secure in the knowledge that Warren's election was assured.[74]

To counter Warren's support, Carey's forces began a campaign of bluff and newspaper buying. Rumors circulated that Carey had latent strength in every delegation, but Warren correctly dismissed them as without foundation. Carey's representatives managed to purchase a few papers which, on the whole, were sheets with little influence. The bluster of the Carey camp fooled some editors who reported that "the Carey and Warren dogs of war have been turned loose and are snapping at each other's heels," but Warren assured his friends that "Carey is not in the deal."[75]

Warren and Clark's selection became inevitable when J. C. Davis and J. L. Torrey withdrew from the race two days before the legislative caucus convened. At the meeting Warren was named by acclamation, while Clark easily defeated token opposition. "It looked to me," Warren reported, "and to others, as if every republican got off the train here at Cheyenne with the intention of declaring himself for Warren as soon as an opportunity presented itself." Carey's attempts "to break down the effects of the caucus" came to nothing, and two weeks later the legislature elected Warren and Clark to the Senate.[76]

74. Warren to J. D. Woodruff, Dec. 13, 1894, to J. H. Ryckman, Dec. 23, 1894, to M. C. Barrow, Dec. 29, 1894, Warren Papers; Van Devanter to B. F. Fowler, Dec. 8, 1894, to Ed Dickinson, Dec. 30, 1894, to J. M. Thurston, Dec. 30, 1894, Van Devanter Papers.

75. *Carbon County Journal*, Dec. 22, 1894; Warren to J. D. Woodruff, Dec. 13, 1894, to M. C. Barrow, Dec. 29, 1894, Warren Papers.

76. *Leader*, Jan. 8, 1895; *Sun*, Jan. 8, 1895; Warren to H. L. West, Jan. 18, 1895, to S. N. Wood, Jan. 21, 1895, to W. F. Wakeman, Jan.

The action of the legislature completed the rout of the Democratic Party and installed Warren, Clark, and Mondell as the custodians of Republican fortunes. With Clark's dominance in the west, Mondell's preeminence in the north, and Warren's supremacy in the east, Wyoming Republicans had seen the establishment of the pattern which was to govern their party until 1910. Only the seat on the national committee remained in Carey's possession, but with the coming of an election year, a change could be made at the national convention. Warren resolved to oust Carey and put Van Devanter in his place, thereby eliminating the last obstacle to an orderly flow of patronage in Wyoming.

Warren's triumph over Carey marked the transition in Wyoming politics from the heyday of the officeholder whose power rested on his own personal influence, his length of residence in the state, and his economic eminence to the era of the professional politician with a machine which dispensed patronage and cash at predictable intervals. Despite his years on the national committee, Carey never created a viable organization of loyal associates who could advance his career in Wyoming. This oversight hardly mattered before 1890 in the context of the personal nature of poiitics, but with Warren's elevation to the Senate, Carey faced a new kind of challenge. Where Carey openly disregarded the fortunes of his party when they conflicted with his own ambitions, Warren succeeded in giving the impression that he was placing party above self when, in fact, the precise opposite was true. To succeed in this masquerade, Warren needed order and stability in Wyoming politics, and after 1892 he set about attaining it.

28, 1895, to H. R. Mann, Jan. 30, 1895, to J. D. Gill, J⸏⸏ Warren Papers.

In a larger sense, then, Warren's election represents the passing of the era of undisciplined frontier politics in Wyoming that had persisted since the founding of the territory in 1868. After 1894 Wyoming politics lost the flamboyant character associated with the Johnson County War and the cattle business. Under Warren's benevolent eye, the politics of development acquired coherent focus, system, and efficiency.

CHAPTER NINE. SILVER AND POPULISM: THE ELECTION OF 1896

ARREN'S senatorial victory climaxed a hectic year of political activity, and since Congress would not meet until December 1895, the months following his election saw a marked decrease in overt partisanship. In contrast to its predecessor, the 1895 legislature adjourned with its members "pretty generally good natured and satisfied." They had reason to be content. Their labors had produced the first state action under the Carey Act, created the Wyoming State Historical Society, provided for statute revision, and reshaped the county system. "The Legislature," Warren remarked, "has done a very large amount of excellent work and very little bad work."[1]

The Senator himself did not wait for the convening of Congress to open his lobbying efforts for his state. In the course of the year he traveled to Washington three times to speed action on requests for land under the Carey Act. When Congress met, he asked for a set of committee assignments which would enable him to oversee the state's interests and was pleased with his chairmanship of the Committee on Arid Lands, as well as his seats on the Claims, Military Affairs, Public Buildings and Grounds, and Agriculture committees. From these strategic positions, he renewed his interrupted campaign for irrigation legislation by seeking appropriations for the single most expensive

1. Warren to Clarence D. Clark, Feb. 20, 1895, Warren Papers.

reclamation facility, the storage reservoir. Promotion of all his manifold legislation schemes, including appropriations for Fort D. A. Russell, subsidies for public buildings, and pension bills, caused Warren to note on February 10, 1896, "I have been beset on all sides with pressing duties which have nearly overwhelmed me with hard labor."[2]

Warren's predominant concern, however, remained his political goals for the presidential election year of 1896. Wyoming had to be carried for the Republican candidate to insure that Warren would continue to supervise the patronage. Before that, Wyoming Republicans must endorse the eventual nominee to prevent Carey from exploiting any discontent between the national and state parties. During a normal presidential year, such a task would have been comparatively simple, but 1896 was hardly typical.

After 1894 free silver sentiment continued to grow in Wyoming; if the Republican party made a pro-gold race, the Democrats would win easily, especially if a silver candidate headed their ticket. Yet Warren realized that there was no chance that the Republican national convention would support silver and very little hope that any but a "goldbug" nominee would be chosen. With all this in mind, Warren believed that there was

but one course to pursue and that is, send men to Sheridan [the location of the state convention] who believe that we should support both silver and tariff, expecting of course that all Republicans can agree upon tariff while there may be trouble about getting a na-

2. Warren to Elwood Mead, Aug. 9, 1895, to E. F. Best, Aug. 9, 1895, to Senator John Mitchell, Chairman of the Committee on Committees, Dec. 6, 1895, to Richard J. Hinton, Feb. 10, 1896 (the quotations are from this letter), Warren Papers.

tional agreement on silver, but get the most we can in a national way and each state keeping strong in the faith in its state work, calculating to cling to the ship until we get in port with silver, no matter what rough water we encounter in the mean time.[3]

At no point did Warren contemplate a bolt from the Republican party if the national convention nominated a gold candidate. Instead he wanted to keep the Wyoming party "regular" but friendly to silver. The problems involved in the adoption of this strategy contrasted sharply with the situation in other Republican parties in the West. In Colorado, for instance, Senator Edward O. Wolcott, trying to follow a similar course, faced the resolute opposition of the free silver wing of the party led by Senator Henry M. Teller. Wolcott found it impossible to hold his moderate position under the pressure of the Republican silverites, and the Colorado state convention ultimately gave implied permission to Teller and his delegation to bolt if the national candidate proved unsatisfactory. Other Republican organizations in the Rocky Mountain states were subjected to identical tactics by friends of the white metal.[4]

The main thrust against Warren's position in Wyoming did not come from the free silver wing but from Carey and his small coterie of gold men. Through his newspaper, the *Wyoming Tribune,* Carey kept up a barrage of attacks against silver and stressed his allegiance to the eastern posi-

3. Warren to J. F. Crawford, Feb. 12 and March 16, 1896 (the quotation is from this letter), to E. A. Slack, Mar. 5, 1896, Warren Papers; Van Devanter to Warren, Mar. 3, 1896, Van Devanter Papers.
4. Joel F. Vaile to Edward O. Wolcott, Mar. 6, 1896, Joel F. Vaile Papers, Denver Public Library; Elmer Ellis, *Henry Moore Teller: Defender of the West* (Caldwell, Idaho, 1941), pp. 252–53.

tion on the gold standard that he had adopted in 1893. Warren had little to fear from Carey on the state level; the danger of his editorials emerged in the context of national politics. If the convention did name a gold man, Carey would claim that this faction alone had represented the true faith in Wyoming, but if Warren capitulated to the *Tribune's* demands, he would provide Carey with new leverage within the party.[5]

Even if Warren had wanted to surrender to Carey, a possibility which was never considered, the action of the Democrats would have made it politically risky. After the disastrous campaign of 1894, ex-Governor Osborne rallied the party behind silver, distributing letters and pamphlets around the state; and in July 1895 he wrote William Jennings Bryan that "the Democracy of Wyoming are for Free Silver Coinage and can be trusted to advocate this as the ratio of '16 to 1' first last and all the time in our next Natl convention." By the spring of 1896, the Democrats were in the hands of the silver forces; any Republican faltering on the issue would be used as evidence of the G.O.P.'s lack of fidelity to bimetallism.[6]

Warren also wanted to remove Carey from his position as national committeeman. Backed by Mondell and Clark, who had no love for Carey, Warren wanted the state convention, which would choose delegates to the national convention, to endorse Van Devanter in place of Carey. "The Judge has been one of the hardest workers in our party and all things considered the most liberal contributor finan-

5. *Wyoming Tribune,* Mar. 17, 1896.

6. John E. Osborne to William Jennings Bryan, July 27 and Nov. 7, 1895, and Apr. 28, 1896, William Jennings Bryan Papers, Manuscripts Division, Library of Congress; A. L. New to Grover Cleveland, May 25, 1896, Cleveland Papers.

cially. We need a man who is both able and willing to go east, west, north or south, wherever necessary, paying his own expenses as he would have to do to be present at the meetings of the National Committee, etc., etc. and the Judge is exactly that kind of a man."[7]

Within this context, the candidacy of William McKinley suited the needs of Warren precisely. McKinley was known for his advocacy of the protective tariff and was moderate on the monetary issue. These qualities made him popular in southern Wyoming among the railroad workers, miners, and laborers, all sources of new Republican strength, while sheep growers praised him for his stand on a wool tariff. The union of protection and silver appealed to Wyoming Republicans, aware by 1896 that Wyoming had no silver mines of its own and conscious that the state was dependent to a significant degree on the fortunes of certain protected industries like coal, wool, and iron. The evidence suggests, moreover, that little of this sentiment was fostered by the Union Pacific or its agents. "The Union Pacific people are probably strongly for McKinley," Van Devanter wrote in April 1896, "but not a single one of them has asked or suggested that I should do anything in Wyoming for McKinley."[8]

By supporting McKinley, Warren's machine thus took the candidate with the proper ideological leanings and the greatest appeal to most segments of the party. In early

7. Warren to W. W. Gleason, Feb. 4, 1896, to E. P. Mather, Mar. 31, 1896, Warren Papers.

8. Van Devanter to Clarence D. Clark, Apr. 1, 1896, Van Devanter Papers; Herbert Croly, *Marcus Alonzo Hanna: His Life and Work* (Hamden, Connecticut, 1965), p. 194; H. Wayne Morgan, *William McKinley and His America* (Syracuse, 1963), pp. 183–208; Stanley L. Jones, *The Presidential Election of 1896* (Madison, 1964), pp. 128–38.

March Van Devanter reported that "McKinley sentiment is rapidly growing here and elsewhere in the State." McKinley's campaign against the eastern "bosses," Matthew Quay of Pennsylvania and Thomas C. Platt of New York, also placed him in at least implicit support of Warren's movement against Carey. These anti-McKinley leaders hoped to obtain a majority of the Republican national committee against the seating of McKinley delegates from contested states at the St. Louis convention. Warren's desire to replace Carey, an opponent of the Ohioan, with Van Devanter thus harmonized perfectly with the strategy of Mark Hanna and the McKinley camp. Warren's faction had an even larger claim on McKinley's backing; it represented the wishes of the bulk of Wyoming Republicans.[9]

The campaign to unseat Carey began in December 1895, and by March 1896 the effort had become linked to the McKinley canvass. Other candidates, especially William Boyd Allison of Iowa, had scattered pockets of supporters, but none even aproached the popularity of the McKinley candidacy. This feeling increased when Carey used his newspaper to publish pro-gold, anti-McKinley editorials in February and March.[10]

To maintain his control in Wyoming, Warren, through Van Devanter, opened a concerted political offensive to dominate the state convention in May. They had to see that each county convention in March and April endorsed Van Devanter as national committeeman, named delegates favorable to McKinley, and approved the preselected slate of delegates to the St. Louis convention in June. While working toward these goals, Van Devanter had to be alert for any

9. Van Devanter to Warren, Mar. 3, 1896, Van Devanter Papers.
10. Van Devanter to Warren, Mar. 3 and 22, 1896, Van Devanter Papers.

attempt by Carey to retain his seat on the national committee.

Characteristically, Carey's reaction was too little and too late. He allowed Van Devanter to operate almost unhindered until April. After consulting with Sheridan County Republicans, Van Devanter scheduled the state convention there to give northern party members a sense of belonging to the state party. He also initiated an extensive letter-writing campaign among prominent Republicans in each county to secure their support for his candidacy.[11]

While lining up the county conventions behind McKinley and his own candidacy, Van Devanter also had to choose the six delegates and six alternates who would represent Wyoming at St. Louis. Here the sectional divisions in state politics posed a problem. Every county wanted the prestige of having a delegate, and those that could not be satisfied must be pacified with a proper alternate. At the same time, those counties which had not had delegates in 1892 must be given first consideration. Finally, all five southern counties wanted to be represented, an arrangement which was out of the question.

Laramie County must have one, probably Van Devanter, if he won the endorsement of the county convention. Albany County was entitled to a delegate, and Warren decided that Otto Gramm would be better than M. C. Brown, a perennial maverick who this year favored Thomas B. Reed of Maine. Allocating these two places was relatively simple, as were the designations of the state's attorney general, B. F. Fowler, from Crook and J. C. Davis from Carbon County. In Natrona County, Van Devanter favored Bryant B.

11. Van Devanter to E. F. Cheyney, Mar. 4, 1896, Van Devanter Papers.

Brooks, who had taken defeat of his ambitions for Congress in 1894 with good grace.[12]

The demands of Senator Clark confused matters on the sixth delegate. He wanted a representative from Uinta County, his own district; but Uinta was the center of Wyoming's silver agitation, and Warren remained reluctant to give it a delegate and deprive more solidly Republican counties of recognition. The compromise solution was to make C. C. Hamlin, a close friend of Clark's and a leader from Sweetwater, the last member of the delegation. Clark continued to hope that Uinta might get a place, but in the face of Warren's determination he had to settle for the arrangement decided upon by the Cheyenne leaders.[13]

While the delegation was being assembled, the question arose of whether or not it should be instructed for McKinley. As it became evident that the Ohioan would almost certainly be nominated on the first ballot, the more volatile state Republicans urged that the Sheridan convention bind the delegates to support McKinley. Because it would curtail their freedom to maneuver, Warren and Van Devanter were originally hesitant; but events in March and April 1896 gradually convinced them that it would be best to instruct.[14]

12. Van Devanter to Bryant B. Brooks, Feb. 19, 1896, to Warren, Mar. 3, 1896, to Mondell, Mar. 20, 1896, to Otto Gramm, Mar. 21, 1896, to Clarence D. Clark, Apr. 1, 1896, Warren to Van Devanter, Apr. 23, 1896, Van Devanter Papers; Warren to Van Devanter, Apr. 1, 1896, Warren Papers.

13. Warren to Van Devanter, Apr. 23, 27, and 29, and May 2, 1896, Van Devanter to Warren, Apr. 27, 1896, to Mondell, Apr. 19, 1896, to Clark, Apr. 19, 1896, to C. C. Hamlin, Apr. 19, 1896, Van Devanter Papers.

14. Van Devanter to J. S. Clarkson, Mar. 4, 1896, to Warren, Mar. 22, 1896, to J. M. Thurston, Mar. 22, 1896, Van Devanter Papers.

WYOMING: A POLITICAL HISTORY

Senator Clark did not share this view. Because of his own preference for William B. Allison and his sensitivity to the silver sentiment in Uinta, Clark hoped that the state convention would keep away from an endorsement of McKinley. But in Van Devanter's opinion McKinley's popularity was so widespread that it would be simply an act of charity to give Allison any delegates. "Wyoming being unquestionably a McKinley state, it results that any Allison delegates elected from here are elected by sufferance merely, and if McKinley is to be nominated we ought not to permit any apathy here or inaction to place us in a position different from the actual sentiments of the republicans of the state."[15]

The most important factor in favor of an instructed delegation was Carey's opposition to it. When the anti-McKinley camp began making overtures to Carey to aid in procuring an unaffiliated slate of delegates, Warren and Van Devanter decided that there was no alternative to instructions. On March 27, 1896, Van Devanter was summoned to Denver by James S. Clarkson for a discussion of the presidential situation. Clarkson and a Pennsylvania state senator, W. H. Andrews, were traveling through the West in an attempt to win backing of the Republican national committeemen for the anti-McKinley disputed delegations at St. Louis. Clarkson also hoped to convince Republicans in the western states to send unpledged delegations to the convention. Endowed with ample funds from Thomas C. Platt, Matthew Quay, and Grenville M. Dodge, Clarkson had asked Carey to come to Denver for talks as well.[16]

15. Van Devanter to Warren, Mar. 22, 1896, Van Devanter Papers; Warren to Van Devanter, Apr. 18, 1896, Warren Papers.
16. Van Devanter to Warren, Mar. 28, 1896, Van Devanter Papers; Frank Trumbull to Grenville M. Dodge, Apr. 11, 1896, Box 26, Dodge Papers; Jones, *Presidential Election of 1896,* pp. 151–52.

This was Clarkson's crucial error. As soon as Van Devanter learned of Carey's presence, his slight interest in Clarkson's cause disappeared completely. He told Clarkson that Carey was the man to see about an anti-McKinley delegation. When Andrews promised financial support for an uninstructed slate, Van Devanter informed him that if the anti-McKinley elements continued their agitation in Wyoming, they would make it absolutely necessary to send a McKinley delegation. Despite his assurances to his associates of his success in the West, Clarkson's maneuvers had strengthened Van Devanter's resolve to see that Carey's views did not prevail and that the state convention endorsed McKinley delegates.[17]

When Warren learned of the Denver meeting, he seconded Van Devanter's action and gave his approval of a pledged delegation. To Governor Richards Warren outlined his willingness to have the convention commit the delegates, as long as the instructions did not eliminate any chance to capitalize on events as they developed at St. Louis:

> I see no reason why if the people of the state feel that way they should not express themselves accordingly, though it is not always best to have a delegation surrounded with iron clad instructions, but if in their opinion McKinley is the best man and they say so leaving the delegates to feel that their constituents have confidence in them and expect in case of accident or change that the delegates will avail themselves of any benefit that can enure to Wyoming through wise and skillful action on their part, then we are in the best possible fix, but of course things cannot be always manipulated to exactly the fine point desired.[18]

17. Van Devanter to Warren, Mar. 28, 1896, Van Devanter Papers.
18. Warren to W. A. Richards, Apr. 16, 1896, Warren Papers.

By April 1, 1896, Van Devanter had the situation under control. The county conventions would favor his designation, the projected slate of delegates had aroused no discernible discontent, and the possibility of an instructed delegation met opposition only from Carey. All this had been accomplished without alienating any Republicans whose support would be vital in the fall election, and Warren assured Mark Hanna on April 8 that "I am now of the opinion that when the time comes there will be a harmoneous [sic] solid vote from Wyoming."[19]

One obstacle did remain, however. If Carey entered the Laramie County primaries with a set of candidates for the county convention and won, it would make the Sheridan convention much more difficult to manage. A Carey triumph would also eliminate Van Devanter from consideration as a delegate and seriously weaken his chances to replace Carey. As a result, Warren urged Van Devanter to redouble his exertions in Cheyenne, even at the cost of wounding the feelings of some Laramie County Republicans who would not understand "the reason for contention and difference." Warren believed that

> While we must take note of this and guard against it, yet there must be no halt, no falling down, no rest, no let up in fact, until he is out of the saddle of Committeeship and until we have the state shaped right as to candidates throughout for the next election. I grant that we should do as much as possible of it by diplomacy and easy quiet ways without clubbing or spilling fore [sic] more than necessary. The result we must obtain and this granted let us arrive at it walking on velvet and with velvet touches as much of the ways

19. Warren to Marcus A. Hanna, Apr. 8, 1896, Warren Papers.

as possible and with velvet hand whenever and wherever possible.[20]

Aware of all this, Van Devanter started, in his usual thorough way, to line up all the political factions in Cheyenne behind his cause. His attempt to do this encountered no resistance because Carey, for reasons which are now unclear, had angered most of his former lieutenants in Cheyenne, and his effort to recapture their backing in the few days before the primaries failed dismally. Some of Carey's friends told him that he would surely lose, but in much the same way as he had acted in 1894, Carey went ahead blindly. Printed tickets with Carey delegates were distributed in the days before the election, which was set for the evening of April 16, 1896. In light of this belated activity from Carey, Warren reminded Governor Richards of the necessity for victory: "I hope everybody is on deck and at work and that you are all alert and watching every straw. I shall want to eat my shirt, boots and saddle even, if we shall fail there at Cheyenne."[21]

The night was cold, snowy, and slushy, but a large turnout buried Carey's hopes. In all three wards Carey got less than fifty votes, and Warren, learning of the defeat, was ecstatic: "Yours of the 17th inst just to hand this evening and I read with relish all the interesting (disgusting to Carey) details of your very marked and commendable victory at the Cheyenne primaries. I do not now recollect among our many fights and scrimages anything more decided or more neatly done than the killing, skinning and burying of 'his nibs.' "[22]

20. Warren to Van Devanter, Apr. 9, 1896, Warren Papers.
21. Van Devanter to Warren, Apr. 2, 1896, Van Devanter Papers; Warren to W. A. Richards, Apr. 12, 1896, Warren Papers.
22. Warren to Van Devanter, Apr. 20, 1896, Warren Papers; Warren to Van Devanter, Apr. 23, 1896, Van Devanter to Mondell, Apr. 17,

An indication of the shift in leadership was Van Devanter's reception of numerous apologies from Carey followers, who now pledged themselves to work for the interest of the triumphant faction. Warren was not surprised. "With things looking as they do now and with the walloping you are giving Carey all the rats and mice, yes, and monkeys, too, will leave the sinking ship." As for Carey, "now when we come to cut around him, leaving nothing of him from last Fall's election, and then not leave even a grease spot of him in this last fight you can rest assured he will not cause much trouble for some time to come in the way of opposing or being able to influence any formidable number of votes."[23]

With victory assured, Warren told Mark Hanna to "put Wyoming down for six votes on your private tab and kindly inform Maj. McKinley what he can depend upon, absolutely from Wyoming." All that remained to be done was to see that silver was provided for in the convention's platform. After some thought, Warren decided to combine an endorsement of the tariff with a reaffirmation of the Casper platform of 1894. Such a middle course would not satisfy either the rabid silver men from Uinta County or the gold standard supporters like Carey, "But since we had silver in the Casper platform, since we are surrounded by silver states, since Carey's Tribune has been pounding us claiming that we do not mean what we say, and the state platform is the one we stand upon in electing our member of Con-

1896, to Warren, Apr. 17, 1896, to J. M. Thurston, Apr. 19, 1896, Van Devanter Papers; *Cheyenne Sun-Leader,* Apr. 17, 1896. E. A. Slack had acquired the *Leader* early in 1895.

23. Warren to Van Devanter, Apr. 20, 1896, Warren Papers; Warren to Van Devanter, Apr. 23, 1896, Van Devanter Papers.

gress and legislature, it seems to me we have got to keep tolerably near the Casper declaration."[24]

When the Sheridan convention met on May 14, 1896, it brushed aside Carey's plea for an uninstructed delegation and gave unanimous approval to resolutions binding the delegates to McKinley and Van Devanter. On silver, the convention reiterated its "allegiance to the principles of bimetallism as enunciated in the Republican state platform adopted at Casper in 1894," and commended "the record of our senators and representatives in congress in maintaining these principles, and we instruct our delegates to the St. Louis convention to take like action when the financial plank of that convention is being made."[25]

For Warren's purposes, "the *outcome* at Sheridan was exactly right. The enthusiasm shown there for Judge Van Devanter found as ready and as hearty an echo in my breast as it could possibly have met in the bosom of Van himself." The silver plank was "just enough, not too little or too much," and the completed slate of delegates was satisfactory. Warren believed that all in all the result of the convention and the imminent nomination of McKinley offered the best hope for Republican success in Wyoming in November 1896.[26]

The pre-convention campaign for McKinley in Wyoming was decided on local issues. If the McKinley camp had backed Carey, it is possible that Warren and Van Devanter would have swung behind Allison. Happily, this choice

24. Warren to Hanna, Apr. 24, 1896, to Van Devanter, Apr. 29, 1896, Van Devanter Papers.

25. *Wyoming Tribune,* May 15 and 16, 1896; *Sun-Leader,* May 15 and 16, 1896.

26. Warren to R. H. Repath, May 25, 1896, Warren Papers; Warren to Van Devanter, May 20, 1896, Van Devanter Papers.

never presented itself. McKinley was by far the strongest candidate on the basis of his tariff and silver views, but his real appeal lay in his willingness to support the anti-Carey struggle. This allowed Warren to complete his take-over of the Republican party in Cheyenne and Laramie County which he had begun in 1893.

As the McKinley campaign in Wyoming indicates, Wyoming politics still turned on narrow issues of personality and individual success. With a small electorate, this would remain true for many years. Yet Warren and Van Devanter had demonstrated on the local level, as the Republicans were to show in 1896 in the nation, that organizational ability and thoroughness would replace and surpass mere personal appeals and individual campaigns in the future. The techniques that had brought Carey victory in the 1880s were inadequate to the political demands of the 1890s, and his failure to realize this accounts for his political eclipse.

In May 1896 the first half of the election struggle had ended in total victory for the Warren forces. A deceptive confidence pervaded the Republican ranks in Wyoming as they prepared for McKinley's selection at St. Louis. This euphoria was not to last. By mid-June a series of calamities had befallen Republican chances in Wyoming, and Warren had to fight a desperate battle alone to salvage the gains made in the spring of 1896. With Van Devanter sick and absent, Warren had to face the rejuvenated Democrats and Populists gathered under the banner of William Jennings Bryan.

Van Devanter had exhausted himself during the winter of 1896 with his political work, his law practice, family worries, and the burden of arguing the Race Horse Indian case for the state of Wyoming before the United States Supreme

244

Court. This rigorous schedule caught up with him in May, and he contracted typhoid fever. A month's illness brought Van Devanter near death, but the crisis passed in June; his physicians, however, advised a long period of recuperation. Consequently in early July Van Devanter departed for a tour of the Pacific Northwest which kept him out of Wyoming until the end of September. Events during Van Devanter's absence demonstrated how important his talents had been to Warren's success. With his reliable aide away, Warren found himself burdened with the innumerable details of organization that Van Devanter had handled so capably from 1890 to 1895.[27]

While the state chairman began his recovery, the results of the two national conventions transformed the Wyoming election of 1896 from a sure Republican triumph into a close and bitter contest. McKinley's nomination satisfied Warren, but the money plank in the platform put the Wyoming party in a difficult position. In July the selection of William Jennings Bryan by the Democrats compounded the problem, for now the Wyoming party could boast of a candidate wholeheartedly devoted to free silver. A wave of enthusiasm for Bryan swept the state in July and August as free silver Republicans went over to the Democrats.[28]

"Bryan Republicans were almost as numerous as spears of grass in a meadow after the Chicago meeting," Warren told eastern Republicans, "and Bryan buttons on Republican coat lapels are still distressingly frequent." When the federal

27. Gould, "Willis Van Devanter in Wyoming Politics, 1884–1897," pp. 222–28, 247–51.
28. The Republican monetary plank is available in H. Wayne Morgan, *William McKinley and His America* (Syracuse, 1963), p. 214.

judge who had supported the Union Pacific workers in 1894 in their fight against wage cuts endorsed the Democratic platform, there were further defections in southern Wyoming. At a Laramie ratification meeting, a speaker told an excited crowd, "We have found a young champion that will win more votes for our cause than Mark Hanna can buy for McKinley with all his millions, and it is evident that we have found him none too soon. (cheering). I am happy to say that our young hero is the Honorable William Jennings Bryan, (cheering,) of Nebraska, the 'boy orator of the Platte'. (Great applause)."[29]

Warren found the roots of this sudden frenzy for Bryan in the hard realities of geography:

> Our state is once and a half as large in area as all the New England states; we have many towns off the railway—in fact, have county seats 150 miles from the railway; our border line, nearly 1,500 miles, abuts up, every inch of the way, against bolting silver states or localities where Populists control. The western end of Nebraska has been represented in Congress a long time by Kem, a Populist; and South Dakota, Montana, Idaho, Utah and Colorado complete the circle. Denver newspapers are in Cheyenne and adjoining towns in the southern portion of the state before breakfast on the day of their issue; Salt Lake papers are over the western portion of the state before dinner; Montana papers are in from the north earlier than any other, and with the exception of a few localities reached by Omaha papers, all parts of the state are covered by either Populists,

29. Warren to Moses P. Handy, July 29, 1896, Van Devanter to Joseph P. Smith, Oct. 17, 1896, Warren Papers; Laramie *Daily Boomerang,* July 13, 1896.

silver Democrats, or seceding Republican newspapers.[30]

Warren conceded that if the election had been held the
week after Bryan's nomination Wyoming would have gone
for the Democratic candidate by three thousand votes, but
he believed that the Republicans could make up the lost
ground by November. To stem the silver tide, Warren im-
plored Mark Hanna to send money and campaign literature.
He wanted newspapers, speakers, and pamphlets, but most
of all Warren pleaded for cash. "With only two state candidates to assess, no wealthy candidates, no large corpora-
tions, and our people mostly poor, we cannot raise sufficient
cash for necessary election expenses."[31]

The exact amount that Warren received from eastern
sources cannot be determined. He asked Henry Clay Payne
for ten thousand dollars on September 12, and his papers
disclose a check from Senator Redfield Proctor for five
thousand dollars which came in early October. The president of the Chicago and Northwestern Railway Company
added another thousand dollars, and a Boston source contributed an additional three hundred, for a total of sixty-
three hundred dollars. As the campaign drew to a close,
Warren asked McKinley headquarters for five thousand
dollars more, promising to repay the full amount if Wyoming did not go for McKinley.[32]

---

30. Warren to Hanna, July 13, 1896, Warren Papers.

31. Warren to Hanna, July 13, 1896, to Moses P. Handy, July 29,
1896, Warren Papers.

32. Warren to S. H. H. Clark, Sept. 7, 1896, to Clarence D. Clark,
Oct. 9, 1896, to Henry Clay Payne, Oct. 16, 1896, to Marvin Hewitt,
Oct. 20, 1896, to E. F. Atkins, Oct. 20, 1896, Van Devanter to Joseph P.
Smith, Oct. 17, 1896, Warren to George B. Cortelyou, Oct. 6, 1904,

Available records suggest, however, that the Republicans had ample funds with which to wage the campaign. In the four counties for which even partial indications remain, Sheridan, Sweetwater, Carbon, and Uinta, Warren sent out a total of ten thousand dollars. It seems plausible to assume that the Wyoming Republican Party had over twenty thousand and perhaps as much as thirty thousand dollars in its coffers. The Democrats, on the other hand, could not match that amount. In one letter Van Devanter told the national committee that Democratic resources exceeded sixteen thousand dollars, but Warren informed an aide that the enemy did not have more than two thousand dollars in its war chest. While again no firm conclusion is possible, eight to ten thousand dollars seems like the outside limit of the Democrats' expenditures.[33]

Warren would have preferred, like McKinley, to play down the money question and concentrate on the tariff, but he had to recognize the widespread silver sentiment when the Republican state convention met to pick candidates for state offices in August. Some "goldbugs" like Carey wished to stand pat on the St. Louis platform, but Warren decided that the convention must indicate a "friendliness" for silver beyond that granted by the national convention. Warren realized that despite the threats of Carey and his friends, the gold men had no place to go, while Republican adherence to the exact wording of the St. Louis

---

Warren Papers. Warren told Cortelyou that the railroads had contributed three thousand dollars to the Republicans in 1896.

33. Warren to John W. Hay, Oct. 17, 1896, Van Devanter to Joseph P. Smith, Oct. 17, 1896, Warren to C. W. Garbutt, Oct. 24, 1896, to J. C. Davis, Oct. 28, 1896, to Clarence D. Clark, Oct. 29, 1896, to John W. Hay, Oct. 29 and 31, 1896, Warren Papers.

platform would drive all wavering Republicans into the Bryan camp.[34]

In the weeks preceding the convention, Warren solicited drafts from leading Republicans of money planks which would satisfy all factions. At first Warren intended to have the platform assert the party's fidelity to the St. Louis declaration with the exception of the silver question and to express Wyoming's belief in woman suffrage. Warren had slight interest, if any, in women voting, but this would offset Democratic claims that the state Republican party had differed with the national platform only on the monetary issue.[35]

Further consideration led Warren to drop any declaration of discontent with the St. Louis platform. Instead, the Republicans in their convention of August 13, 1896, favored "the free coinage of gold and silver into standard money as expressed in our former platforms under such legislation as will guarantee that all our money shall remain on an equality." As Warren noted, "while this platform means everything for the silver men as it reads—makes our record consistent—we have *never* said anything against free silver —does not surrender to the Carey faction nor endorse him nor his view, and there is nothing in it that can be offensive to reasonable eastern (?) Republicans or other friends elsewhere."[36]

While the Democratic papers castigated the Republican evasion, the platform had furthered Warren's central aim.

34. Warren to Merris C. Barrow, July 26, 1896, Warren Papers.

35. Warren to C. H. Parmelee, July 14, 1896, to Benjamin Howell, July 19, 1896, to J. C. Davis, July 31, 1896, Warren Papers.

36. *Sun-Leader,* Aug. 13, 1896; Warren to Clarence D. Clark, Aug. 3, 1896, to Mondell, Aug. 7, 1896, to C. C. Hamlin, Aug. 19, 1896, Warren Papers.

The party, except for a few dissidents, was united behind McKinley. With Frank Mondell's candidacy for relection, Warren hoped to carry on a vigorous campaign of education to woo back the bolting Republicans and to show the weaknesses of the opposition. "We want to push home the fact that while they may be right on one plank—silver—yet all of their other planks are wrong and that Pefferism, Altgeltism [sic], Tillmanism, Populistism, Anarchy and general cussedness is all hung on to, and done up with, their free silver protestations."[37]

The Democrats held their state convention at Rock Springs while the Republicans met in Cheyenne. After endorsing Bryan and his running mate, Arthur Sewall, the delegates chose John E. Osborne to run against Mondell for Congress and named three candidates for presidential electors, John A. Martin, George H. Cross, and P. J. Quealy. With enthusiasm for Bryan still rampant, the party expected no trouble in carrying the state for the Democratic nominees.[38]

The Democrats reckoned without the Wyoming Populist party. At their state conclave in July they endorsed Bryan but also nominated a set of their own electors, F. M. Matthews, Daniel L. Van Meter, and C. H. Randall, as well as a candidate for Congress, William Brown. The seventeen delegates from five counties who made up the assembled host of Wyoming Populism were divided nine to eight against fusion with the Democrats, and this small majority of a tiny convention meant that if the Populist national convention chose a Populist running mate for Bryan, there would be two sets of Bryan electors on the Wyoming ballot.

37. Warren to Benjamin Howell, July 19, 1896, Warren Papers.
38. Laramie *Daily Boomerang*, Aug. 14, 1896.

The nomination of Tom Watson at St. Louis thus posed the real threat of splitting the Wyoming silver vote and giving the state to McKinley.[39]

By 1896 nuisance value was all that remained of Wyoming Populism. It never exceeded the power which it wielded in the 1892 campaign, and the gradual swing of Wyoming Democrats to silver had deprived the Populists of their one concrete appeal to the voters. The rest of their program remained irrelevant to the economic life of Wyoming; their calls for public ownership of the railroads, repeal of the stock association laws, and attacks against ceding arid lands to the states bear out the conclusion of the party's historian that "Populism in Wyoming was essentially a skin graft that would not take because it was unsuited to the body economic of the state."[40]

If the Populists had no hope of winning in 1896, their separate ticket might still lose the state for the Democrats. The thousand or so votes which the party might get for the Bryan-Watson electors would probably allow the Republicans to sneak through to victory. The Democrats, however, sought fusion on their own terms; when the Populists suggested to the Democratic state convention that they would agree to an electoral ticket fusion if Osborne withdrew in favor of Brown, the Democrats refused. The only concession that the Democrats would make was to give the Populists nominations for some county offices if the Populist electors were removed. Most Populists, more interested in Bryan's success than the preservation of their party, found this ac-

39. *Wyoming Tribune*, July 18, 1896.

40. Kreuger, "Populism in Wyoming," pp. ii, 78–79. As Mr. Kreuger has shown, the loss of Populist newspapers and manuscripts makes it difficult to penetrate the inner workings of the party in 1896.

ceptable; but the tiny clique of middle-of-the-roaders wanted, for selfish reasons, to make their campaign.[41]

Warren saw that the Republicans had everything to gain from a Populist party in the field, and with the aid of the national committee he set about giving the die-hard Populists some inducement to continue. The first necessity was to ensure that the chairman of the Populist state convention, D. W. Elliott, would file the party's nominations, as made at the gathering, on September 4, the earliest date on which the papers could be submitted to the secretary of state. In late August, while Warren sought funds in Chicago, Attorney General B. F. Fowler tried to convince the chairman to send in the certificates.[42]

The Democrats met Republican offers to Elliott with promises that he would receive the fusion nomination for Laramie County attorney. This prospect convinced him not to file the certificates, and September 4 passed with no Populist ticket registered with the secretary of state. In the next several weeks, however, the Republicans dangled more money in front of Elliott while the small group of anti-fusion Populists pressed him to give them a chance to make the race. On September 18, 1896, the Populist electors and William Brown were placed on the ballot to the cheers of the Republicans.[43]

Even before Elliott gave in, the Republicans had taken steps to make sure that there was a Populist campaign. They contacted state campaign chairman, John W. Paterson, who

41. *Sheridan Enterprise,* Aug. 22, 1896, clipping in Warren Scrapbooks, Warren Papers; Kreuger, "Populism in Wyoming," pp. 57–58.

42. Benjamin F. Fowler to Warren, Aug. 23, 26, and 28, 1896, Warren Papers.

43. *Sun-Leader,* Sept. 19, 1896; *Sheridan Enterprise,* Aug. 29, 1896, clipping in Warren Scrapbooks, Warren Papers.

had been selected by the convention because he was not there to decline the honor, and through a Republican relative they arranged to "take care of him." To ensure that Paterson would make a strong canvass, the Republicans gave him a promise of a post-election job, a small supply of operating funds, and railroad passes. By September Warren reported to national headquarters that the "Chairman of the Populist Committee is out over the state with plenty of railway transportation to cover the necessary travel and cash for expenses to keep his party 'in the middle of the road' and away from fusion with the Democrats, but with friendly feelings toward Republicans."[44]

The Republicans also wanted to persuade William Brown, the Populist congressional candidate, to take the campaign trail and draw off votes from Osborne's total. Brown, whose ego was greater than his common sense, let himself be convinced by railroad passes, faked letters of support, and outright donations from Republican sources. Fowler told a Fremont County leader that "Mr. Wm. Brown is at Big Horn and undoubtedly enthusiastic Populists in Fremont county would write similar letters to him encouraging him to remain in the field and to not allow Osborne to side track him, if you would quietly without creating suspicion give the matter some personal attention. I think that you understand the full weight of my suggestions."[45]

Republican sponsorship of Brown's campaign in September intensified the Democratic desire to formalize a fusion agreement on the electoral ticket. Early in October,

44. Fowler to Mondell, Aug. 31, 1896, Warren to Henry Clay Payne, Sept. 12, 1896, Warren Papers.

45. Fowler to C. G. Coutant, Aug. 30, 1896, to John W. Hay, Sept. 5. 1896, Warren Papers; *Sun-Leader*, Sept. 19, 1896.

acting in accordance with the instruction of the Populist national committee, Chairman Elliott obtained declinations from two of the Populist electors, F. M. Matthews and C. H. Randall, while one Democratic elector, George H. Cross, resigned. A combined ticket of Bryan-Sewall electors was formed of two Democrats, John A. Martin and P. J. Quealy, and one Populist, Daniel L. Van Meter. The Republicans responded by circulating petitions among Populists which, when filed by campaign chairman Paterson, put two new Populist electors, Patrick J. M. Jordan and William Simms, back on the ballot. The third Populist elector, Van Meter, was approached about declining the Democratic endorsement, but he turned on the Republicans and revealed their attempt to bribe him. As a result the Wyoming ballot contained at this point two Democratic electors pledged to Bryan and Sewall, Van Meter endorsed by the Democrats and Populists but committed to Bryan and Sewall, and two Populist electors for Bryan and Watson.[46]

Though frustrated in their attempt to have a full slate of Populist electors, the Republicans used their control of the state government to get the most from the existing situation. The secretary of state "had the electoral ticket arranged so that the three Republican electors appeared first, followed by Paterson's three electors [Jordan, Simms, and Van Meter], who in turn were followed by three electors of the Prohibition Party, who in turn were followed by the two Democratic electors [Martin and Quealy]." In this way, the fusion voter would have to mark his ballot with extreme care to avoid wasting his vote, and even under the worst

46. *Sun-Leader,* Oct. 5 and 10, 1896; Warren to Joseph Lytle, Oct. 11, 1896, Warren Papers. Fusion in Wyoming is only briefly noted in Robert F. Durden, *The Climax of Populism: The Election of 1896* (Lexington, Kentucky, 1965), p. 76.

circumstances the Republicans stood a good chance of getting two out of the three electoral votes at stake.[47]

The Democrats retaliated by initiating mandamus proceedings to have the secretary either rearrange the ballot or remove the Populist electors entirely. As Willis Van Devanter, now returned from his recuperative trip, informed the national committee, "the opposition are very disturbed." He promised to "give this litigation my personal attention and will endeavor if possible to keep the disturbing factor still in the ring."[48]

Before the Wyoming Supreme Court, Van Devanter argued that the nominations to fill vacancies could be filed up to the day before election and that the petition met the requirements of Wyoming law. He also upheld the secretary of state's authority to place Van Meter with the electors of the party that had first nominated him. The supreme court agreed. As a result, the Populists would have an electoral ticket on the ballot, but Democratic newspapers cautioned their readers to vote with care so that their ballots would not be squandered. Republican leaders, for their part, notified the county clerks to make sure that the official tickets followed the supreme court's ruling.[49]

Other Republican vote-gathering schemes were even less ethical than the Populist subsidy. As they had in 1894, Republican workers used cash among the foreign miners at the Union Pacific coal camp in Sweetwater County to procure votes. With alien workers, the Republicans paid for natural-

47. Kreuger, "Populism in Wyoming," p. 60.
48. Van Devanter to Joseph P. Smith, Oct. 17, 1896, Warren Papers.
49. *State ex rel. Blydenburg v. Burdick, Secretary of State,* 6 *Wyoming Reports,* 448; Van Devanter to J. W. Hay, Oct. 26, 1896, Warren Papers.

ization proceedings and beat down Democratic attempts to challenge these new citizens. Fowler, in his capacity as attorney general, concluded that the literacy provisions in the state constitution did not specify a knowledge of English, and with the help of Finnish versions of the document, the miners were registered.[50]

The Republicans had no monopoly on these tactics. Warren repeatedly warned his workers not to let the Democrats make sufficient purchases of votes in the hours before elec-. tion to undo all the patient corruption of the Republicans. Acting on the principle that "a dollar the last night is worth several spent earlier in the campaign," Warren cautioned his operatives in Sweetwater to remain alert, even as he sent them a five hundred dollar check. "I am tired of Rock Springs getting lots of money early in the campaign, as in some former years, and then permitting democrats to come in at the last day and catching all of our voters whom we naturalized and guzzled, etc., throughout the entire campaign."[51]

Other railroad workers, captivated by free silver and still upset by memories of the Pullman strike, provided a constant source of worry to the Republicans. Through the general manager, Ed Dickinson, Warren tried to get the Union Pacific to put pressure on the waverers. Whatever their sympathies with McKinley, the quasi-public position of the railroad made it difficult for the management to act overtly, but they did what they could to help the cause. Nevertheless

50. Warren to Van Devanter, Oct. 9, 1896, to John W. Hay, Oct. 10, 1896, to Merris C. Barrow, Oct. 10, 1896, Warren Papers; *Wyoming Tribune,* Oct. 2, 1896. The Wyoming Supreme Court repudiated Fowler's interpretation in *Rasmussen v. Baker,* 7 *Wyoming Reports,* 117.

51. Warren to John W. Hay, Oct. 30, 1896, Warren Papers.

Warren, for all his coercion of railroad men, wrote in October

> It is just H – – l among the railroad employes and I haven't half, nor a quarter, detailed to you the intensity of the difficulty. As I remarked when leaving you at your car in Cheyenne the other day, I am going to do everything I can to carry the State for McKinley and I trust you people will continue to do the same, and *increase and enforce the pressure.* If whipped I shall know that we feel no worse about it here, than you and your associates of the U.P. will feel. I wish I was for the time being an employe of your corporation and in authority, and I would pound some of those fellows on the back, until I either had their votes or their scalps.[52]

The lavish use of money, the subsidization of the Populists, and the equally subtle devices so characteristic of Francis E. Warren seemed to turn the tide in favor of the Republicans by the last weeks of October. While McKinley's victory was not yet certain, Warren felt confident that Mondell would defeat Osborne handily. In the course of asking McKinley headquarters for another five thousand dollars, Van Devanter assured a McKinley aide that while Bryan would surely have carried the state in July, "The improve-

52. Warren to Clarence D. Clark, Aug. 3, 1896, to Ed Dickinson, Oct. 18, 1896, Warren Papers. The evidence seems to show that the Union Pacific reacted very cautiously to Warren's pleas. The granting of free passes to Populists was standard practice. Every legitimate political party received them. As for the coercion of the employees, see the revealing letter of Warren to Van Devanter, Feb. 5, 1897, Warren Papers, which hints that months after the election, the Republicans were still having trouble in convincing the railroad to fire Populists.

ment and tendency toward McKinley since then has been such that if the election were had to-day the result would probably be in doubt, but with changes between now and election like those which have been occuring, we will certainly carry the State."[53]

In the days before the election, Warren authorized some carefully placed bets on McKinley's victory, but he advised caution because the situation was still so confused. Success depended, the Senator believed, on holding the predicted Democratic majority in Uinta County below five hundred votes and swelling the Republican margin in Laramie County above three hundred ballots. "The averaging up of the others," Warren claimed, "will give us some kind of plurality." Election day confirmed the wisdom of hedged forecasts. The two parties exchanged the lead several times in the early returns, and Warren acknowledged that "what little is left of me is now anxiously waiting for returns from the remote precincts."[54]

When all the votes had been received, Bryan electors had carried the state by the narrow margin of three hundred votes on the strength of the fifteen hundred votes that fusion had supplied from the Populists. Osborne defeated Mondell by an even smaller plurality, and the middle-of-the-road Populists managed to gather less than five hundred votes for their presidential electors. Uinta County had delivered landslide majorities of seven hundred to eight hundred votes for Osborne and the Democratic electors. In Laramie County, meanwhile, the Republicans ran only one hundred and ninety votes ahead of their opponents. This, combined

53. Van Devanter to Joseph P. Smith, Oct. 17, 1896, Warren Papers.
54. Warren to S. D. Kilpatrick, Oct. 26, 1896, to H. L. West, Nov. 5, 1896, Warren Papers.

with defeats in Sheridan and Sweetwater, cost the Republicans the election.[55]

The Democrats naturally saw Bryan's victory in the state as a portent of future success. In the face of Warren's schemes and intrigues, they had won a significant triumph:

> The returns prove to the people of the other states that the voters of Wyoming, although apparently dominated by great corporations, cannot be coerced by threats of closing manufactories [sic], checking work in coal mines, or fear of loss of positions, nor can the majority be corrupted by money. This result will put the people of Wyoming in a truer light in the estimation of men of all parties in the older states who have heretofore looked upon the mountain states with small populations, as being pocket boroughs, where the will of corporations is law.[56]

The close defeat gave ample opportunity for Republican attempts to explain away the result. Van Devanter pointed to a county seat fight in the new county of Big Horn which had hurt the Republican majority there; Warren stressed the proximity of Bryan states and blamed Democratic help from Colorado, especially the ubiquitous A. L. New, who had delivered several campaign speeches across the state. The most appealing rationale for Bryan's victory involved Warren's favorite enemy, Judge Carey. In a series of letters, Warren told eastern Republicans that Carey had sabotaged the Republican ticket at his agricultural colony of Wheatland by urging his settlers to vote Democratic. Warren contended that as a result of this subversion, a large Republican

55. Erwin, *Wyoming Historical Blue Book*, pp. 1188–89.
56. Laramie *Daily Boomerang*, Nov. 19, 1896.

triumph had been converted into a Bryan success and had held down the victory margin for the G.O.P. in Laramie County.[57]

All these explanations missed the real reasons for Bryan's achievement. The Democratic nominee's free silver stand had awakened the enthusiasm of Wyoming voters in the summer, and their excitement, particularly in Uinta County, had lasted, though in ever-diminishing amounts, through the election day. It had asserted a more powerful force than all of Warren's attempts to manipulate the election process by bribery and corruption. The key to the personal nature of the 1896 campaign in Wyoming was the failure of the Democrats to extend Bryan's popularity to the legislative and county tickets. There, despite some Democratic gains, Republican dominance persisted. In view of the closeness of the vote and the ephemeral character of the Democratic victory, the election of 1896 must be regarded as an aberrant factor in the political history of Wyoming.

Two years later, aided by the Spanish-American War and the absence of a national race, the Warren organization reasserted its supremacy and overwhelmed the Democrats in the state and legislative contests. The Democrats, preoccupied with silver in 1896, had not exploited the opportunity to build for the future and had tied their fortunes to carrying the state for Bryan. When the frenzy for the white metal passed, they were left with their usual problems—weak leadership, an unappealing program, and a legacy of defeat. For them the election of 1896 was not a prelude to success, but only a temporary reprieve from disaster.

57. Warren to Edward O. Wolcott, Nov. 7, 1896, to William McKinley, Nov. 11, 1896, to W. F. Wakeman, Nov. 15, 1896, Warren Papers; Van Devanter to Mondell, Dec. 16, 1896, Van Devanter Papers.

Warren and his party, on the other hand, displayed a staggering array of effective political tactics in 1896 which, taken together, narrowly failed to wrest victory from the enemy. More important, the machine erected from 1890 to 1894 proved that it could survive an election where the opposition received the greater share of good fortune and even possessed the more appealing candidate. For the next decade and a half, Warren's organization would be threatened only by discord within the Republican party; until the accession of Woodrow Wilson to the presidency and the emergence of John B. Kendrick as a state politician of influence, the Wyoming Democratic Party offered little effective challenge to Republican leadership.

CHAPTER TEN. CONCLUSION

HE winter of 1896–97 was a fretful time for Francis E. Warren. An emergency appendectomy in December confined him to a hospital bed in Chicago where he could do little but worry over the results of Wyoming's failure to support McKinley. He envisioned difficulties over patronage and searched for arguments that might convince the President-elect that a narrow defeat should be waved away. As he wrote Van Devanter before illness overtook him,

> Of course you remember the excuse made by the lady who was guilty of enjoying the pleasures of sexual contact out of wedlock and who unfortunately conceived and bore fruit. She said that as the baby weighed but a little over two pounds she thought it was too small an affair to make any fuss over or to hold her responsible for, and I suppose this is about all the argument I will have in approaching the powers that be in explanation of Wyoming's difficulty. However, I will undertake to make up in earnestness and pathos for the lack of a firmer and more legitimate basis.[1]

Approach of the 1897 legislature also brought political problems for Warren. Sentiment lingered for a resolution on behalf of free silver, while various legislators had pet schemes for local appropriations. The state of Wyoming, however, its finances ravaged by the Panic of 1893, could not stand such expenditures, and the desire for local subsidy had to be curbed. Under the efficient supervision of Willis Van Devanter, the lawmakers proved surprisingly

1. Warren to Van Devanter, Dec. 6, 1896, Van Devanter Papers.

docile. A monetary resolution emerged in an innocuous form, the appropriations were held down, and an investigation of a corrupt Democratic judge embarrassed the opposition.[2]

On the patronage front, President McKinley was willing to forgive Wyoming's apostasy. Warren's appointments were approved, and in the case of Van Devanter, the Senator effected a major coup. His lieutenant wanted to be named solicitor general, but this place had been reserved for an Ohio friend of McKinley. Several months of negotiation and maneuvers, keyed to the formation of the president's cabinet, finally won for Van Devanter a position as the assistant attorney general assigned to the Department of the Interior. The acquisition of this place, a reward for Van Devanter's faithful service and marked ability, demonstrated that Warren had little to fear from the McKinley administration in the distribution of the spoils.[3]

Though held back to a degree by his winter illness, Warren resumed his round of promotional activities in the spring of 1897 with customary verve. Irrigation agitation, appropriations for Wyoming forts, public buildings for the state's towns, and offices for his friends—with a Republican administration in power and with Warren's increasing influence in the Senate, these goals for Wyoming could now be pursued with vigor and effectiveness. For thirty-three years, until Warren's death in November 1929, Wyoming politics would operate within this framework of federal subsidy; and Warren would stamp his personality so firmly on the state's economic and political life that even today his career and achievements are the model for aspiring public servants in the Equality State.

2. Gould, "Willis Van Devanter in Wyoming Politics," pp. 268–79.
3. Ibid., 279–93.

Warren's major successes as a pork barrel artist occurred after 1897, but the history of Wyoming politics from the creation of the territory through the election of 1896 underlined the relevance and need for the kind of system and organization which Warren brought to the politics of development. He understood, well before his colleagues, that Wyoming's demands for a continuous stream of federal money could only be met by the construction of a machine geared to the efficient handling of the appropriation process until self-sufficiency was attained.

In the absence of abundance, then, order and system became the sine qua non of Warren's approach to politics. He rejected the kind of fratricidal skirmishing which had held back the territory in the Campbell years; he distrusted the narrow focus of the Wyoming Stock Growers Association; and he could not understand either the suicidal tendencies of the Wyoming Democratic Party or the individualistic methods of Joseph M. Carey. Possessed of an unerring sense for the location of power, equipped with the talent to use it, and moved by an ability to benefit self and state, Warren looked upon politics as a business and not a diversion to be intermittently practiced. Only thus, Warren reasoned, could Wyoming obtain the substitutes for the economic resources which nature had denied it.

It should now be obvious that the crucial position of a partisan politician like Warren in Wyoming life does not accord with explanations which have placed the WSGA and the Union Pacific at the center of the state's history in these early years. There can be no doubt that these organizations wielded tremendous influence and could usually frustrate attempts to whittle down their power. But the truth is that politics in Wyoming was not framed in these

264

terms; the concern of most people was not with the excessive power of the cattlemen or the railroad, but with their failure to provide, in and of themselves, an economic reward commensurate with the expectations of those who had settled in the West. Existence of the UP and the WSGA was accepted as a given factor, and politics turned on considerations of which faction or party could supply the additional appropriations or facilities needed to spur the state's growth. Promotion, not protest, was the motive that normally animated the electorate.

The Republican Party had most to gain from the presence of this attitude among Wyoming residents. Its doctrines and heritage predisposed its adherents to look favorably on Wyoming's demands for government aid. The notion of positive promotion of economic enterprise evoked a sympathetic response from a party which from 1865 to 1900 supported federal aid to education, irrigation legislation, a protective tariff, and speedy distribution of the public lands. Wyoming's experience bears out the recent contention of historians that the Republicans owed their rise to dominance in the 1890s as much to the nature of their program as to the tactics of their leaders.

Wyoming Democrats, on the other hand, struggled to transform the tenets of their eastern leaders into a form more suited to the requirements of the West. Unhappily, the rise to power of Grover Cleveland and the group he led after 1884 made it very difficult for the local representatives of the Democratic Party to harmonize their strategy and platforms with those of the national party. Faced with the unenviable task of translating a negative program of limited government action into terms that would appeal to the voters, the Democratic Party in Wyoming wasted its energies in factional disputes and patronage battles. In the process it forfeited the initiative to its opponent, and like Republican parties in the South, deteriorated into a shadow structure of state and county committees which existed largely for the rewards that might come if the national party recaptured the presidency.

Historians have puzzled over the failure of western Populism in the Rocky Mountain states, but the rudimentary quality of the Wyoming economy, with its reliance on two basic private industries, goes far toward explaining why the state was so little affected by the social unrest of the 1880s and 1890s. Issues which, as Robert Wiebe has shown,[4] were produced by the shift from a nation composed of "island communities" to an urbanized, industrialized society had slight impact on a state still laboring to emerge into the community-oriented order which had characterized America in the 1870s. Thus questions like labor agitation, Populism, trusts, immigration restriction, or currency reform impinged on Wyoming tangentially and briefly, deflecting but not displacing the continued quest for the bonanza.

Consequently, an examination of Wyoming politics cannot escape an anachronistic aura. The territory and state lingered in a simpler America that had disappeared for the rest of the country, but because of Wyoming's economic situation, its precepts of public policy continued to have relevance for men like Warren. The aridity, distance, and barrenness of Wyoming compromised the usual frontier virtues of individualism and self-reliance, and men looked to Washington for support. Yet with no sense of inconsistency they maintained their allegiance to the frontier spirit even as, under Warren's guidance, they set about fram-

4. Robert H. Wiebe, *The Search for Order, 1877–1920* (New York, 1967), pp. 11–75.

ing institutional arrangements for the smoother flow of federal largesse. This behavior did not appear paradoxical to Wyoming residents. They had had the courage and the desire to succeed in the inhospitable terrain of their state, and they asked only for their fair share of subsidies until they could stand alone.

By 1896 geography and history had made Wyoming a state of contrasts. Fiercely independent and proud, its people were tied, as the inhabitants of few other states were, to the apron strings of Washington. Its political genius, Francis E. Warren, had used his native talents to construct a machine unmatched in the West for effectiveness; yet this organization, the product of innovative skill, kept Wyoming bound to policies which the rest of America had discarded decades before. Deprived of the sustained economic boom which had given the other western states their characteristic tone and unique influence on the nation, Wyoming, through the cattle industry and its cultural byproducts, became by the end of the nineteenth century a symbol of all that the West had meant to America.

In a figure like Warren the tension between these contradictory forces proved to be the impetus for success and achievement. The very nature of Warren's subsequent career, however, demonstrated the diminishing importance of the Wyoming political experience for the nation at large. Despite his crucial positions on the Appropriations and Military Affairs committees of the Senate, the fruit of his massive seniority, Warren contented himself with such feats as raising the number of soldiers stationed in Wyoming from 456 in 1900 to 3,625 in 1910, a total larger than the number of servicemen in all the other Rocky Mountain states combined. Similarly, he gathered more than one million dollars for public buildings within Wyoming between 1902 and

1912.[5] Trapped in this never-ending round of patronage disposal, appropriation decisions, and lobbying sessions, Warren, in his long tenure, left scant positive imprint on American life. He rarely looked up from his pursuit of influence for himself and riches for his state to consider the pressing questions of his time.

This attitude reflected Warren's accurate appraisal of the mood of his constituents, who preferred the concrete rewards of federal projects to the ephemeral satisfaction of having a representative in Washington with direct influence on national politics. An occasional exception like Senator Joseph C. O'Mahoney skillfully managed, for a time, to combine the acquisition of subsidies with an interest in national issues, but even he was temporarily retired because of inattention to local matters. The majority of other Wyoming politicians have been content to imitate the strategy of Warren's career. As a result, the state has not produced figures on the order of Pat McCarran of Nevada or William E. Borah of Idaho. Instead, men in Wyoming public life have paid homage to the precepts of the politics of development and endeavored to emulate the success of such predecessors as Warren. The fidelity to the past of Wyoming politicians consequently gives the formative years of the state's history a relevance which is absent in other western states whose politics have escaped the constricting framework imposed by underdevelopment.

In a larger sense, the history of Wyoming politics between 1868 and 1896 supports those scholars who have argued that the development of the West can best be understood within the context of national patterns rather than by an applica-

5. Arrington, *Changing Economic Structure,* pp. 33–34; Larson, *History of Wyoming,* p. 318; Elting E. Morison, *Turmoil and Tradition* (Boston, 1960), pp. 147–48.

tion of theories premised on the uniqueness of the region. Their contention that the role of the federal government has been underplayed is amply borne out in Wyoming. Indeed, an attempt to penetrate the complexities of the territorial period must begin by considering the strengths and weaknesses of national policy toward the western dependencies. This intimate relationship between federal action and local events suggests that each western territory and state offered a kind of testing ground for native theories of government and that by examining the results of this process historians can, as Wallace Farnham has remarked, discover some of the basic assumptions of American society in the nineteenth century.

Farnham has described the American faith in promotion without regulation as responsible for the "weakened spring of government" which led to the scandals, waste, and inefficiency so typical of governmental behavior from 1865 to 1900. After examining the history of the Union Pacific, Farnham remarks, "Perhaps the study of kindred subjects with this theme in mind will permit us to decide that it was a central fact in the history of the United States in the last century."[6] The record in Wyoming indicates that the implications of these arguments, advanced by Farnham, Earl Pomeroy, and others, deserve testing in every western state in this period. In a federal union such as the United States, national trends are a combination of separate events and developments in each of the states, and like historians of colonial America, students of the West should now turn to intensive study of state and local history for verification of the large generalizations which have been made about the area.

6. Wallace D. Farnham, "The Weakened Spring of Government," p. 680.

The specific conclusions from such an inquiry will, of course, vary from state to state; but in view of Wyoming's experience, historians will probably find that western politics were as complex as the eastern variety, the leaders were equally adept, sophisticated, and responsive to national movements, and much as in the East, the major questions about the future of society were debated and analyzed in the political arena. The two major parties were not simply the tools of unscrupulous economic interests, and political battles were not sham contests designed to mask subterranean intrigues. It is ironic, for instance, that western Populism, with its limited appeal to the electorate, has been the subject of more interest than the Republicans and Democrats, who after all commanded the allegiances of seventy-five to ninety percent of the voters.

In short, western politics in the last three decades of the nineteenth century were part of a broader national picture which, through the efforts of historians of the East and South, is gradually being brought into focus. Fascinated by the problems inherent in industrialization in the East or in the agrarian upheavals in the South, the historical profession has given the West scant attention. Yet as Wyoming's politicians show, the West had to adjust to the birth of modern America like the other regions, and because of its weight in Congress, expressed in the power of Warren, it could influence national decisions on issues like conservation, the tariff, or agricultural policy. In view of these factors, the West surely merits the detailed scrutiny which has been lavished on the other sections of the nation, and if the Wyoming situation is typical, the results should prove as rewarding and stimulating to a better comprehension of American history in the last century.

BIBLIOGRAPHICAL ESSAY

A detailed guide to the sources for a study of the early history of Wyoming in T. A. Larson, *History of Wyoming* (Lincoln, Nebraska, 1965) makes an extended discussion of secondary materials superfluous. Only those books, articles, and theses of special value are listed below. This essay seeks instead to supply a description of the manuscript sources used in the preparation of this volume and to provide an outline of the relevant newspapers consulted.

Manuscripts

The manuscript sources for a history of Wyoming politics in the state's formative years are scattered and diverse. The best place to begin, however, is the Western History Research Center at the University of Wyoming, which contains a number of useful collections, especially the indispensable Francis E. Warren Papers.

The original gift of the Warren family to the University of Wyoming included one hundred and twenty-nine letterbooks spanning the period 1890 to 1929. Despite serious gaps between 1893 and 1896, these volumes thoroughly covered Warren's senatorial career. The next major addition to the collection occurred in 1964 when sixty-odd letterbooks and much business material were added. These new letterbooks, running from 1869 to 1896, filled in most of the major spaces in the record of Warren's public and business life. Finally, since 1964 the collection has been augmented by letters written by Warren to his future wife between 1868 and 1870.

Warren's handwriting was abominable, and the earlier

letterbooks are sometimes difficult to decipher. After 1885, however, the new territorial governor purchased a typewriter, and the problem of reading his voluminous correspondence eases. He was less meticulous about incoming mail. As it accumulated over the course of his life, he destroyed most of it at regular intervals. Fortunately Warren did preserve the letters dealing with such episodes as Rock Springs and the Johnson County War; this compensates, to some degree, for the destruction of other materials. Warren also had his staff compile detailed scrapbooks of newspaper clippings which contain news items and editorials from many journals whose back issues have been lost.

The Warren Papers are a significant, if largely unexplored, lode of important information about Wyoming and national history between 1870 and 1929. Unmatched in their frankness, detail, and completeness, the letterbooks provide, after 1885, insights into the workings of Wyoming legislatures, the internal deliberations of the Republican party, and the development of national policy toward the West. Because of Warren's gift for innuendo and his love for the subtleties of partisan intrigue, these letterbooks also offer fascinating glimpses of the mind of a political virtuoso at work.

Other collections at the Western History Research Center were most helpful. The records the Wyoming Stock Growers Association make clear the extent of their economic power and the limits of their political influence. The Clarence J. Dunder Papers, F. W. Lafrentz Papers, Teschmacher and deBillier Cattle Company Records, and Owen Wister Collection illuminate other aspects of the cattle industry in Wyoming.

Politicians are fairly well represented in the Center's holdings, but the result is disappointing. On the Republican side, the Joseph M. Carey Family Papers have only two or three letters for the period in question. The whereabouts of the bulk of the Carey Papers is dealt with below. The George B. McClellan Papers do not contain letters from the period covered in this volume; the same is true of the William A. Richards letters in the Alice Richards McCreery Papers. The John A. Riner letterbook is unrevealing, while the Jay L. Torrey Collection has nothing of value.

Democrats fare better. The John Hunton Papers mirror the opinions of a conservative Democrat, as do the W. S. Metz letters in the Percy S. Metz Papers. The William Daley Collection has an important letter from George W. Baxter in 1892. The George T. Beck Collection draws on a large spectrum of party sentiment but contains relatively few items.

A few other collections at the University of Wyoming were examined. Little was found in the University of Wyoming archives, the records of Albany County, or the J. S. Casement Papers. The M. A. Chapman Collection has some interesting telegrams about the Johnson County War.

In his effort to build up the manuscript resources of the Western History Research Center, Professor Gene Gressley sought to locate the papers of other prominent Wyoming politicians. Diligent search has revealed, however, that the papers of Bryant B. Brooks, Clarence D. Clark, Henry A. Coffeen, Frank Mondell, and John Charles Thompson, among others, have been lost or destroyed. A similar hunt for manuscripts of Populist leaders also proved fruitless.

As disappointing as these setbacks were, they could not equal the frustration that arose over the absence of the papers of Joseph M. Carey. In 1964 and 1966, during my visits to Wyoming, I approached the descendants of the Senator about the existence and location of the Carey

Papers. An exchange of letters and interviews did not unravel the mystery of what has happened to Senator Carey's manuscripts since his death in 1924. Neither Mr. Robert D. Carey of San Francisco nor Mr. Charles D. Carey of Cheyenne could provide help on the fate of the papers, and as Mr. Charles Carey wrote me on October 6, 1966, he has "exhausted all possible resources here on letters that might be helpful." There the matter rested when the manuscript for this study was completed.

Through Professor Gressley, I did learn of a small collection of the letters of John E. Osborne, the Democratic leader, located at the Carbon County Historical Society in Rawlins. This source consists of letters and telegrams dealing with the election of 1892 and for that purpose is most helpful.

The second most important repository within the state is the Wyoming State Archives and Historical Department in Cheyenne. Among the relevant collections are the papers of territorial governors John A. Campbell, John W. Hoyt, William Hale, Francis E. Warren, and Thomas Moonlight. The Warren letterbooks for his gubernatorial service are also available in the Warren collection in Laramie, while the small group of materials relating to John M. Thayer has nothing of value.

State governors have left some interesting correspondence at the Archives. The incoming letters of Amos Barber and John E. Osborne are available, as well as the letterbooks and letters received of William A. Richards. A collection of private letters sent to John E. Osborne is confined to items from the twentieth century. Other official papers include the State Engineer's letterbooks, which have many letters sent by Elwood Mead, and the State Treasurer's Records, the files of which extend back into the territorial period.

Among the private collections in the Archives are the Frank Bond letterbook, the Gibson Clark Collection, the J. K. Moore Papers, John W. Hoyt's manuscript autobiography, and the E. A. Slack Scrapbook on microfilm. I used the latter in the original through the courtesy of Mr. W. R. DuBois of Cheyenne.

Outside Wyoming many libraries possess items which further an understanding of the state's history. The Bancroft Library, University of California at Berkeley, has the dictations recorded by H. H. Bancroft's researchers from Wyoming residents in the 1880s and one letter from Joseph M. Carey in the Robert Underwood Johnson Papers of vital importance for the Senator's silver stand in 1893.

The Center for the Study of the Western Range Cattle Industry at the Colorado State Historical Society in Denver has the records of the Swan Land and Cattle Company and the F. G. S. Hesse Papers. The John Evans Papers at the Society shed light on the founding of Wyoming Territory. The Henry M. Teller Letters and the Joel F. Vaile Papers in the Denver Public Library cover peripheral aspects of the Wyoming story.

The Grenville M. Dodge Papers at the Iowa State Department of History and Archives in Des Moines are an essential source for the early territorial period. The William Boyd Allison Papers at the Archives have a few letters from William Hale about his appointment as territorial governor in 1882.

At Yale the Silas Reed Papers in the Western Americana Collection provide vital information on the Campbell era. The Andrew Jackson Faulk Papers view the establishment of Wyoming Territory from the Dakota perspective. The J. W. Cook Papers deal with the early days of Cheyenne. The Western Americana Collection also contains political pamphlets and promotional literature from the early days of the territory.

The Manuscripts Division, Library of Congress, has numerous collections of the first importance for this study. The Willis Van Devanter Papers, on deposit with the Oliver Wendell Holmes Devise, are as significant as the Warren Papers for the politics of the 1890s; they contribute letters from Carey and Mondell that are not available elsewhere. Of the presidential papers, those of Benjamin Harrison and Grover Cleveland were the most germane. The papers of Chester A. Arthur, U. S. Grant, Andrew Johnson, and William McKinley contain relatively little on Wyoming. Other manuscripts consulted at the Library of Congress include the papers of William Jennings Bryan, James S. Clarkson, Moreton Frewen, Daniel S. Lamont, Richard Olney, Carl Schurz, and William C. Whitney.

A history of Wyoming politics could not be written without the documents gathered at the National Archives in Washington. The appointment papers for the various federal offices during the territorial and early statehood period are an unexplored cache of valuable sources, especially for the second administration of Grover Cleveland.

The Department of the Interior, Record Group 48, has the appointment letters for the Wyoming territorial governor and secretary, 1873–90, appointment papers for the surveyor-general, 1870–96, and the appointment papers for the Buffalo, Cheyenne, Douglas, Evanston, Lander, and Sundance land offices, 1870–96. The official territorial papers dealing with Wyoming, including executive correspondence, penitentiary reports, and other data, 1870–90, have been microfilmed.

The Department of Justice, Record Group 60, contains the appointment papers for territorial judges, 1869–90, district attorney, 1869–96, and marshal, 1869–96. In addition, the Wyoming chronological files of incoming correspondence, the President's chronological files, and the official letterbooks of the attorney general were consulted. The department also collected correspondence in regard to the Johnson County War which was microfilmed by the University of Wyoming Library.

The nomination files of the United States Senate, Record Group 46, supply information on the conflict over the appointment of William Ware Peck. Records of the Department of State, Record Group 59, provide the appointment papers for the Wyoming governor and secretary, 1869–73. The department's territorial papers on Wyoming, 1868–73, have been microfilmed.

The Treasury Department, Record Group 56, contains the appointment materials for the Colorado collector of internal revenue, 1893–97, which bear on the appointment of A. L. New.

The military correspondence on the Johnson County War is available in the Adjutant General's Office records, Record Group 94, and the records of Army Commands, United States, Record Group 98. Microfilm versions of these materials are on deposit at the University of Wyoming and the State Historical Society.

Newspapers

Of the newspapers examined, the two most important were the *Cheyenne Leader* (1867–95), and the Cheyenne *Sun* (1879–95). The *Leader* became the voice of the Wyoming Democratic Party after 1880, while the *Sun*, under the editorial guidance of E. A. Slack, spoke for the Republicans. The two papers merged in 1895, and the *Cheyenne Sun-Leader* was operated in the interest of Francis E. Warren.

Relatively complete files of the *Leader* are deposited at the Wyoming State Historical Society, but the run of the *Sun* there is broken for 1893 and 1894, and the *Sun-Leader* for 1896 is missing. Consequently, the set of the papers at the Library of Congress should be used.

Unbroken runs of the *Wyoming Tribune* (1869–71, 1892, 1896) have not survived, but scattered copies can be located at the Historical Society and the University of Wyoming. After 1894, the *Tribune* became the organ of Joseph M. Carey in Cheyenne. The *Wyoming Commonwealth* (1890–91) attempted to promote interest in mining and Republicanism in Cheyenne. A microfilm copy of this paper's issues can be found in the Yale University Library.

J. H. Hayford edited the Laramie *Daily Sentinel* (1870–78) and the Laramie *Weekly Sentinel* (1877–95) with his customary flair and devotion to the Republican cause. The Laramie *Daily Boomerang* (1884–96) began as a Republican sheet but was purchased by the Democrats in 1890. Outside Cheyenne, a variety of newspapers carried on the political battle. The *Buffalo Bulletin* (1893–1900, Republican), *Natrona Tribune* (1894–96, Republican), Rawlins, *Carbon County Journal* (1887–97, Democratic), and the *Rawlins Republican* (1892–94), like the *Sentinel* and *Boomerang,* are all available at the Wyoming State Historical Society.

National newspapers of value were the Denver *Rocky Mountain News, Chicago Tribune, New York Times,* New York *World,* and the Washington *Post.*

Public Documents

Federal documents relating to Wyoming may be conveniently located in Ben: Perley Poore, comp., *A Descrip-*

tive Catalogue of the Government Publications of the United States, 1774–1881 (Washington, 1885), and John G. Ames, Comprehensive Index to the Publications of the United States Government, 1881–1893 (Washington, 1905). The Congressional Globe (Washington, 1868–73) and the Congressional Record (Washington, 1874–96) cover matters about Wyoming discussed in Congress. The annual reports of the Wyoming governors appeared in the Annual Report of the Secretary of the Interior (Washington, 1877–90). The reports of the commissioner of the General Land Office, also collected in the reports of the Secretary of the Interior, were especially valuable for the first administration of Grover Cleveland.

The work of territorial and state legislatures is set forth in the Council Journal, Wyoming Legislative Assembly (Cheyenne, 1869–90), House Journal, Wyoming Legislative Assembly (Cheyenne, 1869–90), House Journal of the State Legislature of Wyoming (Cheyenne, 1895–97), and the Senate Journal (Cheyenne, 1895–97). The proceedings of the first two state legislatures were not printed. The Session Laws of Wyoming (Cheyenne, 1869–97) were also helpful, as were the legislative messages of the Wyoming Governor (Cheyenne, Laramie, 1869–90). Judicial actions were followed in Wyoming Reports, volumes 1–7.

Two state documents of special value were Journals and Debates of the Constitutional Convention of the State of Wyoming (Cheyenne, 1893), and Marie H. Erwin, Wyoming Historical Blue Book (Denver, 1946). The latter is a treasure house of biographical information, election returns, and important documents and speeches. Every student of Wyoming history is indebted to the patient and thorough labors of Mrs. Erwin.

Secondary Sources

Professor T. A. Larson has replaced all earlier histories of the state with his one-volume *History of Wyoming* (Lincoln, Nebraska, 1965). His copious bibliography and encyclopedic approach make his book the place to begin any study of Wyoming politics. Second in importance are the articles contained in the *Annals of Wyoming,* published biennially by the Wyoming State Historical Society, which reflect the continuing interest of Wyoming residents in their state. The footnotes indicate how valuable a source this journal has been.

Serious examination of Wyoming's political history started with the pioneering efforts of Professor W. Turrentine Jackson in the 1940s. His most significant articles include "Territorial Papers of Wyoming in the National Archives," *Annals of Wyoming, 16* (1944), 45–55; "The Governorship of Wyoming, 1885–1889: A Study in Territorial Politics," *Pacific Historical Review, 13* (1944), 1–11; "The Administration of Thomas Moonlight, 1887–1889," *Annals of Wyoming, 18* (1946), 139–62; "Railroad Relations of the Wyoming Stock Growers Association, 1873–1890," *Annals of Wyoming, 19* (1947), 3–23; "The Wyoming Stock Growers Association: Political Power in Wyoming Territory, 1873–1890," *Mississippi Valley Historical Review, 33* (1947), 571–94; and "The Wyoming Stock Growers Association: Its Years of Temporary Decline," *Agricultural History,* 22 (1948), 260–70.

A staggering amount of material has been produced on the Wyoming cattle industry. The three indispensable works are E. S. Osgood, *The Day of the Cattleman* (Minneapolis, 1929); Lewis Atherton, *The Cattle Kings* (Bloom-

280

ington, 1961); and Gene Gressley, *Bankers and Cattlemen* (New York, 1966).

As an offshoot of the cattle business, the Johnson County War has claimed the attention of innumerable historians. Helena Huntington Smith, *The War on Powder River* (New York, 1966) is the best single treatment. George T. Watkins, "Johnson County War," *Pacific Northwesterner,* 5 (1961), 17–28 is a sane guide to the literature of the controversy. A. S. Mercer, *The Banditti of the Plains* (Norman, Oklahoma, 1954) has achieved a wide notoriety, which is probably undeserved. This subject is explored at more length in Lewis L. Gould, "A. S. Mercer and the Johnson County War: A Reappraisal," *Arizona and the West,* 7 (1965), 5–20.

To establish the interpretive framework for the study of western political history, the work of Leonard J. Arrington, Wallace Farnham, Howard R. Lamar, and Earl Pomeroy is essential. Wallace Farnham, " 'The Weakened Spring of Government': A Study in Nineteenth-Century American History," *American Historical Review,* 68 (1963), 662–80 and Earl Pomeroy, "Toward a Reorientation of Western History: Continuity and Environment," *Mississippi Valley Historical Review,* 41 (1955), 579–600 are the two most provocative articles written about western history in the last two decades. Leonard J. Arrington, *The Changing Economic Structure of the Mountain West, 1850–1950* (Logan, Utah, 1963) provides invaluable statistical data.

Earl Pomeroy, *The Territories and the United States, 1861–1890* (Philadelphia, 1947), began the intensive study of the territorial system after the Civil War. Pomeroy's analysis has been extended by Howard R. Lamar in *Dakota Territory, 1861–1889* (New Haven, 1956); "Political Patterns in New Mexico and Utah Territories, 1850–1900,"

Utah Historical Quarterly, 28 (1960), 363–387; "Carpet-baggers Full of Dreams: A Functional View of the Arizona Pioneer Politician," *Arizona and the West, 7* (1965), 187–206; and *The Far Southwest, 1846–1912: A Territorial History* (New Haven, 1966).

The national context for western political developments is set forth in Allan Nevins, *Grover Cleveland: A Study in Courage* (New York, 1932); Harold H. Dunham, *Government Handout: A Study in the Administration of the Public Lands, 1875–1891* (New York, 1941); H. Wayne Morgan, *William McKinley and His America* (Syracuse, 1963); Carl N. Degler, "American Political Parties and the Rise of the City: An Interpretation," *Journal of American History, 51* (1964), 41–59; and Stanley L. Jones, *The Presidential Election of 1896* (Madison, 1964).

Several unpublished theses and dissertations added useful information. Lois Van Valkenburgh, "The Johnson County War, The Papers of Charles Bingham Penrose in the Library of the University of Wyoming with Introduction and Notes," unpublished M.A. thesis, University of Wyoming, 1939, is virtually a primary source. John K. Yoshida, "The Wyoming Election of 1892," unpublished M.A. thesis, University of Wyoming, 1956, and Thomas Kreuger, "Populism in Wyoming," unpublished M.A. thesis, University of Wyoming, 1960, are helpful surveys. Kenneth Nelson Owens, "Frontier Governors: A Study of the Territorial Executives in the History of Washington, Idaho, Montana, Wyoming, and Dakota Territories," unpublished Ph.D. thesis, University of Minnesota, 1959, compares Wyoming to its surrounding neighbors.

INDEX

Absentee ownership of cattle, abuses, 67
Adams, Charles Francis, 89, 117
Agriculture. *See* Farming
Agriculture Committee of Senate, 230
Albany County, 13, 36, 57, 92, 99, 121, 125, 135, 162, 164, 172, 185, 208, 209, 236; capital location issue, 100; Republican party of, on successor to Gov. Warren, 124; and apportionment, 127
Allison, William Boyd, 70, 235, 238, 243
American Cattle Trust, 68
American Protective Association (APA), 206–11
American Protective Tariff League, 217
American Railway Union, 213
Ames, Oakes, 4, 30
Andrews, W. H., 238–39
Angus, W. G. (Red), 144
Anti-lottery bill, 59
APA. *See* American Protective Association
Apportionment, 126–27
Appropriations Committee of Senate, 267
Arid lands, 230; economic effect on settlement of Wyoming, 9, 130–31; cession of, 130–33, 251; arid land bill, 136, 160, 161, 169, 172, 202
Arizona, 115, 129

Arthur, Chester A., appoints Warren territorial governor, 73–74
Ashley, James M., 5–7

Baker, L. C., 187
Baker, Nat, disputed legislative seat *(1892)*, 175, 184, 189
Baker, Nathan A., editor of *Cheyenne Leader,* 1, 3, 10
Balch, H. G., 94
Banditti of the Plains, The, 218
Barber, Amos W.: completes Warren's term as state governor, 124, 127; during Johnson County War, 142–48, 150, 159; after Johnson County War, 169–70; role in *1892* election disputes, 177, 180n., 181; acting governor, 190
Barrow, Merris C., 166
Bartlett, I. S., 108
Baxter, George W., 93, 101; brief appointment as governor *(1886)*, 96; gubernatorial candidate, 120–21; conspirator in Johnson County War, 159–60, 185; battle for Senate, 185 and n.
Bear River City, 2
Beck, George T., 93; battle for Senate, 185 and n.
Beckwith, A. C.: appointed to Senate, 194; resigns, 195–96
Bennett, S. B., disputed legislative seat, 176–77, 183

ment for Warren, 124–25; candidate for governor, 135–36, 163-66; loses election, 171–72; ignored by Warren, 204

Jackson, Andrew, 199
Jefferson, Thomas, 199
Johnson, Andrew, signs Wyoming bill, 6–7
Johnson County, 161, 170, 172; founded as Pease County, 51, 54; low population, 128; believed dominated by cattle rustlers, 149–53, 156; seeks dismissal of charges against cattlemen, 157; Populists in, 162, 163, 186. *See also* Johnson County War
Johnson County War, 185, 191, 218, 229; cattlemen's actions, 136–38, 140n., 141, 143; trial of cattlemen, 145–57; political aftermath, 158, 159, 161–63, 167, 168, 172, 190
Jones, William T.: appointed territorial judge, 24; elected delegate (*1870*), 32–33; election of *1872*, 38–41
Jordan, Patrick J. M., 254
Judicial system of territories, 19
Justice Department: and Johnson County War, 167; Rankin resigns, 168

KC ranch, 137
Kelley, A. D., 156
Kem, Nebraska Populist congressman, 246

Kemp, Frank A., 151, 160
Kendrick, John B., 261
Kilpatrick Brothers, 205
Kime, James, 188
Kingman, John W., 24
Kingsbury, D. A., 186n.
Kinzer, Donald, 206
Knights of Labor, 88

Lamar, Howard, 5, 34
Lamar, L. Q. C., 92; rescinds suspension of land acts, 85; overrules Sparks on Desert Land Act, 94
Land policy: reform under Cleveland administration, 85–86, 97, 115; in platform of Democratic convention of *1886,* 95
Lander *Clipper,* 190
Laramie, Wyo., 2, 11, 77, 92, 99, 105, 128, 136, 148, 149, 206; and capital location issue, 13, 36, 45; gets Union Pacific rolling mill, 14; site of penitentiary, 26; site of territorial convention, 32; university proposed, 92; site of Republican convention of *1892,* 164
Laramie County, 57, 58, 121, 135, 162, 172, 174, 185, 205, 236, 240, 244, 252, 258, 260; created, 2; supported by Dakota Territory, 4; political competition with Albany County, 13; increases size, 36; delegation opposes Warren, 60; loses territory, 99; discriminated against in Constitutional convention, 113; and apportionment, 126–27; site of

121; and Johnson County War, 143–49; *1892* election, 159–60, 163–66, 171–72, 174; disputed legislative seats *(1892)*, 175–76, 178, 186–88; *1894* election, 203, 221; and APA, 206–07, 210–11; platform in *1896*, 248–49; subsidizes Populists, 252–54; final weeks of McKinley campaign, 257–58; policies suited to Wyoming, 265

Richards, DeForest, 124, 163, 164, 191; runs for Senate, 174, 184, 186–87

Richards, William A., 163; elected governor, 204–06, 211–12; and APA, 208; and *1896* national convention, 239, 241

Riner, C. W., 207

Robbins, Roy M., 86

Rock Springs, Wyo., 11, 121, 128, 250, 256; riot, 88; site of Democratic convention of *1892*, 161

Rocky Mountain News, 176

Rocky Mountain railroad, proposed, 12

Rocky Mountain region, 129, 232, 266, 267

Rollins House, 35

Ross, S. B., disputed election *(1892)*, 176, 177, 180

Royal Commission on Agriculture, 65

"Rump" legislature of *1873*, 45

Russell, John L., 188

Rustlers, cattle, 137–40, 149, 151–52, 156, 219. *See also* Johnson County War

St. Louis: site of Republican national convention *(1896)*, 235–36, 238, 239, 243, 244, 248, 249; site of Populist convention *(1896)*, 251

Salt Lake City, 131, 246

Schofield, J. M., 23

Schurz, Carl, 53, 58, 60, 62

Scott, John, disputed election of *1892*, 175, 184

Scott, Richard, 156

Secretary, territorial, duties of, 18–19

Sectionalism, in early territory, 13–14, 20

Sener, James B., 57

Settlers: versus Indians, 50; favored after cattle bust, 97–98

Sewall, Arthur, 250, 254

Sheep, place in economy, 130

Sheridan, Wyo., site of Republican state conventions, 216, 231, 237, 240, 243

Sheridan County, 121, 128, 172, 236, 248, 259

Sherman Silver Purchase Act of *1890*, 194; repealed, 196, 198, 200

Silver. *See* Free silver issue

Simms, William, 254

Sioux Indians, 29

"Sioux Indian scrip," 37

Slack, E. A.: editor of Cheyenne *Sun*, 169; supports Carey, 72, 125; work in *1892* campaign, 166; attacks Esteb, 209; buys *Cheyenne Daily Leader*, 218; attacks Carey, 226

Snider, E. U., 186n.

Co., 58; territorial treasurer, 59–62; appointed governor, 71–74, 88–91; union with Carey, 75; on Carey, 78; background, 78–82; on unity of a political party, 80, 82–83; on Sparks' land policy, 87; opposition of Democrats to, 88, 93, 95–96; and northern railroad, 91; and capital location, 91, 100; on Moonlight, 97, 101; on Tenth Legislative Assembly, 98; and formation of new counties, 99; in delegate campaign of *1888*, 102; second gubernatorial term, 103–04, 106–10; and statehood drive, 111–14; attacked by *1890* Assembly, 115–16; first state elections, 117; feud with Carey, 118–19, 125, 172n., 236, 241–44; state governor, 120–21; elected to U.S. Senate, 122–24, 128, 134–36; and apportionment, 126–27; on arid lands, 130–34, 169–70, 172; and Johnson County War, 141–44, 147–55, 158–60, 163; *1892* election, condemned by Democrats, 161–62, 164–66, 170–71; asks Rankin's resignation, 167–68; dispute over *1892* election, 173–75, 177–80, 182; political battle for second Senate term, 184–86, 186n., 187, 188n., 189n., 190; political low point, 191–93; on *1893* Panic, 194; contrasted with Coffeen, 200; political comeback, 201–06; and APA, 208–09; and *1894* election

convention, 211; and free silver issue, 212, 249; and railroad union troubles, 213; financial setbacks, 216–17, 219; runs for Senate (*1894*), 220, 222–27; elected, 227–28, 230; duties as senator, 230–31; working for party solidarity in *1896*, 232–33; supports McKinley, 234–35; and *1896* convention, 236–40; problems in Van Devanter's absence, 245; and *1896* election campaign, 246–53, 256–57, 257n., 258; subsidizes Populists, 252–53; explanation of Democratic victory in Wyoming (*1896*), 259; continued party leadership, 260–61; hospitalized, 262; McKinley approves appointments of, 263; approach to politics, 263–64; summary, 266–68

Warren Land and Livestock Co., 79
Warren Live Stock Co., 110, 160, 170, 216
Warren Mercantile Co., 79
Washington, D.C., 129, 212, 213, 217, 224, 230, 267, 268
Water rights, 112–13
Watson, Tom, 251, 254
Weaver, James B., 162, 173
Webb, Walter P., 9
Wellman, George, 151
Weston County, 128, 162
Wheatland, 259
Whigs, 20
Whitehead, J. R., 2
Wiebe, Robert, 266